*George III and the Satirists
from Hogarth to Byron*

George III
and the Satirists
from Hogarth to Byron

Vincent Carretta

The University of Georgia Press
Athens and London

© 1990 by the University of Georgia Press
Athens, Georgia 30602

All rights reserved
Designed by Nighthawk Design
Set in 11 on 12 Linotron 202 Garamond No. 3

The paper in this book meets the guidelines for
permanence and durability of the Committee on
Production Guidelines for Book Longevity of the
Council on Library Resources.

Printed in the United States of America

94   93   92   91   90   5   4   3   2   1

Library of Congress Cataloging in Publication Data
Carretta, Vincent.
George III and the satirists from Hogarth to Byron /
Vincent Carretta.
p.   cm.
Bibliography: p.
Includes index.
ISBN 0-8203-1146-4 (alk. paper)
1. Great Britain—Politics and government—1760–
1820—Caricatures and cartoons.   2. Great Britain—
Politics and government—1760–1820—Humor.
3. George III, King of Great Britain, 1738–1820—
Humor.   4. Political satire, English—History and
criticism.   5. English wit and humor, Pictorial.
I. Title.
DA505.C36   1990
941.07′3—dc19   89–4778   CIP

British Library Cataloging in Publication Data available

For Pat and Sal

Contents

Illustrations

Preface

This book is an attempt to describe and analyze the satiric career of George III, the first such effort since Thomas Wright's *Caricature History of the Georges* (1868). Only incidentally is this a study of the relationship between verbal and visual political satire in Britain and colonial America during the late Georgian period (approximately 1760–1820). As the last British monarch who fully ruled as well as reigned and as the last king of America, George III was the target of many satiric attacks. Concentrating on his reign has enabled me to analyze the development of British regal satire as it changed in the face of the American and French revolutions, the Napoleonic Wars, and the romantic movement. Soon after I had begun to research this subject, I recognized that, although George III was to be its focus, it should begin by considering the developing institution of early modern monarchy in England (Britain after 1707) established at the Restoration of 1660 and the tradition of regal satire that developed in response to that changing institution.

The satiric career of George III was determined more by the accident of his person than by deliberate attempts to instill the masses with a false consciousness designed to consolidate cultural hegemony. For example, the convergence of the king's two bodies during the 1790s into the satiric character of Farmer George–John Bull, so effective in anti-French satires, would have been impossible without the actual character of George the man. George III was the first British monarch to have a public family life and the first to have a practical interest in agriculture. His supporters certainly took the opportunity to exploit the shift in circumstances that turned erstwhile private follies into public virtues, but no amount of government propaganda could have transformed his Hanoverian predecessors or successor into such a fictional character. Contemporary eighteenth-century suggestions that the king was unduly influenced by his mother or Lord Bute, charges that the government was trying to indoctrinate the ruled with Scottish principles of Stuart despotism in the 1760s or with German despotism in the 1790s, Thomas Paine's accusation that religion was abused as "a political machine," and what I refer to as unexamined premises of monarchy could all be described in terminology that I have eschewed to avoid the deterministic and teleological implications such phraseology can convey. At least for the sake of argument, we should entertain the possibility that amidst the circumstances of history religion may be a repository of truth.

I am very grateful to the Henry E. Huntington Library, the National Endowment for the Humanities, the National Humanities Center, the Yale Center for British Art, and the John Carter Brown Library for fellowship support that made research for this project both possible and enjoyable. A generous award for research support from the American Philosophical Society allowed me to purchase photographs for study. A sabbatical leave from the University of Maryland enabled me to learn much from the leader and my fellow members in J. G. A. Pocock's seminar, "Political Thought in the English-Speaking Atlantic, 1760–1820," at the Folger Shakespeare Library while I completed the book. My debts to major collections and their staffs are equally great: the British Library and British Museum in the United Kingdom; in the United States, the Library of Congress and the Library Company of Philadelphia, the Folger Shakespeare Library, the Henry E. Huntington Library, the Lewis Walpole Library, the Beinecke Library, the Sterling Library, the Yale Center for British Art, the John Carter Brown Library, the Pierpont Morgan Library, the Colonial Williamsburg Foundation, the Paul Mellon Collection, and the university libraries of Brown, Duke, Maryland, and North Carolina at Chapel Hill. A shorter version of chapter 2 appeared in *The Age of Johnson* 1 (1987); I thank the editor for permission to reprint the essay.

I gladly acknowledge my debts to the people who assisted me at various stages of my work. Without the support of Robert D. Hume and Paul J. Korshin from the inception of this project, the book would probably never have been completed. I thank as well William J. Romanowski, Jr., who aided me at an early stage of my research, and those who read and helpfully commented on the manuscript in whole or in part: Lance Bertelsen, Neil Fraistat, Brenda W. Kolb, David Lampe, F. P. Lock, Robert L. Patten, Tony Rosso, Joseph Sitterson, and Joseph Wittreich. The anonymous readers for the University of Georgia Press gave me much useful advice and criticism. In a more general way, I am indebted to the encouragement and scholarship of Ronald Paulson. Publication of this book was partially supported by a generous book subsidy award from the General Research Board of the University of Maryland.

Abbreviations

APW	*American Political Writing during the Founding Era, 1760–1805,* ed. Charles S. Hyneman and Donald S. Lutz, 2 vols. (Indianapolis, Ind.: Liberty Press, 1983).
Blackstone	William Blackstone, *Commentaries on the Laws of England,* 4 vols. (London, 1765–69; Chicago: Univ. of Chicago Press, 1979). Unless otherwise indicated, all quotations are from volume 1.
Blake	William Blake, *The Poetry and Prose of William Blake,* ed. David V. Erdman (Berkeley and Los Angeles: Univ. of California Press, 1982).
BMC	*Catalogue of Prints and Drawings in the British Museum: Division 1. Political and Personal Satires,* ed. Frederic George Stephens, Edward Hawkins, and Mary Dorothy George, 11 vols. in 12 parts (1870–1954; London: British Museum Publications, 1978).
Byron	George Gordon Byron, Sixth Baron Byron, *Byron,* ed. Jerome J. McGann (Oxford: Oxford Univ. Press, 1986).
Chatterton	Thomas Chatterton, *The Complete Works of Thomas Chatterton,* ed. Donald S. Taylor and Benjamin B. Hoover, 2 vols. (Oxford: Oxford Univ. Press, 1971).
Churchill	Charles Churchill, *The Poetical Works of Charles Churchill,* ed. Douglas Grant (Oxford: Oxford Univ. Press, 1956).
Common Sense	Thomas Paine, *Common Sense and the Crisis* (Garden City, N.Y.: Doubleday, 1973).
Cowper	William Cowper, *The Poems of William Cowper,* ed. John D. Baird and Charles Ryskamp (Oxford: Oxford Univ. Press, 1980–).
Dryden	John Dryden, *The Works of John Dryden,* ed. E. N. Hooker et al. (Berkeley and Los Angeles: Univ. of California Press, 1956–).

Goldsmith   Oliver Goldsmith, *The Collected Works of Oliver Goldsmith*, ed. Arthur Friedman, 5 vols. (Oxford: Oxford Univ. Press, 1966).

Johnson   Samuel Johnson, *The Yale Edition of the Works of Samuel Johnson*, ed. John H. Middendorf et al. (New Haven, Conn.: Yale Univ. Press, 1958–).

Junius   Junius, *The Letters of Junius*, ed. John Cannon (Oxford: Oxford Univ. Press, 1978).

POAS   *Poems on Affairs of State: Augustan Satirical Verse, 1660–1714*, ed. George deForest Lord et al., 7 vols. (New Haven, Conn.: Yale Univ. Press, 1963–75).

Pope   Alexander Pope, *The Twickenham Edition of the Poems of Alexander Pope*, ed. John Butt et al., 11 vols. (New Haven, Conn.: Yale Univ. Press, 1939–69).

Reflections   Edmund Burke, *Reflections on the Revolution in France*, ed. Conor Cruise O'Brien (Harmondsworth: Penguin, 1969).

ROM   Thomas Paine, *Rights of Man*, ed. Henry Collins (Harmondsworth: Penguin, 1969).

Smith   Adam Smith, *The Glasgow Edition of the Works and Correspondence of Adam Smith*, ed. David Daiches Raphael et al., 6 vols. (Oxford: Oxford Univ. Press, 1976).

Thoughts   Edmund Burke, *Thoughts on the Cause of the Present Discontents*, in *Party, Parliament, and the American Crisis, 1766–1774*, vol. 2 of *The Writings and Speeches of Edmund Burke*, ed. Paul Langford et al. (Oxford: Oxford Univ. Press, 1981–), pp. 241–323.

Wolcot   John Wolcot, *The Works of Peter Pindar*, 5 vols. (London, 1812).

Chapter 1

The Tradition
of Regal Satire

The King can do no wrong.

In 1760 King George III inherited two legacies from the Restoration of
1660: his crown and a tradition of regal satire. The civil war during the
1640s produced both. Prior to the struggle between Charles I and Parliament over the premises of power, satires against kingship are virtually
unknown, in large part because the theoretically unlimited divine right
by which monarchs ruled made such attacks sacrilegious. In the words of
James I, the king was as inviolable as God himself:

> That which concerns the mystery of the King's power is not lawful to
> be disputed; for that is to wade into the weakness of princes, and to
> take away the mystical reverence that belongs unto them that sit in the
> throne of God. . . . As for the absolute prerogative of the Crown, that
> is no subject for the tongue of a lawyer, nor is lawful to be disputed.
> It is aetheism and blasphemy to dispute what God can do; good Christians content themselves with his Will revealed in his Word; so it is
> presumption and high contempt in a subject to dispute what a King
> cannot do, or say that a King cannot do this or that, but rest with that
> which is the King's revealed will in his law.[1]

Events of the 1630s and 1640s demonstrated, however, that power indeed
limited theory. The direct, though gradual, result was what George III
would later call "this excellent Constitution . . . the most beautiful Combination that ever was framed."[2]

By 1750, Britain was firmly committed in theory and fact to a balanced
system of government, codified and celebrated by the orthodox Whig Sir
William Blackstone in his Vinerian lectures delivered at Oxford and later
published as *Commentaries on the Laws of England* (1765–69).[3] The excellence of Britain's constitution lay in its combining the three recognized

pure forms of government—democracy (rule by many), aristocracy (rule by few), and monarchy (rule by one)—so as to achieve the optimum balance between the power of the state and the liberty of the subjects. In its pure form, each has merits and drawbacks:

> In a democracy, where the right of making laws resides in the people at large, public virtue, or goodness of intention is more likely to be found, than either of the other qualities of government. Popular assemblies are frequently foolish in their continuance, and weak in their execution; but generally mean to do the thing that is right and just, and have always a degree of patriotism or public spirit. In aristocracies there is more wisdom to be found, than in the other frames of government; being composed, or intended to be composed of the most experienced citizens: but there is less honesty than in a republic, and less strength than in a monarchy. A monarchy is indeed the most powerful of any; for by the entire conjunction of the legislative and executive powers all the sinews of government are knit together, and united in the hand of the prince: but then there is imminent danger of his employing that strength to improvident or oppressive purposes. (Blackstone, pp. 49–50)

Because of man's postlapsarian nature, each pure form, according to Niccolo Machiavelli, would naturally corrupt or degenerate—monarchy into tyranny, aristocracy into oligarchy, and democracy into ochlocracy or anarchy. Only periodic *ricorsi,* or renewals, of first principles could approach the pure forms with their separate perfections and imperfections.[4] The British constitution's mixed form came as close to being a self-correcting mechanism as man was thought likely to devise. Excellent though the balance of the British constitution was held to be, it was threatened by the encroachment of any one constituent part on the powers of another. To avoid the danger of absolute monarchy, for example, the king was at once part of and separate from Parliament: "In all tyrannical governments the supreme magistracy, or the right both of *making* and *enforcing* the laws, is rested in one and the same man, or one and the same body of men; and whenever these two powers are united together, there can be no public liberty. . . . With us therefore in England this supreme power is divided into two branches; the one legislative, to wit, the parliament, consisting of king, lords and commons; the other executive, consisting of the king alone" (Blackstone, pp. 142–43).[5]

Because of his "attribute of *sovereignty,* or pre-eminence, . . . by law the person of the king is sacred, even though the measures pursued in his reign be completely tyrannical and arbitrary: for no jurisdiction upon earth has power to try him in a criminal way; much less to condemn him to punishment." Consequently, "the king himself can do no wrong; since it would be a great weakness and absurdity in any system of positive law, to define any possible wrong, without any possible redress." As for private injuries, should a subject have, "in point of property, a just demand upon the king, he must petition him in his court of chancery, where his chancellor will administer right as a matter of grace, though not upon compulsion." Quoting John Locke, Blackstone dismisses as remote the likelihood of suffering personal wrong at the king's hands. "As to cases of ordinary public oppression, where the vitals of the constitution are not attacked," his ministers bear responsibility for evil measures, "for as a king cannot misuse his power, without the advice of evil counsellors, and the assistance of wicked ministers, these men may be examined and punished. The constitution has therefore provided, by means of indictments, and parliamentary impeachments, that no man shall dare to assist the crown in contradiction to the laws of the land" (pp. 234–37). In addition to the idea that "whatever is exceptionable in the conduct of public affairs is not to be imputed to the king, nor is he answerable for it personally to his people," the maxim "the king can do no wrong . . . means that the prerogative of the crown extends not to do any injury. . . . The king, moreover, is not only incapable of *doing* wrong, but even of *thinking* wrong; he can never mean to do an improper thing: in him is no folly or weakness" (pp. 238–39).

Because the monarch exercises his sovereign power as King-in-Parliament, "the supposition of *law* . . . is, that neither the king nor either house of parliament (collectively taken) is capable of doing any wrong; since in such cases the law feels itself incapable of furnishing any adequate remedy. For which reason all oppressions, which may happen to spring from any branch of the sovereign power, must necessarily be out of the reach of any *stated rule,* or *express legal* provision: but, if ever they unfortunately happen, the prudence of the times must provide new remedies for new emergencies" (pp. 237–38). Blackstone warns, moreover, that if the sovereign should "invade the fundamental constitution of the realm," as in the case of James II, the people "will not sacrifice their liberty by a scrupulous adherence to those political maxims, which were originally established to preserve it" (p. 238).

In Blackstone's theory of the constitution, shared by most Hanoverian politicians, direct popular involvement should occur only at times of extraordinary danger to the constitution. In normal times, the vast majority of disfranchised Britons enjoyed virtual rather than direct representation by members of Parliament, whose independence assured their refusal to truckle to popular opinion: "And every member, though chosen by one particular district, when elected and returned serves for the whole realm. For the end of his coming thither is not particular but general; not barely to advantage his constituents, but the *common* wealth. . . . And therefore he is not bound, like a deputy in the united provinces to consult with, or take the advice of, his constituents upon any particular point, unless he himself thinks it proper or prudent so to do" (p. 155).

The constitution qualifies its ascription "to the king, in his political capacity, [of] absolute *perfection*" by recognizing the right of both houses of Parliament to remonstrate and complain "to the king even of those acts of royalty, which are most properly and personally his own; such as messages signed by himself and speeches delivered from the throne." So great is the reverence of the two houses for the royal person that "they usually suppose them to flow from the advice of the administration. But the privilege of canvassing thus freely the personal acts of the sovereign (either directly or even through the medium of his reputed advisers) belongs to no individual, but is confined to those august assemblies, and there too objections must be proposed with the utmost respect and deference" (pp. 238–40).

Another attribute of the king's majesty alluded to in satires of George III is "his *perpetuity*. The law ascribes to him, in his political capacity, an absolute immortality. The king never dies. Henry, Edward, or George may die; but the king survives them all. . . . In consequence of the disunion of the king's natural body from his body politic, the kingdom is transferred or demised to his successor; and so the royal dignity remains perpetual" (p. 242). Hence the saying, The king is dead—long live the king.[6]

But what of the king's actual role in government as observed in practice? Blackstone's description leaves out such practical problems as the roles in government of parties, prime ministers, organized oppositions, and the "People," all of whom restricted the freedom of individual kings to exercise their royal prerogative to choose their own ministers.[7] Because so much of the British constitution consists of the *lex non scripta,* the unwritten, or common, law, in addition to the *lex scripta,* the written, or statute, law, its character is more prescriptive than positive. That is, what is constitutionally correct more often reflects what has traditionally been done for time immemorial than what specific legislation has formulated on precise dates. As a result, political innovations, such as the development of the office of prime minister or the later expectation that the prime minister become first lord of the treasury, innovations not of positive law but of new custom, could only very gradually win public acceptance and constitutional legitimacy. Consequently, any description of the present constitution, such as Blackstone's in the 1760s, was necessarily outdated in relation to current political practices. A prescriptive constitution, as George III and his people increasingly discovered, is much more an informer of the past than a guide to the present or a revealer of the future. Although the gap between constitutional theory and practice was certainly not as wide at the beginning of George III's reign as during the civil war, the space was quite sufficient to exercise the energies of satire.

From 1660 until the appearance of Andrew Marvell's *Second Advice to a Painter* in 1665, Restoration satirists granted the reconstituted monarchy a brief honeymoon, acknowledging the king's right to rule. Marvell's satire, like that of most of his contemporaries, contains the rhetoric of disappointment, not disobedience.[8] In the envoi to *Second Advice,* he chides Charles II for being ineffective:

> Imperial Prince, King of the seas and isles,
> Dear object of our joys and Heaven's smiles:
> What boots it that thy light does gild our days
> And we lie basking in thy milder rays
> While swarms of insects, from thy warmth begun,
> Our land devour and intercept our sun?   (*POAS,* p. 52)[9]

The king only implicitly shares responsibility for his ministers' actions, and his right to rule is admitted:

> Since both from Heav'n thy race and pow'r descend,
> Rule by its pattern, there to reascend:
> Let justice only draw and battle cease;
> Kings are in war but cards: they're gods in peace.   (*POAS,* p. 53)

The satirists tended to concentrate on the king's body natural, as Marvell does in *The Last Instructions to a Painter* (1667), where we find the king's love of body obscuring his love for country in the painting of the visionary woman:

> The object strange in him no terror mov'd:
> He wonder'd first, then piti'd, then he lov'd
> And with kind hand does the coy vision press
> (Whose beauty greater seem'd by her distress),
> But soon shrunk back, chill'd with her touch so cold,
> In his deep thoughts the wonder did increase,
> And he divin'd 'twas England or the Peace.   (*POAS,* p. 136)

By the end of the decade, the king's body natural had become a familiar object of attack. In *The King's Vows* (1670), about the only consistency found in Charles is his devotion to whores. Even John Dryden has to concede the satirists' point in his royalist satire *Absalom and Achitophel* (1681), which opens with a jocular reference to the monarch's status as *parens patriae,* or parent of his country (Blackstone, 3:427).[10]

Dryden is most explicit about the dichotomy between the king's two bodies halfway through the poem, when he describes "the Solymaean

Rout," "Who follow next, a double Danger bring, / Not only hating David, but the King" (511–13). They despise the man and the monarch. The poem opens with a mildly satiric treatment of the failings of David's body natural—"But since like slaves his bed they did ascend, / No True Succession could their seed attend" (15–16)—which gravely endanger the body politic—"That Kingly power, thus ebbing out, might be / Drawn to the dregs of a Democracy" (226–27). David himself recognizes that the conflict between his two bodies is partially responsible for the current threat to his regal body:

> Thus long have I, by native mercy sway'd,
> My wrongs dissembl'd, my revenge delay'd:
> So willing to forgive th' Offending Age,
> So much the Father did the King asswage.   (939–42)

In Dryden's moving the focus from Charles the man to Charles the monarch, both the poem's typological conception and its *deus ex machina* conclusion reflect the perpetuity of the king's political body. The poem's concluding verse paragraph also serves to validate Dryden's ideological position that Charles II rules *jure divino,* by divine right, and that James II's right to the throne is indefeasible, incapable of being annulled or voided by any human agent.[11] The closing couplet ends with a secular/divine pun on the proper object of allegiance/worship, underscored by the consonance of the final two words: "Once more the Godlike *David* was Restor'd, / And willing Nations knew their Lawfull Lord" (1030–31). Even Absalom recognizes the principle of indefeasibility:

> His Lawfull Issue shall the Throne ascend,
> Or the Collateral Line where that shall end.
> His Brother, though opprest with Vulgar Spight,
> Yet Dauntless and Secure of Native Right,
> Of every Royal Vertue stands possest;
> Still Dear to all the Bravest, and the Best.   (351–56)

Fortunately, in Dryden's eyes, James II's human virtues reinforce his indefeasible "Native Right" to the throne. Thus James II is the proper heir to Charles II in his bodies natural and politic. To attack his right to the throne not only questions the political wisdom of allowing him to succeed his brother but, more importantly, is a sacrilegious assault on the "Ark" of the governmental covenant between God and man represented by "Kings . . . (the Godheads Images,)." To tamper with the succession of James II in his body natural is to tamper with the body politic and ultimately to challenge the cosmic order:

Nor only Crowds, but Sanhedrins may be
Infected with this publick Lunacy:
And Share the madness of Rebellious times,
To Murther Monarchs for Imagin'd crimes.
If they may Give and Take when e'er they please,
Not Kings alone, (the Godheads Images,)
But Government it self at length must fall
To Natures state; where all have Right to all.

. . . .

All other Errors but disturb a State;
But Innovation is the Blow of Fate.
If ancient Fabricks nod, and threat to fall,
To Patch the Flaws, and Buttress up the Wall,
Thus far 'tis Duty; but here fix the Mark:
For all beyond it is to touch our Ark.
To change Foundations, cast the Frame anew,
Is work for Rebels who base Ends pursue:
At once Divine and Humane Laws controul;
And mend the Parts by ruine of the Whole.
The Tampering World is subject to this Curse,
To Physick their Disease into a worse.   (787–810)

Insofar as contemporaries believed that "there was something divine in this right [of kings to rule], and that the finger of Providence was visible in its preservation," public satires of either of the king's two bodies were highly unlikely, but in the wake of the Exclusion Crisis and the Glorious Revolution, Englishmen increasingly came to accept the monarchy to be "though a wise institution . . . clearly a human institution; and the right inherent in him no natural, but a positive right" (Blackstone, p. 202). As Dryden had feared, they had learned that "they might ruine him they could create" (*Absalom,* 65). Blackstone traces the now unquestioned right of Parliament to determine the defeasibility of regal inheritance to the Exclusion Bill (p. 203).[12] After the convenient legal fiction of James II's abdication in 1688 and Parliament's redirection of the hereditary monarchy in 1689, only a reactionary could call a future monarch what Dryden calls Charles II in *Threnodia Augustalis: A Funeral-Pindarique Poem Sacred to the Happy Memory of King Charles II* (1685): "That all forgiving King / The type of him above" (257–58).

The events of 1688–89 also showed that what man could create and undo, he could mock: William III and his supporters attempted to portray James II and his heir as corruptions of the body natural and the body politic. Of the graphic satires, most are Dutch, but one of the most comprehensive in its charges is the English *England's Memorial: Of Its Wounder-full Deliverance from French Tiranny and Popish Oppression, Performed through Allmighty Gods Infinite Goodness and Mercy. By His Highness William Henry of Nassau, the High and Mighty Prince of Orange, 1688* (fig. 1).[13] The design is organized around the central orange tree, emblem of the House of Orange since 1641 and implicitly a substitute for the royal oak associated with the House of Stuart. A new family tree has been planted in England, and the defeasibility of James II's hereditary right to the throne is iconographically represented by the orange dropping from the tree to knock the crown from his head. Louis XIV's advice to James, allegedly a proponent of absolute monarchy, to "Tread on my Stepps and be great" represents the kind of corruption of the body politic charged against the ousted king. Jesuits and Papists, supporters of absolutism, flee from the tree, crying, "Hye for France," "This is a deadly Plant," "How strong it Smells of a free Parlement," "And thats a rank poison to a Jesuits nose."

Contemporary slander labeled James a cuckold, "his" son actually that of a miller (other accounts said that the baby, smuggled in in a warming pan, was a priest's son). Corruption of the body natural implied that of the body politic. Questions about the paternity of James's son and mockery of Charles's bastard making disguised challenges to both kings' patriarchal authority. The dubious paternal claims of their mortal bodies symbolized the claims of their regal bodies.[14] If a king could not guarantee his physical offspring, how could he be trusted to perform as father of his country?

As *England's Memorial* illustrates, attacks on James II's legitimacy were often coupled with attempts to enhance William III's claims. William's partisans faced the tricky problem of diminishing James the man as much as possible while diminishing his office as little as possible. And the more generally recognized became the concept that a monarch ruled by positive rather than divine or natural right, the more available he became as an object of satire. The almost universal relief felt at the removal of James II and his replacement by William III probably accounts for contemporary satirists' failure to take full advantage of their new ideological opportunity. F. P. Lock nicely sums up the implications of the Glorious Revolution for the concept of English kingship:

> After the Revolution, it was less easy to treat the office of kingship so reverently as Dryden had been able to. The reality of the post-1688 monarchy was unglamorous, neither William nor Queen Anne (nor George I) having any taste for the theatrical pageantry that had contributed so much to the public image of the earlier Stuart courts. . . . Of much greater practical significance than the essentially symbolic aspects of monarchy was the fact that both William and Anne were forced, though with great reluctance, to take sides in party strife.[15]

Figure 1. *England's Memorial* (BMC 1186). Reproduced by permission of the Trustees of the British Museum.

The involvement of monarchs in party strife and the increasing recognition that monarchs were not divine but human creations accelerated
the development of the modern regal satire traceable through George III's
reign. With the establishment of the Crown-in-Parliament as the center of
power, attention shifted from a fear of tyranny achieved through prerogative to a fear of legal tyranny achieved through corruption. The diminution
of the monarch's status implicit in the Glorious Revolution became mark-
edly more obvious to contemporary observers with the accession of the
House of Hanover in 1714.[16] In George I (and George II), Great Britain
had a ruler who, unlike Mary and Anne, was not a descendant of James II,
not a native Briton, not an Anglican from birth, and not a native of a
constitutional monarchy. As everyone knew, the first two Georges, though
expected to govern as limited monarchs in Britain, were experienced absolute rulers in their native Hanover. And no one could ignore their being
monarchs of Britain by positive right alone. The first two Georges' intimate
involvement with party politics made their subjects less prone to accept the
political convention that the king could do no wrong and therefore wielded
authority and exerted power yet bore no responsibility for government.
Experience, however, showed that the royal prerogative to choose ministers, unrestricted in theory, was quite limited in actuality. Opponents of
the king's ministers embraced the political fiction that they attacked measures, not men, and that while the king had a right to choose his own men,
only they were responsible for the measures the government pursued.

By the end of George II's reign almost all the tactics and topics of
verbal and visual satire to be used against his grandson had already appeared on the British political stage. One such tactic questioned which
politicians as a group were most loyal to the concept of the mixed British
constitution and the heritage of the Glorious Revolution. The group of
politicians who had consolidated power as the Old Corps of Whigs by the
beginning of George III's reign had convinced the first two Georges that
the seventeenth-century party opposition between Whigs and Tories was
still in effect and that the Tories were crypto-Jacobites favoring the restoration of the House of Stuart, while the Whigs were the true friends of the
House of Hanover.[17] Henry St. John, Viscount Bolingbroke, and his Country party allies, a loose group of Hanoverian Tories and dissident Whigs,
denied that the old party labels of Tory and Whig were any longer useful
because Sir Robert Walpole had subverted the principles of the Glorious
Revolution and because many of those who now upheld true Whig principles had formerly been called Tories. The Country party in the 1720s and
1730s, so its members claimed, was a party only in the sense that it was
formed to deny the validity of party government as espoused by Walpole.
Almost all political commentators and theorists denounced the concept of

party, identifying it with factional pursuit of self-interest at the expense of national interests. Not until 1770 did Edmund Burke advocate the need for organized, or "formed," parties of rule and opposition.[18] The disfavor in which organized opposition was held prior to the 1760s led Bolingbroke and his associates to develop a "patriotic" rhetorical strategy of attacking measures, not men, while remaining loyal to the throne. In practice, of course, opponents of the early Hanoverian ministries frequently found the monarch and particular ministers to be at fault.

Most of the charges made against the early Hanoverians were indirect, accusing them of condoning, if not directing, their ministers' attempts to subvert the British constitution either by corrupting one or more of its constituent elements or by introducing a new Jacobitism or new Toryism, expressed in the allegedly absolutist tendencies of the first two Georges. For example, William Shippen was sent to the Tower of London for implying in a speech to the House of Commons on 4 December 1717 that George I intended to introduce Hanoverian absolutism into Britain. Shippen was a true Jacobite in that he supported James II's son as the proper heir to the limited monarchy of Britain, but the advocacy of absolutism that Walpolean Whigs identified with Jacobites like Shippen was turned against the ministry by its opponents. Jacobitism became an all-purpose pejorative label: politicians in power were accused of a new Jacobitism because they supported such indicators of absolutist tendencies as the standing army and septennial parliaments; politicians in opposition, including Sir Robert Walpole in 1719, were accused by the currently ruling ministry of being at least crypto-Jacobites because, in challenging the measures of the ministry, they allegedly challenged the legitimacy of the Hanoverian succession, thereby trying to reimpose James II's absolutism. Indirect attacks on George I's supposed absolutism can be found as well in Jonathan Swift's works. In *The Drapier's Letters* (1724), William Wood "is described in terms of an absolute despotic monarch, and in these passages he is clearly intended to stand as a surrogate for the king himself," and in *Gulliver's Travels*, George I is one of the examples Swift had in mind in his satire on absolutism.[19]

Compared to satires of George I, those aimed at George II were more frequent and often more direct, but the maxims that the king can do no wrong and that measures, not men, were being attacked usually restrained the satirists from being overly bold. Satires of George II may be divided into three broad and overlapping categories: George as a good king victimized by his ministers, particularly Walpole and, later, the Pelhams; George as a would-be absolute monarch; and George as a fool, particularly in his body natural.

Let us consider the last first. Tobias Smollett's description of George II, "under the name of Got-hama-baba," in *The Adventures of an Atom* (1769) summarizes many of the contemporary satirists' charges that "this emperor became a cipher":

> He was rapacious, shallow, hot-headed, and perverse; in point of understanding, just sufficient to appear in public without a slavering bib; imbued with no knowledge, illumed by no sentiment, and warmed with no affection; except a blind attachment to the worship of Fakku-basi [the white horse, emblem of Hanover], which seemed indeed to be a disease in his constitution. His heart was meanly selfish, and his disposition altogether unprincely.
>
> Of all his recreations, that which he delighted in most, was kicking.[20]

That the character traits Smollett and others identified reflected the generally held view of George II is supported by Horace Walpole. In his *Memoirs of the Last Ten Years of the Reign of George the Second,* Walpole distinguishes between the king's two bodies, but he clearly implies that the man's faults have contributed to "the diminution of Majesty":

> His faults were more the blemishes of a private man than of a King. The affection and tenderness he invariably showed to a people over whom he had unbounded rule, forbid our wondering that he used circumscribed power with moderation. Often situated in humiliating circumstances, his resentments seldom operated when the power of revenge returned. He bore the ascendant of his Ministers, who seldom were his favourites, with more patience than he suffered any encroachment on his will from his mistresses. Content to bargain for the gratification of his two predominant passions, Hanover and money, he was almost indifferent to the rest of his royal authority, provided exterior observance was not wanting; for he comforted himself if he did not perceive the diminution of Majesty, though it was notorious to all the rest of the world.[21]

Horace Walpole's summary judgment touches on the overlapping categories of George II as victim of his ministers and as would-be tyrant. Perhaps *interconnected* is a more appropriate adjective than *overlapping* because, especially before Sir Robert Walpole's fall, references to ministerial sins reflected on the creator of the ministers. Walpole allegedly corrupted the British constitution by assuming the office of prime minister, a position not recognized in constitutional theory until long after the publication of Blackstone's *Commentaries*. As prime minister, Walpole was said to undermine the independence of Parliament from the executive through the granting of places and bribery of members. This charge is illustrated in the colossal print *Idol-Worship; or, The Way to Preferment,* advertised in *The Craftsman* and published in 1740.[22] The subscribed quotation parallels George II and Henry VIII to make the king bear responsibility for his minister's actions: "And Henry the KING made unto himself a great IDOL, the likeness of which was not in Heaven above, nor in the Earth beneath; and he reared up his Head unto ye Clouds, and extended his Arm over all ye Land; His Legs also were as ye Posts of a Gate, or as an Arch stretched forth over ye Doors of all ye Publick Offices in ye Land, and whosoever went out, or whosoever came in, passed beneath, and with Idolatrous Reverence lift up their Eyes, and kissed ye Cheeks of ye Postern" ("Chronicle of the Kings," p. 51).

In 1742, just after Walpole's fall from power, the ex-minister and the king appear in double-face as coconspirators against the constitution. The reference to Cardinal Wolsey in the verses accompanying *Touch me not: or B{o}bs Defiance* again parallels George II and Henry VIII:

Behold two Patriots of our British Land,
Join'd Head to Head, instead of Hand to Hand!
When two such Noddles are laid close together,
What tempests in ye State can Shatter Either?
I and the K{in}g the haughty W{ol}sey cry'd,
And All ye Malice of his Foes defy'd;
But R{obi}n, haughtier still, (t'evade Disaster)
Cries, Touch me if you can,—and not my Ma{ste}r.[23]

The print satirizes the king, by associating him with Walpole, Wolsey, and Henry VIII, and defends him, by having Walpole assert that attacks on the minister are attacks on the king. *The Craftsman* 85 (17 February 1728) accuses Walpole of using this tactic to screen himself from accepting ministerial responsibility by directly involving the king in the making of measures as well as men.

While satirizing the king's two bodies, another print, advertised in the *Daily Post,* 26 September 1740, also accuses George II of helping Walpole corrupt British politics: "*This Day is published,* A Political Medley [i.e., a collage of various prints laid one atop another]; or The Champion loaded with his Honour's Creed, or Political Faith: Being a Curious Print, or Deceptio Visus [an optical illusion]; with the King and ——— of Diamonds, the Curse of Scotland [Walpole], the Knave of Diamonds. With a Letter to the Electors of Great Britain on the Importance of an uncorrupted Parliament" (fig. 2).

The satire on the king's body natural appears on the left, where the king partially covers the "——— of Diamonds," or Amelia Sophia Walmoden, created countess of Yarmouth on 24 March 1740 but here referred

Figure 2. "A Political Medley" (BMC 2453). Courtesy of the Library of Congress.

to as "————" because she assumes the position, though not the title, of queen. Having the king partially cover her has obvious sexual implications but also acts as a visual pun. In their relationship, she, legally a *feme sole* (i.e., single), is in practice a *feme covert* (i.e., married). She is only partially *covert,* just as she is only partially a wife and queen. Lines inscribed beneath the king refer to their illicit relationship: "Give not thy Strength unto Women, nor thy Ways to that which destroyeth Kings. Prov. 31:3." The same theme appears in *Solomon in His Glory,* a print of 19 December 1738, which shows George dallying with Madame Walmoden amidst reminders of Queen Caroline's recent death (fig. 3).

"His Political Creed," a blasphemous example of the medieval *parodia sacra* ("sacred parody") mode applied to a political context in rebusses subscribed to "a political medley" (see fig. 2), reveals that George threatens Britain's religion and constitution and thus challenges his right to rule as defender of the Protestant faith. Hence, the legitimacy of the Hanoverian dynasty, like that of Walpole's birth, is undermined:

> I believe in King George the Second, the greatest captain, and the Wisest Monarch, between heaven and earth, And in Sir Robert Walpole, his only son our Lord, who was begotten by Burwell the Attorney, born of Mrs. Walpole of Houghton accused of corruption, expelled and imprison'd he went down into Norfolk the third year he came up again, he ascended into the Administration, and sitteth at the head of the Treasury, from thence he shall pay all those who Vote as they are commanded.
>
> I believe in Horatio Walpole's treaties the Sanctity of the bishops, the Independancy of the Lords, the Integrity of the Commons, a Restitution from the guarda-coastas, and a discharge of the Public Debts Amen.
>
> N.B. Whoever would be in Office should above all things Profess this Political Faith. (see fig. 2)

Charges of complicity in corruption are summarized in the 1743 engraving *A Cheap and Easy Method of Improving English Swine's Flesh by a German Method of Feeding; Also a Proper Material for Smoaking It, Whereby in a Short Time We May Emulate, If Not Exceed Westphalia Bacon. By a Norfolk Man for the Use of the Royal Society* (fig. 4). As the subtitle indicates, the print's organizing principle is the charge that George II seeks to introduce his native German absolutism into the British constitution through the use of various forms of corruption. George, holding a whip, is the overseeing farmer who regulates the distribution of bribes and places, which are discharged and devoured by succeeding swinish supplicants of the ministerial filth distributed by Carteret, Newcastle, and Pelham. Two hogs in

Figure 3. *Solomon in His Glory* (BMC 2348). Reproduced by permission of the Trustees of the British Museum.

Figure 4. *A Cheap and Easy Method of Improving English Swine's Flesh by a German Method of Feeding* (BMC 2604). Courtesy of the Library of Congress.

the foreground bear "H-A-N-[OVE]R" rings in their noses; the number 271 on the lefthand sty refers to the members of the House of Commons who voted to maintain Hanoverian troops in British service. The constitutional implications of George II's Hanoverian obsession appear on the right, where flitches of meat representing newly created peers—Orford, Bath, Ilchester, Edgecombe, and Ombersley—are smoke-cured with the sacred texts of Britain's mixed government—"Mag[na] Char[t]er," "Habeas Corpus," and "Bill of Rights."

To his opponents, George II's obsession with his Hanoverian connection led to perhaps his most blatant abuse of power. Many agreed with James Ralph's judgment in *A Critical History of the Administration of Sir Robert Walpole. . . .* (1743) that "what we call the Opposition to the late Minister, precisely speaking, should not, perhaps, be dated farther back than the Year 1725, when the famous Treaty of Hanover was made" (p. 504). The German issue, a recurring subject in *The Craftsman* (e.g., appendix to vol. 6, no. 396, 12 February 1734), became a central issue in the 1740s, when Walpole's pacific policies were replaced by prolonged involvement in continental wars where, opponents said, George sacrificed the interests of Britain to those of Hanover. The appeal of the Hanoverian connection to satirists is easy to understand. It provoked traditional British xenophobia and fears of absolutism. The earl of Chesterfield and Edmund Waller, coauthors of *The Case of the Hanover Forces in the Pay of Great-Britain, Impartially and Freely Examined. . . .* (1743), perceive the connection as fundamentally threatening Britain's economy and body politic:

> Upon the whole, the present deplorable and melancholy Situation of Europe, the Causes to which it was owing, the constant and uniform Conduct and Considerations of all our Ministers in our foreign Affairs ever since 1714, and the present Contest whether we shall sacrifice the true Interest of this Nation and all it's [sic] remaining Substance to the little, low Interest of Hanover, for ministerial Views, conspire to make the Determination of this Question of the utmost Importance: For the Interests of this Island must, for this once, prevail; or we must submit to the Ignominy of becoming only a Money-Province to that Electorate, and rush upon the Danger of being sundered into two more opposite and irreconcileable Parties, viz. Englishmen, and Hanoverians. (p. 80)[24]

Henry Fielding makes the same points in his allegorical satire *An Attempt towards a Natural History of the Hanover Rat* (1744), which includes a direct swipe at George II: "When in a passion it [i.e., the Hanover Rat] gets on hind legs and kicks" (p. 12). Like the designer of *A Cheap and Easy Method,* Fielding blames the Hanoverian connection for the corruption of Parliament: "Whether allured by the Smell, or what other Temptation I cannot discover, they immediately fell to undermining such a solid Foundation that nothing could hurt it; and had always before served as a safe Retreat for our English Rats when exposed to any extraordinary Danger" (p. 16). The bugbear of Jacobitism was enlisted on both sides of the issue. The anonymous author of *Warning to the Whigs and the Well-Affected Tories* (1744) charges anti-Hanoverians with inciting rebellion against the House of Brunswick. In his pamphlet *The Peace-Offering: An Essay Shewing the Cession of Hanover to Be the Only Probable Means for Extinguishing the Present Rebellion, without Farther Blood-shed, and for Securing These Nations, Forever, from Rebellions and Invasions in Favour of the Pretender or his Descendants . . . To the Anonymous Author of an Apology for the Conduct of a Late Celebrated Second-Rate Minister. . . .* (1747), the pseudonymous Methuselah Whitelock suggests that the Hanoverian connection serves the Pretender's cause so well that George I himself must have been a Jacobite when he came to the throne in 1714.

Of the many engraved satires on the connection, the most striking is *The Conduct, of the two B*****rs,* published in 1749 (fig. 5). The last word of the title may be "B[rothe]rs" or "B[utche]rs," or both, because the print shows the duke of Newcastle wearing a ribbon identifying him as "Undertaker General" and his brother Henry Pelham performing an "anatomy," in which Pelham disembowels Britannia. In the foreground, the white horse, emblem of Hanover, drinks Britannia's blood. Next to the horse are limbs marked "Gibraltar" and "Cape Breton" because the Treaty of Aix-la-Chapelle returned the latter to France and the cession of the former had been considered. The German soldier on the left, pointing to the statue of a Roman emperor, implicates George II. The accompanying verses assert the corruption of the whole political system by the choice of evil ministers:

> O England how revolving is thy State!
> How few thy Blessings! how Severe thy Fate
> O destin'd Nation, to be thus betray'd
> By those, whose Duty 'tis to serve and aid!
> A griping vile degenerate Viper Brood,
> That tears thy Vitals, and exhausts thy Blood.
> A varying Kind, that no fixt Rule pursue,
> But often form their Principles anew;
> Unknowing where to lodg [*sic*] Supreme Command
> Or in the King, or Peers, or People's Hand
> Oh Albion, on these Shoulders ne'er repose
> These are thy dangerous intestine Foes.

Another anti-Hanover print, *St. James's; In October, The K{ing} at H{anover}, MDCCL* (fig. 6), appeared during George II's long visit to Hanover from 16 April to 4 November 1750. By illustrating the effects of court,

The Conduct, of the twoB*****rs.

Figure 5. *The Conduct, of the Two B******rs* (BMC 3069). Reproduced by permission of the Trustees of the British Museum.

Figure 6. *St. James's; In October* (BMC 3083). Reproduced by permission of the Trustees of the British Museum.

or high, politics on the trading and even lower classes of London, this print anticipates the subject matter of a growing number of engravings in George III's reign, when political forces outside the walls of Westminster and St. James's gained increasing recognition. To be sure, *St. James's* depicts the traditional direct dependence of a segment of the London economy on the court trade, but it also particularizes the claim that satirists had been making for a quarter-century: the Hanoverian connection was impoverishing the whole British economy and posed a threat to the British social fabric.

However, as we should expect in a context where legally the king can do no wrong, George II very often appears as a good king and a positive alternative to the evil around him or at worst as a victim of bad advice and political corruption. *The Craftsman* distinguished between good sovereigns and bad ministers on several occasions before the accession of George II (nos. 51, 60, 71, and 72), when the opposition still expected the incoming sovereign to replace Walpole. Disappointed, *The Craftsman* returned to the subject in numbers 84, 88, 305, and 445. *The Craftsman* 124 (16 November 1728), a letter parodying the bishop of London's *Pastoral Letter to the People of His Diocese,* uses a rhetorical tactic repeated in Anglo-American satires against George III—the argument that the people and the king, the bottom and the top of the political pyramid Blackstone discusses (p. 153), are natural allies against a corrupt ministry: "Many excellent Books, Pamphlets, and papers have been published . . . in Defence of the *British Constitution;* but as these Writings are, many of them, either too large or too learned for the Generality of the People, and consist of such a Chain of Reasoning as persons of common Capacity cannot easily follow and comprehend; I have thought it incumbent upon me to draw up, for your Use, Means to preserve every sincere Lover of his *King* and his *Country* from these dangerous Infections."

The idea of the king as the people's ally recurs in a 1733 print, *Britannia Excisa. Part 2,* which includes another rhetorical tactic employed increasingly after 1760—the combination, in a satire, of appeal and threat directed at the sovereign.[25] The appeal occurs in the verse of *Britannia Excisa:*

> 20. Our GEORGE, for his Fame sake,
> Will behave like his Name-sake,
> He came over this Dragon to quell;
> Set firm on his Steed
> Of true English Breed,
> He'll drive all such Monsters to Hell.

The engravings strongly suggest that should George not quell the "Dragon of Excise," his fate will parallel those of Walpole overturned in his coach and his regal predecessor Charles I. To verbally point his visual threat, the satirist says, in *Excise Congress,* that Hanoverian George, unlike his namesake, is an ally of the dragon:

17. Saint GEORGE as they say,
    The DRAGON did slay,
    But our Kn[igh]t both older and wiser,
    To keep us all Quiet,
    Prescribes a Low DIET,
    And lets loose the fell Dragon, EXCISE, Sir.

Because, in Blackstone's words, "with regard to foreign concerns, the king is the delegate or representative of his people" (p. 245) in times of great external threat, George II often received unqualified praise. A good example is the 1745 engraving *The Rebellion Displayed. Most Humbly Inscribed to His Sacred Majesty King George* (fig. 7), which opposes Stuart absolutism to Hanoverian constitutionalism. On the left, we see James II seated upon the throne of "Hereditary right." Underfoot is "Magna Charta." He greets a monk, who steps on "the Holy Bible." In contrast, on the right, we find a temple of liberty founded by the House of Hanover. The sword of divine justice threatens the absolutists.

George II could also be praised for what the satirists considered a significant domestic victory, as in the 1756 engraving *Optimus, Britons Behold the Best of Kings* (fig. 8), which celebrates the dismissal of the Newcastle administration. Beneath the laureated George II's profile, we read:

Beloved by the bravest of People,
Justly admired by all,
By his Enemies Dreaded,
May he live long and happy.
No Evil and Corrupt Ministers
Dare to Approach his Sacred presence;
Let none but such as Imitate his Virtues
have any power.
Then shall Britannia be Blest for Ever.

But such victories over his evil ministers were quite rare until the last five years of George II's reign. The far more common tradition of seeing British monarchs as misled or controlled by their ministers is illustrated in *The Tale of the Robbin, and the Tom-Titt, Who All the Birds in the Air Have Bitt,* a woodcut on a broadside published in the late 1720s (BMC 1839). The subscribed beast fable traces the development of ministerial power from the Protectorate down to contemporary times, when the reigning "Eagle" (George II) has "turn'd Tommy-Titt [Charles Townshend?] out" but has

Figure 7. *The Rebellion Displayed* (BMC 2662). Reproduced by permission of the Trustees of the British Museum.

Figure 8. *Optimus* (BMC 3537). Reproduced by permission of the Trustees of the British Museum.

left "Robbin" (Walpole) in place. The poem ends with a conventional plea for regal independence from evil ministers: "O! let us no more, such times see again; / But pray for the Eagle, with his Feathered Train."

The Craftsman 206 (13 June 1730) illustrates Walpole's alleged usurpation with an ironic gloss on an engraving, *To the Glory of the Rt. Honble. Sr. Robert Walpole* (fig. 9), published about a month earlier. The print shows, surmounting the arches, "A. Great Britt[ania]. alluding to ye Motto of G. R. W. [Sir Robert Walpole's] Arms. He procures me all the advantages wch he Speaks & thinks." Minerva offers Walpole a ducal coronet as she helps him to mount the rock. "W[al]polius" tells *The Craftsman,*

> I am inform'd that, in the first Draught of this Piece, the Figure of his Majesty King *George* supply'd the Place of Britannia; but that the *Authors* were prevail'd upon to alter it as it stands at present, lest the Appearance of the *Prince* should eclipse the *Glory* of the *Minister;* for though Cardinal *Wolsey* was modestly contented with only placing Himself *before his Master;* yet it is certainly more glorious for a *Minister* to appear *singly* in a Panegyrick, without any visible *Dependance,* or *Support;* and instead of writing, as the *Cardinal* did, *Ego & Rex meus;* I and my King; it would run much better thus; *Ego sine Rege meo;* I by myself, I.

Opposition satires liken the perverted paradigm of a king who rules his minister to analogous perversions of the king-queen, husband-wife, and man-mistress paradigms. *The Craftsman* 499 (24 January 1736), under cover of discussing Spain, implies that Britain, too, has a "petticoat government," whereby the queen and evil prime minister rule the king. Until her death in 1737, Queen Caroline was frequently said to be the means Walpole used to rule the king and thus the nation. *The Craftsman* 376 (15 September 1733) and 456 (2 March 1735) are but two examples of this idea.[26]

The relationship among Caroline, Walpole, and George is depicted in *The Festival of the Golden Rump,* "Design'd by the Author of Common Sense" (fig. 10), published in 1737. The 19 March issue of *Common Sense* explicates the design. To our right of the idol (George II) stands the "TAPANTA" (Caroline), who controls the kicking behavior of the satyr-idol by administering timely enemas of "*Aurum potabile* [drinkable gold]." On our left of the idol is "the CHIEF MAGICIAN, or VICAR-GENERAL" (Walpole), whose cassock has "embroidered these Words in Gold Characters: AURI SACRA FAMES [*Aeneid* 3:57, "O sacred hunger of pernicious gold," in Dryden's translation]." Around the idol gather worshipping clergymen and peers wearing the insignia of the golden rump. For the meaning of the inscription on the altar, *Common Sense* directs us to Charles Cotton's translation

Figure 9. *To the Glory of the Rt. Honble. Sr. Robert Walpole* (BMC 1832).
Reproduced by permission of the Trustees of the Pierpont Morgan Library.

Figure 10. *The Festival of the Golden Rump* (BMC 2327). Reproduced by permission of the Trustees of the British Museum.

of Virgil's *Aeneid* 1:85 in *Scarronides: or, Virgile Travestie* (London, 1664), where Aeolus responds with flatulence to Juno's request for wind: "He let at once his General Muster / Of all that ere could blow, or bluster" (p. 14).

After her death, satirists replaced Caroline as intermediary between minister and monarch with Lady Walmoden, a woman who had even less right to rule a man, husband, or king. In the 1740 print *Bob's the Whole* (fig. 11), the moral corruption of the king's body natural is the subject of this tripartite design's first section. George II, Walpole, and Lady Walmoden appear, the last holding in one hand a Yarmouth herring (George created her countess of Yarmouth on 24 March 1740). The herring's mouth holds the label "landed on horn Fair day," which refers to the horns she presented her husband when she became George's mistress. George stands behind her, his hat in his mouth alluding to his habit of kicking. Before him, a drapery displays the names of the nine German electorates. George, seeking to keep the connection secret, tries to conceal the name "Hanover." The blasphemous rebus-parody of the Athanasian Creed beneath the design professes belief in the trinity of the king, his mistress, and his minister:

> And the political Faith is this; that we serve and obey one Monarch in a triple Conjunction. NEITHER confounding the Conjunction tripartite; nor dividing the Persons in Triplicity. For there is one Body of the Monarch, another of the prime minister, and another of the Countess of Yarmouth. But the Interest of the Monarch, of the minister, and of the Countess is all One: Their Pride equal, and their Honour coeval. SUCH as the Monarch is, such is the minister, and such is the Countess . . . THE Monarch corrupted, the minister corrupted, and the Countess corrupted. AND yet they are not only Three corrupted; But one Body corporate corrupted.

The title of the 1742 engraving *Magna Farta or the Raree Show at St. J{ames'}s* (fig. 12) indicates the irreverence with which the king's body natural could be treated. George exposes himself at a window in the palace; a document marked "Magna farta" is to be used for toilet paper. Below the king, the raree-show satirizes the ministry for opportunism and the opposition for hypocrisy. In the 1743 print *The Court Fright* (fig. 13), physicians bleed the king's body while Britannia, crying "Alas I'm Weak," languishes at his feet. His ministers Newcastle and Carteret confess to incompetence, as the crudely caricatured George exclaims, "Bon Dieu! Est il possible? [Good God! Is it possible?]." Among the surrounding icons, two link *The Court Fright* with prints discussed earlier. On the wall behind the physicians, a picture of a spaniel swimming toward a woman, entitled "Promotion," suggests that fawning on Lady Walmoden is the way to get ahead at

Figure 11. *Bob's the Whole* (BMC 2464). Reproduced by permission of the Trustees of the British Museum.

Figure 12. *Magna Farta or the Raree Show at St. J{ames'}s* (BMC 2575).
Reproduced by permission of the Trustees of the British Museum.

Figure 13. *The Court Fright* (BMC 2606). Reproduced by permission of the Trustees of the British Museum.

court. At the right, the Hanoverian horse, a map of Britain on its back, tramples a fallen "Bankrupt" to express the Hanoverian connection's effects on trade. The most scatological print attacking George and his ministers is the 1744 *A Very Extraordinary Motion,* in which a possibly caricatured George excretes the former minister Lord Hobart, while Newcastle and Pelham prepare to force Sir John Hynde Cotton down his throat, thereby illustrating the repeated charge that the king had relinquished his prerogative to choose his own ministers by allowing others to "storm his closet," that is, compel him to accept unwanted subordinates. Future ministers lie on a table, awaiting their turns to be processed through the king's body.[27]

The conflation of the king's two bodies is an element of several prints about the "king in toils," or at the mercy of his ministers. One is the 1755 *A Goose of Old Did Save a State* (fig. 14), in which the king's bodies natural and politic combine in the image of the British lion to show that diminishing Newcastle's power (the goose) reconciles the monarch's personal interest (the Hanoverian horse) and the national interest (promoted by Henry Fox). The point is explicit in the accompanying verse:

A Goose of Old did save a State
It was not so with Goose of late
For Passive Goose, let Foes deride
And Factious Partys did divide
But now since F[ox] has chang'd ye Scene
And Goose Inactive now is Seen
We hope true Courage will advance
And once more Crush ye Pride of France.

With the loss of Minorca in 1756, however, the hopes expressed in *A Goose of Old* were at least temporarily frustrated, and when George II again appears as the national lion, in *Britannia's Revival, or The Rousing of the British Lyon* (fig. 15) of 1756, the lion is asleep. We see, her genius weeping beside her, a despairing and defeated Britannia. She rejects a written address from the courtiers who have enchained the dormant British lion. Instead, she accepts London's address requesting an investigation of the loss of Minorca and calling for a militia. French ships blockade English vessels in port. The designer of *Britannia's Revival* visualizes the relationship between monarch and ministers that many observers and even the king himself believed accurately described the constitution's corrupt state, dating at least to George II's "forced" dismissal of Walpole in 1742. From George's Hanoverian perspective, his prerogative *was* restricted; from a British perspective, however, he remained very much the chief executive of a personal monarchy. The earl of Hardwicke's notes of his audience with

Figure 14. *A Goose of Old* (BMC 3330). Reproduced by permission of the Trustees of the British Museum.

Figure 15. *Britannia's Revival, or The Rousing of the British Lyon* (BMC 3377). Reproduced by permission of the Trustees of the British Museum.

Figure 16. *The Downfall* (BMC 3480). Reproduced by permission of the Trustees of the British Museum.

the king on 5 January 1745, in which they discussed the "forced" dismissal of Carteret the previous November, relay the king's sentiments:

> *K*[ing]: I have done all you ask'd of me. I have put all power into your hands and I suppose you will make the most of it.
>
> *Ch*[Lord Chancellor Hardwicke]: The disposition of places is not enough, if your Majesty takes pains to shew the world that you disapprove of your own work.
>
> *K: My work!* I was forc'd: I was threatened.
>
> . . . .
>
> *Ch:* . . . Your Ministers, Sir, are only your instruments of Government.
>
> *K:* (smiles) Ministers are the Kings in this Country.[28]

The Downfall as It Will Shortly Be Performed, to the Tune of M{urra}ys Delight (fig. 16), a 1756 engraving, expresses the wishful thinking that the king and consequently the nation will be able to throw off ministerial shackles. The blank space in the title invites the reader to see that the tune of "M{urra}ys Delight" and the theme of "M{ajest}ys Delight" are interchangeable. In the print, the British lion kicks Henry Fox, Hardwicke, and Newcastle off his back into "the Bottomless PITT," representing the soon fulfilled expectation that William Pitt would enter the administration. The lion exclaims, "All three!—All three!—All three! And so my old Boys off you go by Jupiter, and the next time you catch me carrying Treble, spit in my face and call me Ass."

The Mirrour: or The British Lion's Back Friends Detected (fig. 17), a 1756 print, celebrates the short-lived defeat of the Newcastle ministry. Here the fetters on George, the British lion, are broken, but as the radical Tory publication, *The Monitor,* shows him in a mirror, Fox, Hardwicke, Lord Anson (the sea lion), and Newcastle (an old woman) are ready to fetter him once again: "Look in this Glass, you'll see your back friends have forged a strong Iron Chain to enslave you! Beware of them. Hear the groans of the People and Redress them Punish the guilty—discard—the Luxurious, the Avaricious, the Gamester &c." The lion's speech is that of a "Patriot King" who places his people's interests above his ministers': "The good People of England have always had the first place in my Paternal affection & Esteem: I am now convinced by their numerous Addresses and Remonstrances that their complaints are not groundless; there shall be a speedy Enquiry and the injured Nation shall be redressed of all the grievances complain'd of, occasioned by bad M[ini]st[eria]l measures; delinquents in high Stations shan't escape punishment, tho' from a sence of conscious fault they want to resign, yet be assured the guilty shant escape with impunity."[29] The subscribed verses celebrate the same theme of regal authority restored:

Figure 17. *The Mirrour: or The British Lion's Back Friends Detected* (BMC 3487). Reproduced by permission of the Trustees of the British Museum.

The Lion, Type of royal Power Behold!
(No longer by insidious Wiles controll'd)
Attentive hears the Pleas of patriot Zeal,
Assures Redress and ev'ry Wound to heal;
His Eye regards with a vindictive Ray,
Men rais'd to save, but studious to betray:
A Monitor, in faithful Mirrour shews
Who are the truest Friends, the basest Foes,
Discovers Chains for royal Hands design'd,
And Councils to misguide, and mists to blind;
Shews the false Daw in Patriot feathers drest,
While keen Resentment fires each zealous Breast,
But ev'ry Art of treach'rous Men shall fail
No Stone uplifted for our Hurt avail.
Britain shall ever great and Free remain,
And all her ravish'd Honours soon regain.

Fox and Newcastle's inability to form a stable ministry in 1757 without Pitt is the subject of *The Present Managers* (fig. 18), which shows a prostrate British lion–George crying, "I am Vastly like a Horse, Methinks Neighing is better than Roaring—O my head." Fox, as if illustrating Hardwicke's response to George II (in the conversation cited above) that "Ministers are the Kings in this Country" only "if one person is permitted to engross the ear of the Crown and invest himself with all its power," pours into the king's ear a "Nostrum to Distemper the Brain." Fox exults, "Why now my Golden Dream is out. Pell Mell I have them now. O they shall be Paid while I am Master. Now for a Ready Scribe who Through any Dirt holds out with me untir'd. None are for me that will pry into my Deeds with thinking Eyes." The political uncertainty this print reflects was soon replaced by the stability of the Newcastle-Pitt ministry of 1757–61, which combined regal support for the Old Corps Whigs with the Great Commoner's popular support. The coalition's political strength, reinforced by the military successes of 1759, Britain's *annus mirabilis,* enabled George II to end his reign at the peak of his people's esteem.[30]

In the century between the Restoration and George III's accession, Great Britain developed a tradition of royal satire paralleling the growth of a recognized opposition loyal to the premise of monarchy. The most important historical event in this tradition's development was the Glorious Revolution of 1688, arguably a more thoroughgoing counterrevolution than the Restoration itself. The events of 1688–89 better enabled satirists to exploit the separation of the king's two bodies by more firmly establishing the king's right to power as positive rather than divine in origin. The House of Hanover's succession in 1714 accelerated the satiric tradition's de-

Figure 18. *The Present Managers* (BMC 3589). Reproduced by permission of the Trustees of the British Museum.

velopment, as contemporaries watched kingship grow less mysterious and less sanctified due to political realities and the characters of the Hanoverians, particularly George II, whose moral faults in his body natural were convenient analogues to increasingly obvious flaws in the body politic. When George III came to the throne in 1760, he confronted at once a tradition of royal satire ready for use and unusually high expectations created by his own personal qualities and the nation's recent and unprecedented military success.

Chapter 2

"The Royal Dupe"

Whoever, or whatever is sovereign, demands the respect and
support of the people.
  —John Horne [Tooke] to Junius, 31 July 1771

When George III succeeded George II on 25 October 1760, he began his
reign at the age of twenty-two and amidst great anticipation. As Horace
Walpole observes in his *Memoirs of the Reign of King George the Third*:

> No British monarch has ascended the throne with so many advan-
> tages as George the Third. Being the first of his line born in England,
> the prejudice against his family as foreigners ceased in his person.
> Hanover was no longer the native soil of our Princes; consequently,
> attachment to the Electorate was not likely to govern our councils,
> as it had done in the last two reigns. This circumstance, too, of his
> birth, shifted the unpopularity of foreign extraction from the House
> of Brunswick to the Stuarts. In the flower and bloom of youth, George
> had a handsome, open, and honest countenance; and with the favour
> that attends the outward accomplishments of his age, he had none of
> the vices that fall under the censure of those who are past enjoying
> them themselves.
>
> The moment of his accession was fortunate beyond example. The
> extinction of parties had not waited for, but preceded, the dawn of
> his reign.[1]

In his person, the new king promised a striking contrast to his boorish
predecessor. He was expected to inaugurate a reign of politeness because,
when he came to the throne, "it was already well known that he was a lover
of art, music, and literature."[2] His new subjects had already seen him as
an exemplar of grace and taste in a later version of Hogarth's *Analysis of
Beauty, Plate 2* (fig. 19), which the artist had probably altered to celebrate
the Prince of Wales's coming of age on 4 June 1756. In his design *Frontispiece to the Artists Catalogue, 1761* (fig. 20), engraved by Charles Grignion,
Hogarth expresses the widespread hope for a cultural renaissance under
the new king, whose royal fountain sustains the arts.[3]

Figure 19. William Hogarth, *Analysis of Beauty, Plate 2* (BMC 3226).
Reproduced by permission of the Trustees of the British Museum.

FRONTISPIECE TO THE ARTISTS CATALOGUE 1761.

Published by Longman, Hurst, Rees, & Orme, March 1, 1807.

Figure 20. Hogarth, *Frontispiece to the Artists Catalogue, 1761* (BMC 3808).
Reproduced by permission of the Trustees of the British Museum.

To Horace Walpole's contemporaries such a renaissance appeared possible because Britain's constitutional monarchy seemed more secure against internal and external threats than at any time since the Restoration in 1660. As the 1760 engraving *Long Live His Most Excellent Britannic Majesty King George the Third, or Down with the Devil, Pope, French King and Pretender* (fig. 21) illustrates, the abortive rebellion of 1745 had eradicated the Jacobite and popish threats, and France was losing the Seven Years' War (known in America as the French and Indian Wars).[4] George III inherited from his grandfather a wartime administration that combined the talents of the "Great Commoner," William Pitt, with those of the duke of Newcastle, leader of the Old Corps of Whigs that had administered Britain since 1714.

George's subjects who had been dissatisfied with the system of court Whiggery or the personality of his grandfather hoped that the new king would restore the "royal dignity," tarnished under George II, by separating himself from bickering political factions and becoming a "Patriot King." Horace Walpole predicted to Sir Horace Mann (27 January 1761) that "services will be pretensions in this reign."[5] The concept of a patriot king had gained widespread currency in 1749 with the publication of Bolingbroke's *Idea of a Patriot King,* dedicated to George's father, Frederick, Prince of Wales (1707–51). The model of the patriot king had influenced the rhetorical pronouncements of the opposition to Walpole since about 1738, when Bolingbroke's political allies began to circulate his manuscript among themselves. Central to Bolingbroke's idea are beliefs in the "royal dignity" and "the king's two bodies." To become a patriot king, a monarch must extricate himself and his office from the clutches of self-interested ministers.[6] Only such a king, Bolingbroke asserts, can command the "royal dignity" fundamental to Blackstone's description of a successful monarchy:

> First, then, of the royal dignity. Under every monarchical establishment, it is necessary to distinguish the prince from his subjects, not only by the outward pomp and decorations of majesty, but also by ascribing to him certain qualities, as inherent in his royal capacity, distinct from and superior to those of any other individual in the nation. For, though a philosophical mind will consider the royal person merely as one man appointed by mutual consent to preside over many others, and will pay him that reverence and duty which the principles of society demand, yet the mass of mankind will be apt to grow insolent and refractory, if taught to consider their prince as a man of no greater perfection than themselves. The law therefore ascribes to the king, in his high political character, not only large powers and emoluments, which form his prerogative and revenue, but likewise certain attributes of great and transcendent nature; by which the people are

Figure 21. *Long Live His Most Excellent Britannic Majesty King George the Third, or Down with the Devil, Pope, French King and Pretender* (BMC 3732). Reproduced by permission of the Trustees of the British Museum.

led to consider him in the light of a superior being, and to pay him that awful respect, which may enable him with greater ease to carry on the business of government. (Blackstone, p. 234)

Even the self-styled republican Thomas Hollis hoped that the new king would reassert the "royal dignity" by exercising his prerogative to choose ministers who would pursue popular measures to serve the nation rather than merely themselves.[7] Hollis's desire that George III, as the king's apologists had promised, would indeed dismantle the political machine of the Old Corps Whigs was shared by Hollis's acquaintance Samuel Johnson, who wrote to Guiseppe Baretti in Italy, in June 1761, "You know that we have a new King. . . . We were so weary of our old King that we are much pleased with his successor; of whom we are so much inclined to hope great things, that most of us begin already to believe them."[8] William Hogarth, Robert Lloyd, Sir Joshua Reynolds, and Horace Walpole expressed similar wishes for a patriot king who would rise above political factionalism to appoint ministers on the basis of merit alone, and by 1760 the professed desire for such a figure had become a commonplace in political discourse. One suspects, however, that at least some of those calling for such a ruler knew that, given the realities of eighteenth-century politics, George III could not be so benignly disinterested a ruler and that, consequently, George or any other monarch could be attacked for failing to measure up to the unattainable ideal. Because patriot princes were restricted to visionary realms, we find the image of the patriot king most fully developed in the third book of Charles Churchill's *Gotham* (1764), where the poet imagines himself in the role that he implies George III fails to play:

> A PATRIOT KING—Why 'tis a name which bears
> The more immediate stamp of Heav'n, which wears
> The nearest, best resemblance we can shew
> Of God above, thro' all his works below.
>
> To still the voice of discord in the land,
> To make weak faction's discontented band,
> Detected, weak, and crumbling to decay,
> With hunger pinch'd, on their own vitals prey;
> Like brethren, in the self-same int'rests warm'd,
> Like diff'rent bodies, with one soul inform'd,
> To make a nation, nobly rais'd above
> All meaner thoughts, grow up in common love;
> To give the laws due vigour, and to hold
> That sacred ballance, temperate, yet bold,

With such an equal hand, that those who fear
May yet approve, and own my justice clear;
To be a Common Father, to secure
The weak from violence, from pride the poor;
Vice, and her sons, to banish in disgrace,
To make Corruption dread to shew her face,
To bid afflicted Virtue take new state,
And be, at last, acquainted with the great;
Of all Religions to elect the best,
Nor let her priests be made a standing jest;
Rewards for Worth, with lib'ral hand to carve,
To love the Arts, nor let the Artists starve;
To make fair Plenty through the realm increase,
Give Fame in War, and happiness in Peace,
To see my people virtuous, great and free,
And know that all those blessings flow from me,
O 'tis a joy too exquisite, a thought
Which flatters Nature more than flatt'ry ought.
'Tis a great, glorious task, for Man too hard,
But not less great, less glorious the reward,
The best reward which here to Man is giv'n,
'Tis more than Earth, and little short of Heav'n;
A task (if such comparison may be)
The same in nature, diff'ring in degree,
Like that which God, on whom for aid I call,
Performs with ease, and yet performs to all.   (63–102)[9]

Such a monarch was needed to correct a perceived imbalance in the
state. Many of George III's subjects believed in 1760 that the major threat
to the balanced constitution was the aristocracy, not the king, and that the
monarch was the natural ally of the people in the struggle to avoid what
Edmund Burke dismisses, in *Thoughts on the Cause of the Present Discontents*
(1770), as "a phantom of tyranny in the nobles" (p. 269). The prediction
of *The Craftsman* 304 (29 April 1732)—that the current trend of acquisition of power and property by a small minority of Whig lords would
lead to oligarchic government—seemed perilously close to realization. On
9 November 1762, for example, Horace Walpole told Sir Horace Mann
that he hoped "the Crown can reduce the exorbitance of the peers." [10]

On 16 October 1762, the radical weekly *The Monitor, or British Free-
holder* observed "that very dangerous innovations have been introduced,
that the just balance of power in the British constitution is destroyed, that
the free popular system, has been compelled to yield almost to the Aristo-

cratical, is evident to any one, who reflects but a moment on the nature of our government, what a House of Commons was in its original institution, and what it is in its present state." *The Monitor* implies that history enables us to predict the results of oligarchic government:

> From a very small knowledge of the history of our own kingdom, we may learn what desolation and distress, the power and pride of the old barons, brought upon this country, during the contest of the houses of York and Lancaster, as well as before that period. Full of their own importance, big with ambition, how have they presumed to alter, and reform, make and unmake kings at will: while the unhappy people, labouring under the oppression of feudal tenures, were too often compelled to take a part, and abet the lawless pretensions of their haughty rulers.

For Oliver Goldsmith, in *The Traveller, or A Prospect of Society* (1764), the king is clearly the counterbalance to the power of the nobles:

> Calm is my soul nor apt to rise in arms,
> Except when fast-approaching danger warms;
> But when contending chiefs blockade the throne,
> Contracting regal power to stretch their own;
> When I behold a factious band agree
> To call it freedom, when themselves are free;
> Each wanton judge new penal statutes draw,
> Laws grind the poor and rich men rule the law;
> The wealth of climes, where savage nations roam,
> Pillaged from slaves to purchase slaves at home;
> Fear, pity, justice, indignation start,
> Tear off reserve and bare my swelling heart;
> Till half a patriot, half a coward grown,
> I fly from petty tyrants to the throne.   (379–92)

Charles Churchill, too, preferred the power of the throne to that of the aristocracy, even though when he wrote the following lines of *The Farewell* in 1764 he had become quite disillusioned by the present king:

> Let not a Mob of Tyrants seize the helm,
> Nor titled upstarts league to rob the realm,
> Let not, whatever other ills assail,
> A damned ARISTOCRACY prevail.
> If, all too short, our course of Freedom run,
> 'Tis thy ["God above"] good pleasure we should be undone,
> Let us, some comfort in our griefs to bring,
> Be slaves to one, and be that one a King.   (361–68)

But who were the "people" whose virtual representative the king was to be when the corrupt influence of the Old Corps Whig aristocracy ruled the House of Commons? As Johnson reminds us, in a general sense "the people is a very heterogeneous and confused mass of the wealthy and the poor, the wise and the foolish, the good and the bad" (10:393). But in political discourse, particularly that of a conservative cast, *people* commonly had a narrower meaning to differentiate its constituents from those of the *mob,* whose lack of a material investment in society caused mobility and volatility. One widely acceptable political definition of the people appears in Goldsmith's *Vicar of Wakefield* (1766):

> But there must still be a large number of the people without the sphere of the opulent man's influence, namely, that order of men which subsists between the very rich and the very rabble; those men who are possest of too large fortunes to submit to the neighbouring man in power, and yet are too poor to set up for tyranny themselves. In this middle order of mankind are generally to be found all the arts, wisdom, and virtues of society. This order alone is known to be the true preserver of freedom, and may be called the people. . . . In such a state . . . all that the middle class has left, is to preserve the prerogative and privileges of the one principal governor with the most sacred circumspection. For he divides the power of the rich, and calls off the great from falling with tenfold weight on the middle order placed beneath them. . . . What they may then expect [should his power be diminished], may be seen by turning our eyes to Holland, Genoa, or Venice, where the laws govern the poor, and the rich govern the law. I am then for, and would die for, monarchy, sacred monarchy; for if there be any thing sacred amongst men, it must be the anointed sovereign of his people, and every diminution of his power in war, or in peace, is an infringement upon the real liberties of the subject. (4:99–103)

Samuel Johnson criticized the first two Georges for isolating themselves from the "middle order of mankind," and in his *Thoughts on the Coronation* (1761) he hopes that George III will establish a closer bond between himself and the people.

The people were a middle state between the "tyranny in the nobles" and "the horrors of mob-government" (Burke, *Thoughts,* p. 269). No significant sentiment existed for universal suffrage or even adult male suffrage; the king's most vehement opponents acknowledged the danger of the mob, who had no financial or social investment in the stability of the state and therefore lacked political *independence,* as contemporaries usually understood the term. Twice in *Common Sense* (1776), even the radical Thomas Paine warns of the dangers of the mob:

If we omit it [forming "a constitution of our own in a cool deliberate manner"] now, some Massenello may hereafter arise, who laying hold of popular disquietudes, may collect together the desperate and the discontented, and by assuming to themselves the powers of government, may sweep away the liberties of the continent like a deluge. . . . We ought to reflect, that there are three different ways, by which an independancy may hereafter be effected; and that one of those three, will one or other, be the fate of America, viz. By the legal voice of the people in Congress; by a military power; or by a mob. (pp. 41, 59)

The conservative, prominsterial *Briton* of 11 September 1762 distinguishes between "the people" and those who would constitute a "mob-ruled commonwealth." For the Country Tory Smollett, political power should be reserved for those who own property and thus have a vested interest in a stable society:

As these Reformers have, upon all occasions, assumed the title of free-born Englishmen, and denominated themselves the good people of England; it will not be amiss to enquire who the individuals are that compose this respectable community. Are they persons of wealth, property, or credit?—No.——Have they distinguished themselves as valuable members of the commonwealth, by their industry, probity, or learning?—No such matter.——Do they contribute to the necessities of the public, or of the poor, by paying scot or lot, King's-tax, or parish-tax?—Not a farthing. They reverence no King: they submit to no law: they belong to no parish. Have they a right to give their voice in any sort of election, or their advice in any assembly of the people? They have no such right established by law; and therefore they deduce a right from nature, inconsistent with all law, incompatible with every form of government. They consist of that class which our neighbours distinguish by the name of Canaille, forlorn Grubs and Garetteers, desperate gamblers, tradesmen thrice bankrupt, prentices to journeymen, understrappers to porters, hungry pettifoggers, bailiff-followers, discarded draymen, hostlers out of place, and felons returned from transportation. These are the people who proclaim themselves free-born Englishmen, and transported with a laudable spirit of patriotism, insist upon having a spoke in the wheel of government, who distribute infamy among the great; calumniate their S[overeig]n, asperse his family, condemn his ministers, criticise his conduct, and publicly declaim upon politics, in coffee houses, ale-houses, in cellars, stalls, in prisons, and the public streets. And indeed, if we reflect, that this division of the species among us, are neither electing nor elected, neither representing nor represented in any national, provincial, municipal or parochial assembly: it is proper they should enjoy some extraordinary privilege to ascertain their title of free-born Englishmen.

The last truly personal monarch who fully ruled as well as reigned, George was not about to play the part of an idealized patriot king, standing aloof from practical politics as head of state and intervening on the side of the people only in extraordinary circumstances. As a result, settlement of the dynastic question, which had appeared to be cause for celebration in 1760, quickly became George's curse. Attention shifted from concern about the throne's rightful heir to greater scrutiny of the office itself. Britons now had the security needed to examine more closely the premise of monarchy. And where discontents were found, causes were sought. However, if the king could do no wrong, someone less obvious must be to blame; the stage was set for the politics of paranoia to enter.

Expectations that George III would be all things to all men were bound to be disappointed. The political honeymoon between George III and the satirists was remarkably brief, and its brevity was largely unavoidable, as Johnson had predicted in his letter to Baretti cited above: "The young man is hitherto blameless; but it would be unreasonable to expect much from the immaturity of juvenile years, and the ignorance of princely education. He has been long in the hands of the Scots, and has alredy favoured them more than the English will contentedly endure. But perhaps he scarcely knows whom he has distinguished, or whom he has disgusted." [11]

Unfortunately, as Johnson recognized, George III was an innocent who seemed to believe that the British constitution operated in practice just as in Blackstone's description of its underlying theory. [12] The consensus reached by twentieth-century historians about George's character mirrors the view most of his subjects had come to accept by the end of his reign:

> What emerges, then, from the recent biographical writing, is a portrait of a shrewd, cultivated, well-meaning, honest individual; conventional and conservative in outlook, even stubbornly prejudiced, and yet with a strong streak of intellectual curiosity; no scholar himself but honouring scholarship in others; widely read and able to discuss his reading intelligently; well-informed about the history and the constitutional law of his country; sincere in his religious beliefs, and with a strong moral sense; a man dedicated to the duties of the monarchy to which he had been born. [13]

Acting on his belief that politicians were sincere when they said the king's prerogative included free choice of his own ministers, George III almost immediately antagonized the Old Corps of Whigs by going outside their ranks to choose ministers. When the king's preference for his former

tutor, the Scotsman John Stuart, earl of Bute, became clear, Pitt and Newcastle both felt compelled to resign from the ministry, respectively, in
October 1761 and in May 1762. By choosing Bute, George III squandered
much of the political capital with which he had begun his reign. From a
political perspective, the elevation of Bute in May 1762 to first lord of the
treasury, in effect prime minister, was disastrous. Unlike Pitt, Bute had no
popular support; unlike Newcastle, Bute had no parliamentary support.
All he had was the king's support. To Burke, Bute lacked "the *two only
securities for the importance of the people; power arising from popularity; and power
arising from connexion*" (*Thoughts,* p. 264; Burke's italics). The attacks on
Bute were swift and unrelenting, as Horace Walpole indicated to Sir Horace
Mann (20 June 1762): "The new administration begins tempestuously. My
father [Sir Robert Walpole] was not more abused after twenty years than
Lord Bute is in twenty days. Weekly papers swarm, and like other swarms
of insects, sting." A month later (31 July 1762) he added, "Parallels, you
know, are the food of all party writings: we have Queen Isabel and Mortimer, Queen Margaret and the Duke of Suffolk, every week. You will allow
that abuse does not set out tamely, when it even begins with the King's
mother." [14]

As Walpole's comments indicate, important differences existed between the satiric campaign against Bute and earlier attacks on Sir Robert
Walpole.[15] In large part, these differences were linked to changes in the
media and electorate in the twenty years between the two ministries.
Samuel Johnson's view of the state of national political awareness given in
his "Observations on the Present State of Affairs" (1756) is at once descrip-
tive and normative: "The time is now come in which every Englishman
expects to be informed of the national affairs, and in which he has a right to
have that expectation gratified" (10:185). The means for such gratification
were at hand: "In 1760 London had four dailies, and five or six tri-weekly
evening papers which were circulated in the country on the three main post
days; in all there were eighty-nine papers paying advertising revenue in the
metropolis." Besides the newspapers, the growing number of weekly and
monthly periodicals that appeared after 1731 exposed citizens to politics.
These periodicals often reproduced in whole or in part previously published political pamphlets as well as excerpts from newspapers and other
periodicals. There also existed "the publishers' twilight zone of printed
ephemera—squibs, handbills, songs, affiches"—and, of course, political
cartoons.[16]

By 1760, formal verse satire had been tarnished by its identification
with politics during the 1730s and 1740s. At the same time, developments
in historiography and iconography encouraged the rise of verbal and visual
caricatures, which were well on their way to becoming the dominant form

of political satire in Britain. They served as a political *biblia pauperum*, familiarizing the populace with the actors on the political stage. Especially for most Londoners, satiric engraving served a purpose analogous to state portraiture on a higher level. Ample evidence exists to show that political engravings brought politics out of Parliament and into the streets, where even the mob was able to see its king and his ministers displayed. For the first time, the development of caricature had made possible a satiric cult of personality in British politics.

On 18 June 1757, the paper *Con-Test* (no. 31) observed, "We may suppose that the press, and the print-shops will swarm with productions both grave and comic: that venal rhetorick, will turn prostitute in the service of disappointed ambition; and that buffonry [*sic*], capped like an ideot [*sic*], will ring her bells, to tickle vulgar ears, with the silly chimes of ridicule." Six years later, the anonymous poet of *Folly, a Satire on the Times. Written by a Fool, and Younger Brother to Tristram Shandy* (1763) has the publisher John Pridden advise a would-be author:

"If then a fortune woulds't atchieve [*sic*],
Write, write politic rhymes, and thrive:
Abuse the Ministers, and whirl
Keen venom at a certain Earl;
Invent new slanders, forge fresh hints
For blasphemy—to aid my prints;
Write Histories, and Libels, too,
And copious Novels not a few."

By 1763, engraved prints had become an essential expression of political satire. In a letter to Hardwicke on 30 September 1762, Newcastle, now in opposition to the Bute ministry, acknowledged the influence of political cartoons: "I own, I don't understand any of those Prints, & Burlesques; I am too dull to taste them; And, if they are not decypher'd for Me, I could not in the least guess, very often, what they mean. . . . They have their real Consequences, And there is an amazing Tameness, in not daring to take Notice of any of Them." [17] The accessibility of the engravings led to "real Consequences." The conservative *Briton* of 11 September 1762, noting that "the most indecent prints which obscenity and impudence can contrive were available to any passerby in London," calls on the proper authorities to prosecute the creators of these "ingenious and significant hieroglyphics, displayed in all the print-shops, from Temple-Bar to the Royal Exchange."

The great rise in political interest and information outside of Parliament's walls was not matched by an increase in direct political participation. Indeed, relative to the growth of the population, the extent of the franchise shrank between Walpole's fall and George III's accession. Some evidence suggests that the shrinkage was even absolute.[18] Popular political tension was inevitable, and politicians in and out of government attempted to exploit extraparliamentary forces.

As the most influential minister of the first Hanoverian king not identified with the Old Corps of Whigs, Bute started a press campaign in 1761 to discredit his rivals within and without government.[19] By 1762, Charles Churchill and John Wilkes's antiministerial *North Briton* was answering Arthur Murphy's prominsterial *Auditor* and Tobias Smollett's *Briton*.[20] Both sides employed the rhetorical strategy developed against Sir Robert Walpole and George II, but with some significant transformations. Supporters of George III's ministers, who served the first anti-anti-Tory Hanoverian, now argued that the continuation of party labels by ministerial opponents was an attempt to promote factionalism.[21] By the end of the 1760s, the Opposition was, for the first time in recent decades, openly arguing that political parties were both necessary and good. And, as we shall see, opponents of the ministry were by the end of the first decade openly questioning and sometimes repudiating the political conventions of ministerial responsibility, of attacking measures, not men, and ultimately of the king's inability to do wrong.

Bute's relationship with the verbal and visual political press is the subject of the 1762 etching *The Hungry Mob of Scriblers and Etchers* (fig. 22), attributed to Alex.[r] MacKenzie, in which Bute distributes coins to his needy supporters. Among them, Samuel Johnson holds a scroll marked "300 pr Ann," referring to the pension recently awarded him. Among the others in the crowd are probably Dr. John Shebbeare, a reactionary Tory pamphleteer, and Matthew Darly, a print designer and publisher. An engraving of "the Screen" identifies Darly, here acting as Bute's observer rather than his follower. A would-be client offers Bute an "Etching in Genl by W. A."

Foremost among visual satirists supporting Bute was William Hogarth, whose 1762 print, *The Times, Plate 1* (fig. 23), comprehends the significant issues of the early 1760s.[22] Nearly at the center of the print, standing on the solid base of the "Union Office," is a fireman. The "G. R." and the royal crown on his badge identify him as George III. He acts as a transformative power uniting the three streams of attack directed at him from the "Temple Coffee House" (representing Earl Temple and his clients Churchill and Wilkes) into one stream that can extinguish the fire of the Seven Years' War that enflames the globe. The fireman's supporters, their hands clasped on the engine, represent a unified Britain of Scots and Englishmen, sailors and soldiers, working together. Images of disruption and instability identify their opponents: the collapsing sign of the "Newcastle Inn"; "the Patriot Arms," with its opposed clenched fists; and the self-created colossus-figure of Henry VIII or Pitt himself, weakly supported on

The HUNGRY MOB of SCRIBLERS and Etchers

Figure 22. *The Hungry Mob of Scriblers and Etchers* (BMC 3844). Reproduced by permission of the Trustees of the British Museum.

Figure 23. Hogarth, *The Times, Plate 1* (BMC 3970). Reproduced by permission of the Trustees of the British Museum.

stilts while the opposition to the Peace of Paris fans the fire of war. The picture of a naked savage with money bags, "Alive from America," reflects the frequent charge that the greed of war profiteers motivated opposition to the peace.

Hogarth's depiction of George III as a fireman is the visual analogue of Blackstone's description of the monarch as "the fountain of justice and general conservator of the peace of the kingdom. . . . He is not the spring, but the reservoir" (p. 257). Hogarth emphasizes the symbolic value of George III's regal body and the royal dignity associated with it to underscore the concept that the king is the "virtual" representative of his people. This concept is repeated in several other prints of the 1760s that implicitly link George III with John Bull, often as victim of his ministers.

One such print is the 1762 *John Bull's House Sett in Flames* (fig. 24), perhaps by Paul Sandby, which prompted publication of Hogarth's *The Times, Plate 1*.[23] A bare-assed Bute fans the flames engulfing St. James's Palace while he farts in the direction of "Brother SMALL WIT [Smollett]" and Henry Fox. Fox was the ministerial spokesman in the House of Commons, whose members he bribed to support the Peace of Paris. George's use of the shamelessly corrupt Fox quickly led to charges that Bute and the king's public proclamation of setting government on a new moral basis was hypocritical. In this anti-Bute but promonarchical print, Pitt is the fireman supported by Newcastle, Churchill (carrying a water bucket marked "North Briton"), and the duke of Cumberland, the king's uncle. In Paul Sandby's untitled 1762 "Satire on Lord Bute, the Duke of Bedford, Earl Talbot, Lord Mansfield, Hogarth, Smollett, and Others" (fig. 25), Bute and Bedford, in front of St. James's Palace, try to force a scroll marked "Peace" down the throat of John Bull while Fox picks his pocket. Cumberland and Pitt come to John Bull's aid.

Bute and his opponents accused each other of posing threats to the monarchy. In the first state of Hogarth's *The Times*, Pitt appears as Henry VIII to indicate that he is a would-be tyrannical alternative to the present king. The charge that Pitt offers an illegitimate (and insubstantial) threat to the British constitution is more explicit in the 1762 print *Sic Transit Gloria Mundi* (fig. 26), where Pitt ascends on bubbles of his own making. The figure on one side, who converts a crown into a Puritan's liberty hat, is more than offset on the other side by the sun, conventional emblem of regal authority, here particularized with George III's face. The soap bubbles of temporary popularity cannot last long in the sunlight of George's reign. In this print, George III as the all-seeing sun fulfills the role Samuel Johnson assigns to him in his sermon number 26: "The king is placed above the rest that he may from his exalted station survey all the subordinations of society, that he may observe and obviate these vices and corruptions by which

Figure 24. Paul Sandby(?), *John Bull's House Sett in Flames* (BMC 3890).
Reproduced by permission of the Trustees of the British Museum.

peace is disturbed, justice violated, or security destroyed; 'he sitteth in the throne of judgment' to scatter 'away evil,' and is required to scatter it away 'with his eyes' by constant care, and vigilant observation" (14:274). Johnson's third definition of *sun* and its illustrative example from the *Dictionary* (1755) are relevant here: "Any thing eminently splendid. I will never consent to put out the *sun* of sovereignty to posterity and all succeeding kings. King Charles."

The inherited satiric tradition available equally to Bute's supporters and to his opponents very soon proved to be especially easily adapted to attacks on the minister. The choice of Bute as first lord of the treasury triggered in England the latent anti-Scot sentiment that had survived the union between England and Scotland in 1707. Scotland became for George III what Hanover had been for his grandfather—a target for the xenophobes who accused the king of slighting his own country in favor of another. In *The Prophecy of Famine. A Scots Pastoral* (1763), Charles Churchill exploits the popular prejudice that the Scots, like the Jews, are an avaricious, dirty, poor, unprincipled, and thieving race of aliens who have descended on England to parasitize her:

> *There,* like the *Sons of Israel,* having trod,
> For the fix'd term of years ordain'd by God,
> A barren desart, we shall seize rich plains
> Where milk with honey flows, and plenty reigns.
>
> . . . .
>
> There shall we, tho' the wretched people grieve,
> Ravage at large, nor ask the owner's leave.   (447–54)

In his notorious letter to the king of 19 December 1769, Junius echoes the parallel between the Scots and the Jews: "Like another chosen people, they have been conducted into the land of plenty, where they find themselves effectually marked, and divided from mankind" (p. 163). Anti-Scot sentiment reappears in Thomas Jefferson's draft of the American Declaration of Independence, where one of the charges against "our British brethren" is that "they are permitting their chief magistrate to send over not only souldiers of our common blood, but Scotch and foreign mercenaries to invade and destroy us." [24]

The notion of the Scots as an alien invading force is a subject of the 1763 print *Scotch Paradice a View of the Bute{eye}full Garden of Edenborough* (fig. 27), which implies that Bute's influence over Augusta, the Princess of Wales and widowed mother of George III, will bring about the Peace of Paris. Bute, sitting atop the apple tree (a reference to the recently passed and unpopular cider tax) of corruption offers fruit to his greedy countrymen. Cumberland ("I'll cut you up Root and branch") chops at the tree

Figure 25. Sandby, "Satire on Lord Bute . . . and Others" (BMC 3910). Reproduced by permission of the Trustees of the British Museum.

Figure 26. *Sic Transit Gloria Mundi* (BMC 3913). Courtesy of the John Carter Brown Library at Brown University.

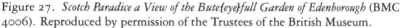

Figure 27. *Scotch Paradice a View of the Bute{eye}full Garden of Edenborough* (BMC 4006). Reproduced by permission of the Trustees of the British Museum.

as Pitt, Churchill, Temple, and Newcastle come over the wall. The princess, as Eve, climbs the ladder to accept a bribe, confessing, "I should like it better if it were a Codling." Her indecent wish is an expression of the stereotype of the Scotsman as an animalistically sexual being, a stereotype found in John Wilkes's *Essay on Woman* and applied repeatedly to Bute.

> Presumptuous Prick! the reason wou'dst thou find,
> Why form'd so weak, so little and so blind?
>
> . . . .
>
> Or ask thy raw-bon'd Scottish Father's Tarse
> Why larger he than Stallion, or Jack-Ass?
>
> . . . .
>
> Then in the scale of various Pricks, 'tis plain
> Godlike erect, BUTE stands the foremost Man.[25]

The accusation, completely untrue, that Bute's rise to power resulted from an illicit sexual relationship with the king's mother is made more explicitly in the 1762 print *The Scotch Broomstick & the Female Beesom: A German Tale, by Sawney Gesner* (BMC 3852), where Bute is identifiable by his Scottish dress and his pendant boots, a visual pun on the Scottish pronunciation of his title.[26] Underlying the print's obvious sensationalistic appeal is a political implication that helps explain the nature of satiric attacks on George III during the first dozen years of his reign. The Princess of Wales reveals that she shares Catherine the Great's absolutist goals as well as her sexual habits: "Heres a beesom for you, the rusian bear is not more carnivorous I love power as well as she."[27]

Attacks on the king's mother and Bute were also at least implicit attacks on George III himself, whose person and position were supposedly protected by conventions of political theory that circumscribed the nature of satiric attacks on a monarch in mid-eighteenth-century Britain. By his actions, George III seemed to many of his contemporaries to ignore the conventions. In a widely known private statement of 1761, he said that Bute's measures were the king's measures and that attacks on the minister were attacks on the monarch. To some, George apparently intended to increase the monarch's personal involvement in governing the country. Such conduct was contrary not so much to constitutional theory as to perceptions of recent political practice. The image of a monarch bent on reestablishing a personal rule like that of the early Stuarts finds its way into the American Declaration of Independence. The declaration, "a piece of propaganda, a recital of the alleged sins of George III to justify the renunciation of his sovereignty," depicts George III as a usurper of the constitution.[28]

In the 1760s, however, Bute's opponents, who covered almost all points of the political spectrum, quickly developed a conspiracy theory that had the appeal of most conspiracy theories. If one accepts the premise, the theory explains all recent political events, and the king remains relatively innocent, albeit through ignorance or stupidity.

The conspiracy theory receives clearest exposition in Edmund Burke's *Thoughts on the Cause of the Present Discontents* (1770). Simply stated, the Princess of Wales and Bute, whose family name was Stuart, actually ruled Britain by teaching the king to espouse Stuart, or Scottish, tenets of absolutist, personal rule and thereby causing him to alienate himself from his subjects. Rather than being the strong "Patriot King" the country wanted and needed, George had allowed himself to become subservient to his mother and her lover. The conspiracy theory easily accommodated Bute's resignation from office in April 1763 and his absence from the country at the end of the decade. Even though he was out of office, he was said to rule from behind the curtain, both because his followers, who eventually became known as the "king's friends," contaminated every succeeding ministry and because the political miseducation he had given the king continued to corrupt the monarch's thinking. Bute's absence was said to be a conscious design to make people think he had lost power. George, like his grandfather, had become a king in toils, and the opposition was patriotically trying to free him. In accordance with the convention that "the king can do no wrong," since George III was not culpable, he usually appears as a fool rather than a knave, and the majority of satiric attacks are on his mortal, not his regal, body.[29]

There was a great deal of truth in the opposition's charge that Bute, a man without popular or parliamentary support, was a favorite as defined by Charles Churchill in *North Briton* 8 (24 July 1763), an ironic defense of Bute against the charge. Noteworthy are the images of blindness and "trifling amusements," images that recur in satires of George III:

Had we seen a man . . . raised to the highest honours and most important places, without any merit to justify his glorification, without any one recommendation but the blind affection of his Sovereign; had we found him solely attached to his own interests, taking advantage of the confidence reposed in him by his master, in order to abuse that sacred trust, tampering with his pliant disposition, making himself necessary to his foibles and passions, separating the interests of king and subject, advising such measures as must naturally estrange the affections of his people, and drawing him into trifling amusements, merely to take off his attention from things of consequence, so that the management and disposition of places might remain intirely in himself and his creatures, such a man would be the first who ought to be branded with the name favourite; a name always attended with odium, and oftentimes with danger.

Churchill's definition elaborates Johnson's second definition of *favourite* and his supporting quotations from Sidney: "One chosen as a companion by his superiour; a mean wretch whose whole business is by any means to please. All favours and punishments passed by him, all offices and places of importance were distributed by his *favourites. Sidney.* I was a Thessalian gentleman, who, by mischance, having killed a *favourite* of the prince of that country, was pursued so cruelly, that in no place but by favour or corruption they would obtain my destruction. *Sidney, b. 1.*"

The charge that Bute was a favorite allowed for another easy adaptation of the strategy against Walpole in the 1730s. Probably in 1762, for example, the 1740 print *The Stature of a Great Man; or, The English Colossus* (BMC 2458) was reproduced as *The Stature of a Great Man; or, The Scotch Colossus* (BMC 4000), with Bute's face replacing Walpole's.[30] Bute's opponents quickly recognized a way to combine effectively the allegation of a sexual affair between Bute and the king's mother with the accusation that Bute was the king's favorite by developing the Walpole-Mortimer analogy available to them. Mortimer and his lover Isabella, wife of Edward II, were thought to have caused the death of the king. Consequently, through his influence with Isabella, Mortimer became the favorite of Edward III, and during his minority the minister and mother effectively usurped the rule of the kingdom. Edward III later realized what was happening, overthrew Mortimer, and went on to defeat France and earn a place as "the Boast of Fame" (Pope, *The First Epistle of the Second Book of Horace Imitated,* 7) in the pantheon of heroes touted by Walpole's Opposition.[31]

On 3 July 1762, John Wilkes demonstrated in the *North Briton* just how tellingly appropriate the Mortimer analogy could be to current prejudices about the king's mother and minister. In 1763 he included an ironic dedication in his republication of a 1731 anti-Walpole play as *The Fall of Mortimer: An Historical Play: Dedicated to the Right Honourable John Earl of Bute.* The Mortimer analogy, with its implications of sensationalism, favoritism, usurpation, and petticoat government, quickly found its way into visual satire as well. *Sawney below Stairs* (fig. 28) celebrates Bute's resignation on 8 April 1763 by imagining his descent into hell, where

> The Spencers, Count Bruhl and Sejanus of Rome
> With Mortimer, Wolsey and Walpole are come
> (All favourite Statesmen to Monarchs of Yore)
> To give his Scotch Lordship a welcome to shore.

Bute says, "The De'el pick mine Eyn but I shall be proud of joining with such a geudly Company." He is about to grasp the hand of Sir Robert Walpole, who greets him with "How is it possible you could bring about the general Excise Bill. I never could accomplish it by Gd my Ld." Mortimer

Figure 28. *Sawney below Stairs* (BMC 4048). Reproduced by permission of the Trustees of the British Museum.

remarks, "I find my Country men have not left off their old Tricks yet, they will be climbing too high till they fall at last as I did." The symbolic significance of the serpent on Bute's leg and apparently about to bite his private parts is obvious. The mirror held by the Devil, overhead, has a twofold meaning: it refers to Bute's widely known personal vanity, and it represents the mirror of satire that reveals truth through apparent distortion (indicated by the angle at which it is held). The devil says, "I have brought you a Looking Glass Mr. Scot, that you may see what a droll Figure you cut now youre on this side the Water."

Verses subscribed to the 1762 print *The Highland Seer, or The Political Vision* (fig. 29) identify Roger Mortimer, earl of March, as one of five ghosts who come to warn Bute to beware their fate. The others are William des Roches, bishop of Winchester; Hubert de Burgh; Simon de Montfort, earl of Leicester; and Robert Devereux, earl of Essex. The anti-Bute weeklies *Monitor* and *North Briton* on the table also act as monitory devices. Bute says, "By St. Andrew, these ill-far'd Ghaists gar my Bleed run cauld with Horrow! gin I were safe in my ain Country, I'se be content to feed on Bannocks & Haggies, as I were wont to do." From behind the curtain, the Princess of Wales advises, "Fly, Sawney, to the Middle of Wallachia & in its blissful Vales forget your Fears." Portraits of Bute and Augusta hang on the wall. Bute's pose, adapted from the famous tent scene of Hogarth's painting and print *David Garrick as Richard III* (1745, 1746), alludes to his usurpation of power and predicts its consequences.

Closely related to the Mortimer-Bute analogy, with its interrelated themes of betrayal, sexuality, and usurpation, are references to Bute as Macbeth and to George III as Hamlet. Bute is likened to Macbeth in the 1762 print *Andrews-Cross* (BMC 3964) and in the closet drama *The Three Conjurors, a Political Interlude. Stolen from Shakespeare* (1763). Literary theft of form reflects the theft of power that is its subject. George's role as Hamlet in *Claudius Pouring Poison into the King's Ear, As He Is Sleeping in the Garden* (fig. 30), engraved for the *Oxford Magazine* in 1769, is a bit more complicated. On one level, the print refers to the amateur theatricals performed at Leicester House during the king's minority, but on a more serious level, George is the analogue to both Hamlet the father and Hamlet the son in Shakespeare's play. Bute and the Princess of Wales are accused of having conspired to kill Frederick, Prince of Wales, first patron of Bute and husband of Augusta until his death in 1751, an accusation Churchill anticipated in *The Conference* (1763):

> HIRCO, who knows not HIRCO, stains the bed
> Of that kind Master who first gave him bread,
> Scatters the seeds of discord thro' the land,

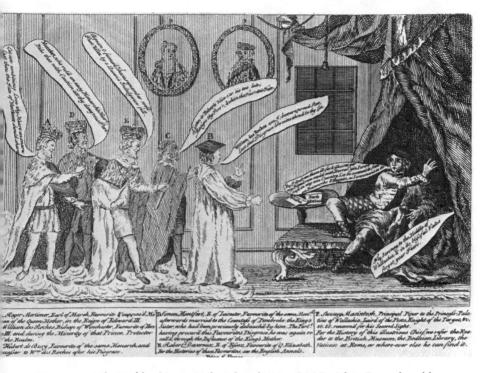

Figure 29. *The Highland Seer, or The Political Vision* (BMC 3867). Reproduced by permission of the Trustees of the British Museum.

Figure 30. *Claudius Pouring Poison into the King's Ear* (BMC 4329). Reproduced by permission of the Trustees of the British Museum.

Breaks ev'ry public, ev'ry private band,
Beholds with joy a trusting friend undone,
Betrays a Brother, and would cheat a Son.   (55–60)

Claudius-Bute cheats George-Hamlet the son by, in Churchill's words, "Pois'ning the royal ear of pow'r" (*The Ghost* 4:1794) with his false doctrines, an image reminiscent of Henry Fox's "Nostrum to Distemper the Brain" in the 1757 print *The Present Managers* (see fig. 18).

Bute and Fox (now Baron Holland), Mortimer and Hamlet all converge in the 1770 print *The R——l Dupe. Eng.d for the Political Register* (fig. 31). Beneath the Hamlet and Mortimer allusions in the paintings on the wall, an infantile and sleeping king George assumes a Pietà-like posture in his mother's arms while Bute usurps his royal scepter and Holland picks his pocket, as he had done in Sandby's 1762 "Satire on Lord Bute, the Duke of Bedford, . . ." (see fig. 25). Bute's pointing to Fox suggests that, though out of office, Bute still directs the corruption of authority. Negative though all these images are, each contains the possibility of positive results—the revenge of Hamlet and Edward III, the resurrection of Christ—so that the print is at once monitory and hortatory. The authority that the present king's mortal body has allowed to lapse remains inherently recoverable by the regal body of his office.

The satirists most commonly undercut the authority of George's mortal body by depicting him in the imagery of blindness (or its variations, such as sleep or nearsightedness) and by associating him with the pursuit of "trifling amusements" to offer the present king as the antithesis of the all-seeing monarchs in *Sic Transit Gloria Mundi* (see fig. 26) and the passage from Johnson's sermon number 26. *Tempora Mutantur* (fig. 32) illustrates its accompanying verse:

Lives there a Briton can with Truth dispute
Pitt's is the Laurel; Fames false Trumpet B[ute's].
Yet fav'rites thrive, by Merit not their own:
What Pity Folly stands so near the [throne].

The consequences of the king's being blindfolded and distracted by "trifling amusements" on the right side of the print are shown on the left side, where the British lion is chained and muzzled while British warships, one of whose flags is falling, have broomsticks tied to their masts to indicate that they are up for sale. As Bute and the princess barter away Pitt's victories, the king's crown slips off his throne.[32]

In *The Masquerade; or The Political Bagpiper* (fig. 33), the princess and Bute have usurped the throne while the king stands and plays the "Scotch fiddle." Iconographically, his status is reduced almost to that of the notori-

Figure 32. *Tempora Mutantur* (BMC 3886). Reproduced by permission of the Trustees of the British Museum.

The MASQUERADE; or the

POLITICAL BAGPIPER.

A New Comic SONG, in the SCOTCH Taste.

By H. HOWARD.

To the Tune of, *The Flowers of* Edinburgh.

Qui Capit ille Facit.

I.

BRA' *John o' Boot* was a bonny muckle Mon,
Frà *Scotland* he came wi his Broadsword in his Hand,
He came at the Head of a bra' bonny Clan,
Who the De'il cou'd his muckle *muckle Suit* withstand?
   He looked so neat,
   And he kissed so sweet,
That a *Dame of Renown* soon gave Ear to his Suit ;
   Then his *Pipe* he lugg'd out,
   And ye need not to doubt,
But in Concert he play'd—with her *German Flute.*

II.

Quoth he bonny Lassie, your *Flute* gangs weel,
   And keeps gude Time wi my *Bagpipe* clear ;
Sic Music as this is, can surely never fail,
   In Time to accord with an *English* Ear ;
   For what Music so sweet,
   Or what Harmony compleat,
As the *Bagpipe* join'd with the *German Flute ?*
   Then turning up her Eyes,
   Strait the muckle Dame replies :
" When the *Bagpipe's* play'd by my *John o' Boot.*"

III.

Play away, bonny Lad, I have good Store of Gold,
   Your *Bag* shall be full, while your *Pipe* it can play,
You ne'er shall return to a Climate so cold,
   For your Kisses are warmer and sweeter than *May* ;
   Quoth he, do not mourn,
   For I ne'er will return,
While here I can taste of the *Golden Fruit :*
   Then his *Pipe* he essay'd,
   And another *Lilt* he play'd,
In Concert sweet—with her *German Flute.*

IV.

Away *English* Fools, ye no more shall pretend,
   In Music to vie with a bonny *Highland* Mon ;
Nor more shall the Lasses of *England* commend,
   The fam'd *Irish Jigg,* when compar'd to my *John* ;
   For a quick merry Strain,
   That enlivens each Vein,
Who the De'el with a *Scotsman* shall e'er dispute ?
   But kis *Bagpipe* alone,
   Has too much of the Drone,
And of Need must be join'd—with my *German Flute.*

V.

Come on, bonny Lads, then with Pleasure advance,
   Your poor empty Scrips, and your Wallets disown ;
John o' Boot bears the Bell, Sir, and leads up the Dance,
   In the *Grand Masquerade* at the *Thistle* and *Crown :*
   There Sweet-meats and Wine,
   Shall intreat you to dine ;
Your Hunger assuage, and your Spirits recruit,
   While more soft to the Ear,
   Hark ! the *Bagpipe* so clear,
In Concert resounds with the *German Flute.*

VI.

A fine *English Fiddle* accords to the Strain,
   A *better,* sure never was *play'd* on before ;
Th' *French-horn,* at a Distance, would join it amain,
   And the *Spanish Guitar* play an Overture in Score ;
   But Woe to the Land,
   If they join in the Band,
Soon the *Fiddle* wou'd be broke, and the *Fiddle*
   For an *Englishman* born,
   Should despise a *French-horn,*
Tho' his Ear may be tickled by a *German*

Sold by the AUTHOR, opposite the Union Coffee-House, in the Strand, near Temple-Bar, and by the Print

Figure 33. *The Masquerade; or The Political Bagpiper* (BMC 3880). Reproduced by permission of the Trustees of the British Museum.

ously venal Henry Fox, who stands on the other side of the throne. The influence of "Scotch politics" is obvious in the scene. The princess wears a plaid bodice and Bute a kilt. The use of the plaid, outlawed in Scotland after the rebellion of 1745, establishes Bute as a criminal even as it identifies him. The motto of the Scotch Order of the Thistle, sometimes called the Order of St. Andrew—*Nemo me impune lacessit* (No One Touches Me with Impunity)—serves a dual purpose: it recalls the Jacobite origin of the order James II founded in 1687, and it reasserts Bute's political status as an untouchable favorite. Scotsmen enjoying the benefits of undeserved patronage surround the throne.

The image of Bute as a usurper who becomes a mock or masquerade king occurs frequently in verbal and visual satires of the time. One example comes from Churchill's 1761 poem *The Apology:*

> But if kind Fortune, who we sometimes know
> Can take a heroe from a puppet-shew,
> In mood propitious should her fav'rite call,
> On royal stage in royal pomp to bawl,
> Forgetful of himself he rears the head,
> And scorns the dunghill where he first was bred:
> Conversing now with well-dress'd kings and queens,
> With gods and godesses behind the scenes,
> He sweats beneath the terror-nodding plume,
> Taught by Mock Honours Real Pride t'assume.
> On this great stage the World, no Monarch e'er
> Was half so haughty as a Monarch-Player.   (244–55)

The representation of Bute as the music master in *The Masquerade* is one of many examples of satiric attacks on the minister's alleged political miseducation of George III. The fiddle in the king's hands has a multilevel significance: first, George actually enjoyed playing the violin; second, he is accused here of foolishly fiddling when he should be ruling; and third, the fiddle is one of many links that can be made between satires of George III and the rich tradition of verbal and visual political satire developed during the first half of the eighteenth century, which produced Alexander Pope's poem about the politics of education in *The Dunciad* 4 (1743). Bute becomes for the satirists of the 1760s the tyrannical archusurper Dulness calls for to reestablish her reign. Dulness admonishes her subjects:

> "Guard my Prerogative, assert my Throne:
>
> . . . .
>
> Others import yet nobler arts from France,
> Teach Kings to fiddle, and make Senates dance.

Perhaps more high some daring son may soar,
Proud to my list to add one Monarch more;
And nobly conscious, Princes are but things
Born for First Ministers, as Slaves for Kings,
Tyrant supreme! shall three Estates command,
And MAKE ONE MIGHTY DUNCIAD OF THE LAND!"

(4:583–604)[33]

The "nobler arts from France" Dulness mentions is simply another phrase for absolutism, like the phrases "Scotch government," "Stuart principles," "petticoat government," and "new Toryism," which are more common in the later satiric vocabulary. In Paine's *Common Sense,* the usurpers of the constitution are "a set of disguised Tories" (p. 47). The theme of political miseducation is repeated in *The Northern Dancing Master or Windsor Minuet* 1762 (fig. 34), which replaces Hogarth's graceful dancer with a clumsy youth. The childish king admits, "I have dancd Scotch tunes from my Infancy." As a result, Bute stands at the formal and political center of the minuet. Amidst the onlookers' sexual innuendos, Bute advises Queen Charlotte that her power over the king will never match the Princess of Wales's: "It cant be expected that you can dance so well as the Lady in my other hand she has had a long experience."

Charles Churchill, the most important verse satirist after Pope, betrays frequently in his poems the influence of *Dunciad* 4 and its theme of political miseducation. Churchill admits that politics pervades his verse:

Whate'er my theme, the *Muse,* who still
Owns no direction but her will,
Flies off, and, ere I could expect,
By ways oblique and indirect,
At once quite over head and ears
In fatal *Politics* appears.   (*The Ghost* 4:699–704)

Churchill organizes *The Rosciad* (1761), a satire on actors, around the political metaphor of legitimate succession, when "The monarch quits his throne, and condescends / Humbly to court the favour of his friends" (5–6). The struggle for succession takes place in an indisputably post-*Dunciad* universe: "A vacant throne high-plac'd in SMITHFIELD view, / To sacred DULLNESS and her FIRST-BORN due" (605–6). The theme of usurpation appears in Churchill's discussion of Falstaff: "Like GOTHS of old, howe'er he seems a friend, / He'll seize that throne, you wish him to defend" (477–78). In his short career, Churchill never quite works out the implications of his political metaphor of succession based on merit rather than heredity, but he returns to it repeatedly. By not following out these implications, he is what I have called elsewhere a protoradical who remains a monarchist.[34]

Figure 34. *The Northern Dancing Master or Windsor Minuet 1762* (BMC 3981).
Reproduced by permission of the Trustees of the British Museum.

In his next poem, *The Apology. Addressed to the Critical Reviewers* (1761), Churchill uses political metaphors of freedom, monarchy, usurpation, and tyranny to attack the critics who reign without legitimate authority in a post-*Dunciad* world:

> UNHAPPY Genius! plac'd, by partial Fate,
> With a free spirit in a slavish state;
> Where the reluctant Muse, oppress'd by kings,
> Or droops in silence, or in fetters sings.
> In vain thy dauntless fortitude hath borne
> The bigot's furious zeal, and tyrant's scorn.
>
> . . . .
>
> How could these self-elected monarchs raise
> So large an empire on so small a base?
> In what retreat, inglorious and unknown,
> Did Genius sleep when Dulness seiz'd the throne?   (71–86)

Political metaphor becomes political subject in *Night. An Epistle to Robert Lloyd* (1761), although Bute's power over the new king is more apparent than real, and the theme of miseducation is not fully elaborated. Churchill can still state with some conviction that Bute, too, has a master:

> THROUGH a false medium things are shewn by day,
> Pomp, wealth, and titles judgment lead astray.
> How many from appearances borrow state
> Whom NIGHT disdains to number with the Great!
> Must not we laugh to see yon *lordling* proud
> Snuff up vile incense from a fawning croud?
> Whilst in his beam surrounding clients play,
> Like insects in the sun's enliv'ning ray,
> Whilst, JEHU like, he drives a furious rate,
> And seems the only charioteer of state,
> Talking himself into a little God,
> And ruling empires with a single nod,
> Who would not think, to hear him law dispense,
> That he had Int'rest, and that they had sense?
> Injurious thought! beneath NIGHT'S honest shade
> When pomp is buried and false colours fade,
> Plainly we see at that impartial hour
> *Them* dupes to pride, and *him* the tool of pow'r.   (139–56)

In *Night,* the baleful effects of Bute's miseducating the king apparently affect only the monarch's mortal body, not the regal body or the body politic. Churchill does not pursue here the implications of the hypocrisy Bute promotes. Before Bute's resignation in April 1763, verbal and visual satirists concentrated on Bute the man, as if hoping measures would change were he removed from office. Before April 1763, the effects of his miseducating the king were usually treated as limited:

> A TUTOR once, more read in men than books,
> A kind of crafty knowledge in his looks,
> Demurely sly, with high preferment blest,
> His fav'rite Pupil in these words addrest:
>
> WOULD'ST thou, my son, be wise and virtuous deem'd,
> By all mankind a prodigy esteem'd?
> Be this thy rule; be what men *prudent* call;
> PRUDENCE, almighty PRUDENCE gives thee all.
> Keep up appearances; there lies the test,
> The world will give thee credit for the rest.
> Outward be fair, however foul within;
> Sin if thou wilt, but then in secret sin.
> This maxim's into common favour grown,
> Vice is no longer vice unless 'tis known.
> Virtue indeed may barefac'd take the field,
> But vice is virtue, when 'tis well conceal'd.
> Should raging passions drive thee to a whore,
> Let PRUDENCE lead thee to a *postern* door;
> Stay out all night, but take especial care
> That PRUDENCE bring thee back to early prayer.
> As one with watching and with study faint,
> Reel in a drunkard, and reel out a saint.
>
> WITH joy the youth this useful lesson heard,
> And in his mem'ry stor'd each precious word,
> Successfully pursued the plan, and *now*,
> "Room for my LORD—VIRTUE, stand by and bow."   (303–28)

Verbal and visual satirists of the 1760s increasingly argued that the influence of Bute over George was one of measures rather than men and that Bute had created a system, a kind of Butearchy, which he directed from behind the scenes just as the "school of Walpole," or "Robinarchy," supposedly continued to operate after Sir Robert Walpole's fall from power in 1742. In *The Conference*, published in November 1763, Churchill imagines the king as a counterweight to the ministerial corruption that remains as Bute's legacy:

'Tis not on Law, a System great and good,
By Wisdom penn'd, and bought by noblest Blood,
My Faith relies: By wicked Men and vain,
Law, once abus'd, may be abus'd again.—
No, on our great Law-giver I depend,
Who knows and guides them to their proper End;
Whose Royalty of Nature blazes out
So fierce, 'twere Sin to entertain a doubt—
Did Tyrant STUARTS now the Laws dispense
(Blest be the hour and hand which sent them hence)
For something, or for nothing, for a Word,
Or Thought, I might be doom'd to Death, *unheard*.
Life we might all resign to lawless Pow'r,
Nor think it worth the purchase of an hour;
But Envy ne'er shall fix so foul a stain
On the fair annals of a BRUNSWICK'S reign.

. . . .

Whilst GEORGE is King, I cannot fear endure;
Not to be guilty, is to be secure.   (325–60)

In another poem Churchill published in November 1763, book 4 of
The Ghost, the satirist is more explicit about the system Bute has created:

But why should the distemper'd Scold
Attempt to blacken Men enroll'd
In Pow'r's dread book, whose mighty skill
Can twist an Empire to their will,
Whose Voice is Fate, and on their tongue
Law, Liberty, and *Life* are hung,
Whom, on enquiry, Truth shall find,
With STUARTS *link'd,* time out of mind
Superior to their Country's Laws,
Defenders of a Tyrant's cause,
Men, who the same damn'd maxims hold
Darkly, which they avow'd of old,
Who, tho' by diff'rent means, pursue
The end which they had first in view,
And, force found vain, now play their part
With much less Honour, much more Art?   (863–78)

The Jacobites, who seek a Stuart restoration, were not decisively defeated
in 1745; they have simply become more subtle in spreading their principles
of absolutism throughout the realm.

Churchill's vision of the present and his remedies for reformation are most clearly expressed in three poems—*The Author* (December 1763), *Gotham* (February, March, August 1764), and *Independence* (October 1764) —related by their use of the image of the poet-king. In all three, Churchill indicates a willingness to change the mortal but not the regal body of the king, the officeholder but not the office. His radical inclinations are increasingly evident in his growing emphasis on merit as the only proper grounds for rule. Whereas in his earliest poem politics was the vehicle and literature the tenor of his organizing principle, in these three late poems tenor and vehicle are reversed. Churchill now offers poetry rather than power as the true, rational standard of natural merit. Like the solitary virtuous voice of Pope's last satires, the poet in Churchill's late poems becomes a majority of one, a moral alternative ruler to the corruption around him:

> He reigns, vain monarch, o'er a barren spot,
> Whilst in the vale of Ignorance below,
> FOLLY and VICE to rank luxuriance grow.   (*The Author*, 8–10)

The Author, which begins and ends with references to miseducation that corrupts both literature and politics—"the slavish drudgery of schools" (15) and "OXFORD . . . sunk in fame" (385)—offers us a glimpse of the political and literary world after Pope's "Universal Darkness buries All":

> But *Now*, when DULLNESS rears aloft her throne,
> When LORDLY Vassals her wide Empire own,
> When Wit, seduc'd by Envy, starts aside,
> And basely leagues with Ignorance and Pride,
> What *Now* should tempt us, by false hopes misled,
> Learning's unfashionable paths to tread;
> To bear those labours, which our Fathers bore,
> That Crown with-held, which They in triumph wore?   (31–38)

Given the explicit post-*Dunciad* setting, "the hardy Poet" referred to in the following passage is most appropriately Alexander Pope.[35] Only the satirist's power can regenerate Britain:

> Is this the Land, where, mindful of her charge
> And Office high, fair Freedom walk'd at large;
> Where, finding in our Laws a sure defence,
> She mock'd at all restraints, but those of Sense;
> Where, health and honour trooping by her side,
> She spread her sacred empire far and wide;
> Pointed the Way, Affliction to beguile,
> And bade the Face of Sorrow wear a smile,

Bade those, who dare obey the gen'rous call,
Enjoy her blessings, which GOD meant for all?
Is this the Land, where, in some Tyrant's reign,
When a *weak, wicked Ministerial* train,
The tools of pow'r, the slaves of int'rest, plann'd
Their Country's ruin, and with bribes unman'd
Those wretches, who, ordain'd in Freedom's cause,
Gave up our liberties, and sold our laws;
When Pow'r was taught by Meanness where to go,
Nor dar'd to love the Virtue of a foe;
When, like a lep'rous plague, from the foul head
To the foul heart her sores Corruption spread,
Her iron arm when stern Oppression rear'd,
And Virtue, from her broad base shaken, fear'd
The scourge of Vice; when, impotent and vain,
Poor Freedom bow'd the neck to Slav'ry's chain;
Is this the Land, where, in those worst of times,
The hardy Poet rais'd his honest rimes
To dread rebuke, and bade controulment speak
In guilty blushes on the villain's cheek,
Bade Pow'r turn pale, kept mighty rogues in awe,
And made them fear the Muse, who fear'd not Law?   (63–92)

The virtuous satirist, even in the land of Dullness, has as much power as a king because the poet can unmake what a king can create—a lord:

What's in this name of *Lord,* that we should fear
To bring their vices to the public ear?
Flows not the honest blood of humble swains
Quick as the tide which swells a Monarch's veins?
Monarchs, who wealth and titles can bestow,
Cannot make Virtues in succession flow.

. . . .
If such thy life, tho' Kings had made thee more
Than ever King a scoundrel made before,
Nay, to allow thy pride a deeper spring,
Tho' God in vengeance had made Thee a King,
Taking on Virtue's wing her daring flight,
The Muse should drag thee trembling to the light.   (157–82)

In *Gotham,* the poet, who is merely an analogue to the king in *The Author,* becomes monarch of a visionary world unlike that over which "Lady DULLNESS with Lord MAYORS / Presides" (1:133–34):

Rejoice, Ye happy GOTHAMITES, rejoice;
Lift up your voice on high, a mighty voice,
The voice of Gladness, and on ev'ry tongue,
In Strains of gratitude, be praises hung,
The praises of so great and good a King;
Shall CHURCHILL reign, and shall not GOTHAM sing?   (1:111–16)

Gotham is Churchill's "Mirror for Magistrates," designed to reeducate those who

. . . like idle monarch Boys,
Neglecting things of weight, . . . sigh for toys;
Give them the crown, the sceptre, and the robe,
Who will may take the pow'r, and rule the globe.   (2:49–52)

Book 2 of *Gotham* is primarily monitory, reminding us of the fallen world of Dullness, where those "Who, bred 'mongst fogs in Academic land, / Scorn ev'ry thing they do not understand" (63–64). Power rather than merit determines the victor in this world. Hence, usurpation is a constant concern because Dullness's universal rules apply as well to Gotham:

The crown of GOTHAM may some SCOT assume,
And vagrant STUARTS reign in CHURCHILL's room.

. . . .

But that the STUART race my Crown should wear,
That Crown, where, highly cherish'd, FREEDOM shone
Bright as the glories of the mid-day Sun,
Born and bred Slaves, that They, with proud misrule,
Should make brave, free-born men, like boys at school,
To the Whip crouch and tremble—O, that thought!

. . . .

Or let, in FREEDOM's seat, a STUART reign.   (240–334)

"ENGLAND's fair records" (338) are searched to trace the development of Stuart tyranny ("The trait'rous doctrines taught by Tories now" {442}) until William III overthrew it. The parallels of the past with current charges against Bute and George are unmistakable. James I was "a tame Tyrant" (344). In his reign, "Turn where You would, the eye with SCOTS was caught / Or *English* knaves who would be SCOTSMEN thought" (367–68). Too cowardly to be a strong ruler, "Vain of the Scholar, like all SCOTSMEN since, / The Pedant Scholar, he forgot the Prince" (379–80). But, as in *Dunciad* 4, he leaves a disastrous legacy:

To answer to that God, from whom alone
He claim'd to hold, and to abuse the throne,

Leaving behind, a curse to all his line,
The bloody Legacy of RIGHT DIVINE.   (417–20)

The closest parallel to George III is Charles I, who "took the Man up, e're he left the child" (428) and was "Tutor'd to see with ministerial eyes" (469) so that he was "most a slave, when most he seem'd to rule" (458), and was "List'ning uxorious, whilst a Woman's prate / Modell'd the Church, and parcell'd out the State" (465–66). Carefully distinguishing between the king's two bodies, Churchill observes the political conventions of ministerial responsibility and regal immunity in his description of George's predecessor:

With many Virtues which a radiance fling
Round private men; but few which grace a King.

. . . .

Unhappy Stuart! harshly tho' that name
Grates on my ear, I should have died with shame,
To see my King before his subjects stand,
And at their bar hold up his royal hand,
At their commands to hear the monarch plead,
By their decrees to see that Monarch bleed.
What tho' thy faults were many, and were great,
What tho' they shook the basis of the state,
In Royalty secure thy Person stood,
And sacred was the fountain of thy blood.
Vile Ministers, who dar'd abuse their trust,
Who dar'd seduce a King to be unjust,
Vengeance, with Justice leagu'd, with pow'r made strong,
Had nobly crush'd; *the King could do no wrong.*   (421–536)

Churchill's remedy for Britain's current ills is his own installation as "a PATRIOT KING" (46) described in book 3, a hortatory call on George III to wake up to what is going on around him—"Sleep was not made for kings" (166). It is implied that George should follow Churchill's example in combining the respective virtues of the king's two bodies:

Be it my task to seek, nor seek in vain,
Not only how to live, but how to reign,
And, to those Virtues which from Reason spring,
And grace the Man, join those which grace the King.   (219–22)

In one passage Churchill recounts the charges verbal and visual satirists had been making for the past four years and concludes, "Kings must be blind, into such snares to run, / Or worse, with open eyes must be undone" (283–84):

Are there, amongst those officers of State,
To whom our sacred pow'r we delegate,
Who hold our Place and Office in the Realm,
Who, in our name commission'd, guide the Helm,
Are there, who, trusting to our love of ease,
Oppress our subjects, wrest out just decrees,
And make the laws, warp'd from their fair intent,
To speak a language which they never meant,
Are there such Men, and can the fools depend
On holding out in safety to their end?
Can they so much, from thoughts of danger free,
Deceive themselves, so much misdeem of me,
To think that I will prove a Statesman's tool,
And live a stranger where I ought to rule?
What, to myself and to my State unjust,
Shall I from ministers take things on trust,
And, sinking low the credit of my throne,
Depend upon dependants of my own?
Shall I, most certain source of future cares,
Not use my Judgment, but depend on their's,
Shall I, true puppet-like, be mock'd with State,
Have nothing but the Name of being great,
Attend at councils, which I must not weigh,
Do what they bid and what they dictate, say,
Enrob'd, and hoisted up into my chair,
Only to be a royal Cypher there?
Perish the thought—'tis Treason to my throne—
And who but thinks it, could his thoughts be known,
Insults me more, than He, who, leagu'd with hell,
Shall rise in arms, and 'gainst my crown rebell.   (235–64)

The way to guard against such Dullness-inspired corruption of the
state is to properly educate the chief magistrate, in part by study of the
past: "Let me the page of History turn o'er, / Th' instructive page. . . .
Be this my Pattern—As becomes a King" (461–62, 505). But, unlike
George III, who was by Bute "into barren theory betray'd" (473), the true
"Patriot King" must "(the weak, dead letter left behind) / Search out the
Principles, the Spirit find" (607–8):

Let me, Impartial, with unweary'd thought,
Try Men and Things; let me, as Monarchs ought,
Examine well on what my Pow'r depends,
What are the gen'ral Principles, and Ends

> Of Government, how Empire first began,
> And wherefore Man was rais'd to reign o'er Man.   (533–38)

Churchill's goal is to teach the king "How Affability becomes a Throne" (642) so that he will remove Bute and the Princess of Wales as barriers between himself and his people:

> In vain my nearest, dearest friend shall plead,
> In vain my mother kneel—my soul may bleed,
> But must not change.   (659–61)

The call is for a strong and independent monarch: "Let me in Peace, in War, Supreme preside, / And dare to know my way without a Guide" (625–26).

Churchill returns less directly to the theme of royal independence in *Independence. A Poem. Addressed to the Minority,* another poem that opens with an image of usurpation, this time by obsequious poets

> Who have conspir'd to seize that sacred hill
> Where the nine Sisters pour a genuine strain,
> And sunk the mountain level with the plain.   (14–16)

Churchill also returns to the subject of aristocracy, which, like bad poetry, is an unnatural creation: "NATURE exclaim'd with wonder—Lords are Things, / Which, never made by Me, were made by Kings" (55–56). As the poem progresses, the independent poet is increasingly identified with the independent king. Here is Churchill's description of "the Majesty of Bards" (284):

> The real *Bard,* whom native Genius fires,
> Whom ev'ry Maid of Castaly inspires,
> Let him consider wherefore he was meant,
> Let him but answer Nature's great intent,
> And fairly weigh himself with other men,
> Would ne'er debase the glories of his pen,
> Would in full state, like a true Monarch, live,
> Nor bate one inch of his *Prerogative.*   (297–304)

In the world of the poem, where "Merit rules here, Be it enough that Birth / Intoxicates, and sways the fools of earth" (209–10), a poet can be as independent as a king, and implicitly the reverse is true as well:

> Bards, if contented, are as great as Kings.
> Ourselves are to ourselves the cause of ill,
> We may be Independent, if we will.
> The Man who suits his Spirit to his state

Stands on equal footing with the Great,
MOGULS themselves are not more rich, and He,
Who rules the English nation, not more free.   (470–76)

The ultimate minority of political virtue in this poem celebrating those who supported in Parliament Wilkes's losing cause is a regenerated George III, fancied ruler of Gotham.

Similar wishful thinking that George III would change sides in the Wilkes affair is depicted in the engraving *The Glorious Minority in 1763, with the Head of the Majority Blason'd* (fig. 35). The "Head of the Majority" is that of Bute impaled on a pole. A label alludes ironically to Joseph Addison's *Cato:* "What pitty [*sic*] it is He can die but Once to serve his Country." The central design of the engraving is a curtain, or "Tappeserie du Roy" (the king's tapestry), which shows several subjects. One is "False Joseph and his Mistress," another reference to the alleged affair between Bute and the Princess of Wales. Above the curtain, the heads of the minority who supported Wilkes include Earl Temple and Wilkes himself. With them, on the right, is George III as an eclipsed sun bearing the inscription "Omen Malvin" or "Malym" (evil omen). However, as subsequent verbal and visual satires demonstrate, hopes that George III would overrule his ministers were short-lived.

Remarkable Characters at Mrs. Cornellys Masquerade (fig. 36), a 1770 print engraved for the *Oxford Magazine*, demonstrates the continuity of the satiric tactics used against George III. The king, whose baby's rattle and dress reflect his subservience to petticoat government and distraction by amusing trifles, looks into a mirror of truth held by a satyr, the conventional emblem of satire. Like Tristram (*Tristram Shandy* 6:15), the as yet unbreeched George is of an age younger than his "seventh year, the period during which women are allowed the sole management of children," according to Mary Wollstonecraft.[36] He remains under his mother's care, not yet having reached the conventional age of reason. George says, " 'Tis a fine Glass, but I do not like anything that reflects." Around his neck is a collar attached to a leash held by Bute, whose widow's snood indicates that his concealed influence still operates through the king's mother. Bute reassures the king, "That's a false Mirror, constructed at the London Tavern [the meeting place of opponents of Lord North's new ministry], it Mis-represents you, you must go North about."

"North" refers to the origin of Scottish principles as well as to the name of Bute's successor. The artist may also be playing on the popular tradition that the North, associated with coldness, lack of sunshine, and wintry death, was the land of the Devil. The theological source for Shakespeare's reference to "the lordly Monarch of the North" (*1 Henry VI,* act 5, sc. 3, line 6) or Milton's locating Satan's base in the "Quarters of the North"

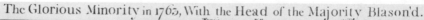

Figure 35. *The Glorious Minority in 1763, with the Head of the Majority Blason'd* (BMC 4034). Reproduced by permission of the Trustees of the British Museum.

Figure 36. *Remarkable Characters at Mrs. Cornellys Masquerade* (BMC 4376).
Reproduced by permission of the Trustees of the British Library.

(*Paradise Lost* 5:689) is Isaiah 14:12. Evildoers were thought to deserve burial on the north, or "Devil's," side of the church, near the small "Devil's door," opened during baptisms and communions to "let the Devil out." The demonic implications are underscored by the appearance in the print of the speaker of the House of Commons, Sir Fletcher ("Bull-face") Norton, who boasts, "I am the Devil of a Speaker and my Needle points to the North." The final figure is the duke of Grafton (horned because of his wife's widely known adultery with the earl of Upper Ossory). In the background, an unattended London burns. Maternal control, Butean influence, and satanic direction presumably offered more palatable conspiratorial explanations for the causes of the present discontents than would a more direct accusation of regal responsibility.

Although the immediate occasion of the print was a masquerade held at Mrs. Cornelly's house in Soho Square on 26 February 1770, satirists exercised their license to alter at will the fictional participants. An anonymous contributor to the third edition of *The New Foundling Hospital for Wit. Being a Collection of Several Curious Pieces, in Verse and Prose. . . .* (London, 1771), for example, sought to attire North, who had become first lord of the treasury on 10 February 1770, in the iconography of Bute: "The Following Illustrious Personages will appear in the under-mentioned dresses and characters, at the subscription masquerade, at Mrs. Cornelly's. . . . His M[ajest]y in a child's frock and bib, followed by L[or]d N[orth], in the habit of an old woman, holding him in leading strings" (p. 47). In both satires, the metaphor of the masquerade displays the reality and not the "inversion of one's nature."[37] Only during an occasional masquerade, say the satirists, do the politicians and the king step out of their usual roles on the stage of state to reveal their true selves.

The print from *Oxford Magazine,* like the frontispiece from volume 3 of *The New Foundling Hospital for Wit* (1768), undercuts the royal dignity. In the engraving, *You Have Got Him Ma'am, in the Right Kew* (fig. 37), the Princess of Wales leads the king by the nose while Bute partially hides his influence behind a tree. In the last two engravings considered here, each of the king's two bodies is shown as being in a condition of arrested development because of his subservience to his mother and to his favorite. A figure of pity, if not contempt, he fails to fulfill his proper roles as a man and a king. The accusation pictured in the 1768 print finds its verbal equivalent two years later in Thomas Chatterton's unpublished "Kew Gardens":

> The Groves of Kew however misapply'd,
> To serve the purposes of Lust and Pride,
> Were by the greater Monarch's Care design'd,
> A place of Conversation for the Mind:
> Where Solitude and Silence should remain,

Frontispiece to part III.

You have got him Ma'am, in the right Kew.

Figure 37. *You Have Got Him Ma'am, in the Right Kew* (BMC 4245). Reproduced by permission of the Trustees of the British Library.

And Conscience keep her Sessions and arraign.
But ah! how fallen from that better state!
'Tis now a heathen Temple of the great;
Where sits the Female Pilot of the Helm
Who shakes Oppression's fetters thro' the realm;
Her name is Tyranny, and in a String,
She leads the shadow of an infant King.   (175–86)

In *Resignation,* another political satire of 1770, Chatterton accuses George of confusing his mortal and regal bodies by allowing his filial duty to his mother to dictate his royal actions. Instead of a "Seraph," he becomes an "Ideot":

Hail, filial Duty: great if rightly usd,
How little when mistaken and abusd
View'd from one point how glorious art thou seen.
From others how degenerate and mean,
A Seraph or an Ideots head we see;
Often the latter stands the Type of thee,
And bowing at his Parents Knee is drest
In a long hood and many color'd Vest:
The sceptred King who dignifys a throne
Should be in private life, himself alone
No Friend or Mother should his conscience scan
Or with the Nation's head confound the Man.   (477–88)

To appreciate how much the satirists we have been looking at and listening to diminish the king's two bodies, we need only reconsider the centrally placed George III as father of his country in *Long Live His Most Excellent Britannic Majesty* (see fig. 21). On the other hand, in the 1771 etching entitled *Farmer G———e, Studying the Wind & Weather* (fig. 38), the king, graphically and symbolically off-center, is merely a child of a larger growth who ignores his paternal and regal responsibilities. George's peering through a reversed telescope is a variation on the theme of his blindness to the state of the nation, a theme reiterated by the torn petition under the dog. His political miseducation is represented by the open book entitled *"The Art of Government by Mecanick Rules,"* which recalls Johnson's observation to Boswell on 14 April 1775 that Bute, "though a very honourable man,—a man who meant well,—a man who had his blood full of prerogative,—was a theoretical statesman,—a book-minister."[38] A portrait of Bute oversees George, dressed in a robe of tartan design to indicate Scottish influence. A monkey imitates the king. The curtain represents Bute's hidden influence, which allows him to possess the king's crown. Samuel Johnson had ample evidence by 1770 to support his charge in *The False*

Farmer G—e, Studying the Wind & Weather.

Figure 38. *Farmer G———e, Studying the Wind & Weather* (BMC 4883). Reproduced by permission of the Trustees of the British Museum.

THE
NEW FOUNDLING HOSPITAL
FOR WIT.

BEING

A COLLECTION OF CURIOUS PIECES

IN VERSE AND PROSE,

SEVERAL OF WHICH WERE NEVER BEFORE PRINTED.

BY

SIR C. HANBURY WILLIAMS,	C. TOWNSHEND,
THE DUKE OF WHARTON,	SOAME JENYNS,
EARL OF CHESTERFIELD,	DR. KING,
————DELAWARR,	DR. ARMSTRONG,
————BATH,	DR. AKENSIDE,
————HARDWICKE,	C. ANSTEY,
————CARLISLE,	T. EDWARDS,
————CHATHAM,	C. CHURCHILL,
LORD VISC. CLARE,	W. SHENSTONE,
LORDS LYTTELTON,	MR. GRAY,
——— HARVEY,	J. THOMSON,
——— CAPEL,	J. S. HALL,
LADY M. W. MONTAGUE,	J. WILKES,
LADY IRWIN,	D. GARRICK,
MISS CARTER,	R. BENTLEY,
HON. C. YORKE,	S. JOHNSON,
———H. WALPOLE,	B. THORNTON,
———C. MORRIS,	G. COLMAN,
SIR J. MAWBEY,	R. LLOYD, Efqrs; &c. &c.
T. POTTER,	

With fome Pieces of MILTON, WALLER, POPE, CON-
GREVE, &c. not in their Works.

Adorned with a curious Frontifpiece.

PART THE SIXTH.

LONDON:
Printed for J. ALMON, in PICCADILLY.
1773.

Alarm that "these low-born railers have attacked not only the authority, but the character of their Sovereign" (10:342).

By the end of the first decade of George III's reign, Johnson's "low-born railers" managed to turn the erstwhile virtuous, independent monarch into a foolish, unwitting tyrant manipulated by his minister and mother. As Junius acknowledges in his notorious "Letter to the King" of 19 December 1769, satirists were still limited by the political conventions of the king's legal immunity, his two bodies, and the notion of ministerial responsibility: "The doctrine inculcated by our laws, *That the King can do no wrong,* is admitted without reluctance. We separate the amiable, good-natured prince from the folly and treachery of his servants, and the private virtues of the man from the vices of his government" (p. 160).[39] Conventions intended to protect the royal dignity, however, enabled the satirists to undermine that dignity by creating what John Wesley calls, in *Free Thoughts on the Present State of Affairs* (1770), "*scandalum regis,* scandalizing the King." In the same pamphlet, Wesley disputes the charges that George III is "a NERO." However, for most satirists, George was still, at worst, an ironic Nero, as shown in an engraving from the 1773 edition of *The New Foundling Hospital for Wit* entitled *Nero* (fig. 39), whose caption reads, "One of the Headmen of Gotham caused a Statue of himself to be erected in the Character of Marcus Aurelius; but the Statuary, knowing nothing of that Prince, took his likeness from NERO." For these satirists, George is a Nero not out of strength but out of weakness; he is an inadvertent, not a willful, tyrant. Behind the powerful figure that the American Declaration of Independence reproaches lies a satiric tradition of diminishing the king's potency. Political miseducation, personal folly, and subservience to ministerial and maternal influence have led to an unwitting Nero who presides over an all too real "absolute Tyranny," under which he is as much victim as villain. As Junius warns George III, "Your Majesty may learn hereafter, how nearly the slave and tyrant are allied" (p. 171).

In his letter of 28 May 1770, Junius summarizes the satirists' view of George III as a cipher whom others have manipulated into playing the tyrant: "Secluded from the world, attached from his infancy to one set of persons and one set of ideas, he can neither open his heart to new connections, nor his mind to better information. A character of this sort is the soil fittest to produce that obstinate bigotry in politics and religion, which begins with a meritorious sacrifice of the understanding, and finally conducts the monarch and the martyr to the block" (p. 202).

Junius's professed and perhaps sincere motivation was the "Present Public Wish," expressed in *The New Foundling Hospital for Wit* (1771), that although "the K[ing] *wishes* to be *quiet*[,] / The people *wish* him to be *great*" (p. 51). Johnson's evaluation of Junius in *Thoughts on the Late Transactions*

Die Zerstörung der Königlichen Bild Säule zu Neu Yorck.

La Destruction de la Statue royale a Nouvelle Yorck.

Figure 40. *La Destruction de la statue royale a Nouvelle Yorck* (Not in BMC).
Courtesy of the John Carter Brown Library at Brown University.

respecting Falkland's Islands (1771) applies as well to other verbal and visual satirists. Junius, Johnson observes, "endeavors to let slip the dogs of foreign or of civil war, ignorant whither they are going, and careless what may be their prey" (10:376). Speaking of the concept of royal dignity, Junius, in his letter of 30 January 1771, recognizes that "public honor is security. The feather that adorns the royal bird supports his flight. Strip him of his plumage, and you fix him to the earth" (p. 224). "Strip him of his plumage," and you increase the chances that the royal icon will be smashed, both verbally on 4 July 1776 and physically five days later in New York City, when the gilded equestrian statue of George III was pulled down (fig. 40).[40]

Churchill had warned in 1763, in book 3 of *The Ghost,*

> For if we Majesty expose
> To vulgar eyes, too cheap it grows,
> The force is lost, and free from awe,
> We spy and censure ev'ry flaw.   (539–42)

As Samuel Johnson recognizes in his twenty-third sermon, the consequences of such diminution of the royalty dignity could be great:

> To be inferiour is necessarily unpleasing, to be placed in a state of inferiority to those who have no eminent abilities, or transcendent merit . . . increases the uneasiness; and every man finds in himself a strong inclination to throw down from their elevated state those whom he obeys without approbation, whom he reverences without esteem. When the passions are once in motion, they are not easily appeased, or checked. He that has once concluded it lawful to resist power, when it wants merit, will soon find a want of merit, to justify his resistance of power. (14:244)

Johnson was surely right: the satirists were "ignorant whither they [were] going." One of their destinations, however, was the American Declaration of Independence.

Chapter 3

"The Royal Brute of Britain"

Every Body Hates a King.
—Blake, "Marginalia on Francis Bacon," *Essays Moral, Economical, and Political,* 1798

Attacks on George III's personal and royal dignity paved the way, especially in America, for more fundamental assaults on regal authority and ultimately on the institution of monarchy itself.[1] Prior to the beginning of hostilities in the 1770s, most colonial Americans shared Samuel Johnson's belief in the significance of royal dignity. In his *Election Sermon* of 25 May 1768, Daniel Shute, a future rebel against the king, expressed the common feeling:

> A respectful treatment of their rulers is also due from the people, and greatly conducive to the end of civil institution. *They* are raised to exalted station by the *people,* under the governance of his providence, who wills the happiness of *all men,* and in promoting which they are to be considered as his viceregents executing his will, and therefore worthy of esteem and veneration. Their success in administration also very much depends upon this respectful deportment toward them: To pour contempt upon rulers is to weaken government itself, and to weaken government is to sow the seeds of libertinism, which in a soil so prolific as human nature, will soon spring up into a luxuriant growth; nor will it be in the power of rulers to stop the growing mischief, or, to keep things in a proper situation, without the concurring aid of the people. (*APW,* pp. 125–26)

By the mid-1770s, such unqualified support for the royal dignity was restricted to American Loyalists like Thomas B. Chandler, who expressed his feelings in *A Friendly Address to All Reasonable Americans* (New York, 1774).

Increasingly, colonial writers accepted Montesquieu's identification of dignity, or honor, as the defining characteristic of monarchy.[2] The anonymous author of *The People the Best Governors: or A Plan of Government Founded on the Just Principles of Natural Freedom* (New Hampshire, 1776) contends "that fear is the principle of a despotic, honour of a kingly, and virtue is the principle of a republican government (*APW*, p. 397). Carter Braxton makes the same distinctions in *An Address to the Convention of the Colony and Ancient Dominion of Virginia on the Subject of Government in General, and Recommending a Particular Form to Their Attention* (Virginia, 1776) (*APW*, p. 330).

By 1770, attacks primarily on his person had undercut George III's royal dignity, or honor. Such diminution of a particular king facilitated succeeding satirists' attempts to undermine kingship's general foundation. However, during the first decade of the new reign, Americans tended to be more loyal than their British cousins to their government and king.[3] Like his countrymen on both sides of the Atlantic, Abraham Williams, in his *Election Sermon* of 1762 (Boston), expresses an Anglo-American's pride in his constitution and optimism about the new reign: "Let us humbly adore and praise the Supreme Lord of the Universe, that he has so remarkably interposed, for the Preservation of our civil Constitution, and that he gives us so reasonably Hopes of its Continuance to the latest Generations. We still enjoy our Liberties and Properties, and the same free and good Government; notwithstanding the Attempts of domestic Traitors, arbitrary bigotted Tyrants, and foreign unrighteous Enemies, in former and later Times" (*APW*, p. 13).

Especially noteworthy in American comments on royal dignity and the British constitution are the frequent references to divine validation of the British political structure. These are expressions not of what Blackstone calls the "wild and absurd . . . doctrine of divine right" (p. 202), but rather of the idea that God ordains some (though not a particular) kind of government, as John Tucker notes in his Boston *Election Sermon* of 1771 (*APW*, p. 161).

In their rhetorical strategies, radicals like Thomas Paine and William Blake took into account the emphasis on God's relationship to government, particularly in colonial America, with its dissenting Protestant tradition of covenant government.[4] Even without specific divine sanctification of monarchy, the great majority of British subjects at the beginning of the new reign agreed with Samuel Johnson's conviction, reported by Thomas Cooper, president of South Carolina College, that Britain had the best of all possible governments: "I believe in no such thing as the jure divino of kings. I have no such belief; but I believe that monarchy is the most conducive to the happiness and safety of the people of every nation, and therefore I am a monarchist, but as to its divine right, that is all stuff. I think every people have the right to establish such government as they may think most conducive to their interest and happiness."[5]

To understand fully colonial satires of George III, we must see them, as their creators and original audience saw them, in a broader Anglo-American context, part of continuous British political, literary, and artistic traditions. Bernard Bailyn and Gordon Wood, among others, have convincingly demonstrated that American political ideology descends directly from the Opposition rhetorical strategy developed against Sir Robert Walpole in the first half of the eighteenth century, a strategy which is traceable back to seventeenth-century republican thought.[6] Colonial American opponents of British rule are rightly seen in the Country tradition of opposition to the court, only further distanced emotionally and intellectually, as well as geographically, from the alleged corruption of the court. As John Brewer points out, "The colonial crisis of the 1760s and 1770s was but the English crisis writ large. Fear of a powerful and corrupt government, fear for the rights of dissenting Protestants, a desire to harness or apprehend the powerful economic forces in the Anglophone world were the mainsprings of radical politics."[7]

The events that triggered the colonial crisis are too varied and complex to be treated here at any length. Alison Olson is surely right in seeing administrative developments in the third quarter of the century as crucial to explaining why the crisis occurred when and as it did.[8] An excessively rigid attempt to rationalize the imperial system of governance superseded the policy of "Salutory Neglect" and flexible response to changing colonial circumstances. The great compromisers, the Walpolean Whigs like Newcastle, passed suddenly from the scene in the mid-1760s, replaced by a new king and ministers less familiar with the importance of colonial interest-group pressures. The impulse toward increased rigidity reflected a larger Enlightenment attitude toward law itself. Beccaria, Hume, and Blackstone, by their writings, and Frederick the Great, by example, sought to make law scientific and predictable rather than random or capricious. In England, unfortunately, the results included the political blunders of prosecuting Wilkes for *North Briton* 45, expelling him from Parliament, and numerous important attempts to limit the freedom of the increasingly powerful press.[9] In almost every case, the government had law but not politics on its side. All these episodes affected the development of Anglo-American political satire.

One visual satire, *Daniel Cast into the Den of Lions, or True Blue Will Never Stain. To John Wilkes Esqr. This Plate Is Humbly Dedicated* (fig. 41), treats the controversial economic and political events of the mid-1760s. It appeared in early May 1763, soon after Wilkes's arrest for publishing *North Briton* 45, in which he implicitly condemns the king by suggesting that George had played Bute's dupe in the king's speech from the throne that had closed Parliament in April:

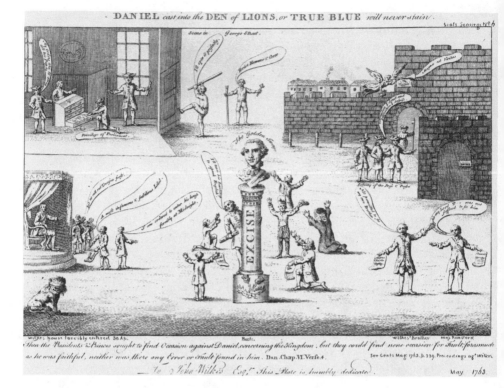

Figure 41. *Daniel Cast into the Den of Lions, or True Blue Will Never Stain* (BMC 4030). Reproduced by permission of the Trustees of the British Museum.

The *King's Speech* has always been considered by the legislature, and by the public at large, as the *Speech of the Minister*. It has regularly, at the beginning of every session of parliament, been referred by both houses to the consideration of a committee, and has been generally canvassed with the utmost freedom, when the minister of the crown has been obnoxious to the nation. . . . The speech at the *close* of the session has ever been considered as the most *secure* method, of promulgating the favourite court creed among the vulgar; because the parliament, which is the constitutional guardian of the liberties of the people, has in this case no opportunity of remonstrating, or of impeaching any wicked servant of the crown.

This week has given the public the most abandoned instance of ministerial effrontery ever attempted to be imposed on mankind. The *minister's speech* of last Tuesday, is not to be paralleled in the annals of this country. I am in doubt, whether the imposition is greater on the sovereign, or on the nation. Every friend of his country must lament that a prince of so many great and amiable qualities, whom England truly reveres, can be brought to give the sanction of his sacred name to the most odious measures, and to the most unjustifiable, public declarations, from a throne ever renowned for truth, honour, and unsullied virtue.

The "most odious measures" included the Peace of Paris and the ministerial attempt to rationalize and systematize repayment of war debts through a policy of "oeconomy," including an excise bill to tax beer, windows, and cider. Opponents charged that the ministry's economy was a false one, designed to profit its friends and oppress the public. According to Wilkes, behind the shameful peace and the impoverishing taxation lay the miseducating tenets of Bute that undercut royal dignity: "A despotic minister will always endeavour to dazzle his prince with high-flown ideas of prerogative and honour of the crown, which the minister will make a parade of firmly maintaining. I wish as much as any man in the kingdom to see the honour of the crown maintained in a manner truly becoming Royalty. I lament to see it sunk even to prostitution."

The theme of prostitution, particularly of education, reappears at the center of *Daniel Cast into the Den of Lions*. Samuel Johnson, identifiable by his pension ("300 pr. An"), offers, "I'll teach his Lordship to speak English." Johnson worships "the Golden Image," Bute's bust on a column marked "EXCISE." A Scottish thistle decorates the column's base, and on its capital are "CYDER," "WINDOWS," and "BEER." Other worshippers include Hogarth, with his print *The Times*, and Murphy, with his *Auditor*. To our left sits a distraught and blindfolded British lion. Behind him,

George III is on his throne. The British monarchy and this particular monarch are distinct here. One man brings George the "North Briton," calling it "a most infamous & seditious Libel." Remaining scenes in the print show the king's messengers seizing evidence in Wilkes's house in Great George Street, Westminster, his imprisonment in the tower (the "den" of the title), and the government's refusal to allow either Wilkes's brother or Earl Temple to visit the prisoner. Wilkes proclaims, "Corruption I detest and Persecution I despise." Ample evidence shows that Americans identified closely with Wilkes in his conflict with the ministry. The Wilkes affair is but a particular instance of the more general identification Americans made between themselves and political events in England during the mid-1760s.[10]

One of the most fruitful periods for studying Anglo-American relations and the influence of politics on art and literature is that of the Stamp Act Crisis of 1765–68.[11] Modern historians frequently locate the beginning of the American Revolution in this period, thereby agreeing with the designer of *The Tea-Tax-Tempest. or Old Time with his Magick-Lanthern* (fig. 42), published in London on 12 March 1783 to commemorate the formal end of the American Revolution. Illustrating the significance of the Stamp Act Crisis and the intimate relationship between words and pictures, this print demonstrates that visual satirists, no less than verbal satirists, worked within a tradition. The engraving is an adaptation of a 1778 print by Carl Guttenberg of Nuremberg, *The Tea-Tax-Tempest, or The Anglo-American Revolution* (BMC 5490), which in turn imitates a 1774 British print by John Dixon, *The Oracle Representing Britannia, Hibernia, Scotia, & America, as Assembled to Consult the Oracle, on the Present Situation of Public Affairs, Time Acting as Priest. Dedicated to Concord* (BMC 5225). The principal addition in the 1783 version is in Time's speech:

> There you see the little Hot Spit Fire Tea pot that has done all the Mischief—There you see the old British Lion basking before the American Bon Fire whilst the French Cock is blowing up a Storm About his Ears to Destroy him and his young Welpes—There you see Miss America grasping at the Cap of Liberty—There you see the British Forces be yok'd and be cramp'd flying before the Congress Men—There you see the thirteen Stripes and Rattlesnake exalted—There you see the Stamp'd Paper help to Make the Pot Boil—There you see &.&.&.

The first Stamp Act print, *The Deplorable State of America or Sc{otc}h Government* (fig. 43), was published in London on 22 March 1765, the day the act received the royal assent. At the center stands America, an Indian, who appeals to Minerva, "Secure Me, O, Goddess, by thy Wisdom: for I abhor it as Death." He refers to the "Pandoras Box," the "S[tam]p Act," that Britannia offers him. Pointing to Liberty, Minerva advises, "Take it not." Crying, "It is all over with Me," Liberty is assaulted by a serpent, whose tail is a Scottish thistle. The French king offers a money bag to an irradiated boot, saying, "Take this and let thy banefull Influence be poured down upon them." The boot's malevolent ray causes Mercury, patron of commerce, to tell America, "It is with reluctance I leave ye." In the background, on the left, stands a gallows, "Fit Entertainment for Stamp Men." Over America's head, an evil wind blows against a tree marked "To Liberty." The wind has already blown the crown off a figure presumably intended to represent George III, resplendent in his robes. Once again, the king, who says of the tree, "Heaven grant it may stand," is imagined as a patriot prince allied with America against his own ministry.

John Singleton Copley crudely adapted this British print for an American audience in *The Deplorable State of America* (fig. 44), published in Boston on 1 November 1765, the day the Stamp Act went into effect.[12] In addition to localizing allusions for the new viewers, Copley makes some significant substitutions: a female emblem of America, pointedly addressed as "Daughter" by Britannia, for the Indian male of the original, and a woman holding a crown for the king. Copley thus taps the rhetorical reservoir Kenneth Silverman labels "Whig Sentimentalism" to present America and the monarchy as helpless victims of ministerial tyranny.[13] Reference to a familial relationship between England and America underscores both the alleged unnaturalness of the treatment America receives and the natural link between the colonies and their mother country. The same sort of rhetorical appeal occurs in the Stamp Act satire *The Times: A Poem. By an American* (probably Benjamin Church), published in Boston in 1765:

> GEORGE! Parent! King! our Guardian, Glory, Pride,
> And thou fair REGENT! blooming by his side!
> Thy offspring pleads a parent's fostering care,
> Reject not, frown not, but in mercy spare;
> Besprent with dust, the lowly suppliant lies,
> A helpless, guiltless, injured sacrifice.   (p. 8)

Copley adds the "Atlantick" separating England and America to balance the mother-daughter relationship uniting them. Copley also adds "W. P[it]t's dog" urinating on a patch of thistles in the foreground, a nicely apt emblem combining fidelity and defiance, the same combination of reactions to the Stamp Act expressed in the 1765 *Oppression, a Poem by an American. With Notes by a North Briton*, published first in London and later in Boston and New York. The message that artist and author convey is that America is capable of responses other than passive suffering.

The most important images Copley retains from his English model are

The TEA-TAX-TEMPEST. or OLL

Figure 42. *The Tea-Tax-Tempest. or Old Time with his Magick-Lanthern* (BMC 6190). Courtesy of the John Carter Brown Library at Brown University.

There you see the little Hot Spit Fire Tea pot that has done all the Mischief — There you see the Old British Lion basking before the American Bon-Fire whilst the French Cock is blowing up a storm about his Ears to Destroy him and his young Welpes — There you see MÿS America grasping at the Cap of Liberty — There you see the British Forces be yokd and be crump'd flying before the Congress Men — There you see the thirteen Stripes and Rattle-Snake exalted — There you see the Stamp'd Paper help to Make the Pot Boil — There you see. &c. &c. &c.

with his MAGICK=LANTHERN.

Figure 43. *The Deplorable State of America or Sc{otc}h Government* (BMC 4119). Courtesy of the John Carter Brown Library at Brown University.

Figure 44. John Singleton Copley, *The Deplorable State of America* (Not in BMC). Reproduced by permission of the Library Company of Philadelphia.

the tree of life, or liberty, and the tree of death, or the gallows tree. As far as I have been able to discover, the first representation of the liberty tree that later became the icon of colonial Americans appears in Copley's English model. Copley, like so many others in and after 1765, appropriated the image because it was rhetorically so well suited to his cause. An organic image, like the mother-child relationship of Britannia and America, the icon of the liberty tree demonstrated that England and America's political relationship was natural and vital, rather than fabricated and unnecessary. Prints and verses repeatedly celebrate this natural justification for the colonists' position. Two such poems include "On Liberty Tree" by "Philo Patriae," which appeared in the *South-Carolina Gazette*, no. 1775 (21 September 1769), and Tom Paine's lines on the subject in the *Pennsylvania Magazine* of June 1775.

The image the anonymous British artist created was certainly a lucky hit for colonial propagandists. Trees had served as emblems of America and to celebrate colonial events since the mid-seventeenth century.[14] The liberty tree and its expression of natural rights complemented and soon replaced the royal oak and its association with regal powers. A quick glance at two more British engravings shows other images Stamp Act satirists could choose to represent the Anglo-American political system. The first print, *The Triumph of America* (1776) (fig. 45), celebrates the repeal of the Stamp Act on 18 March 1766, with Britain conventionally represented by the coach of state, led here by the horses "Crafty" (Lord Shelburne) and "Royal Oak." The subscribed key tells us that "the Horse Prerogative [was] formerly known by the Name of Liberty." The second print, *Samson Pulling Down the Pillars* (1767) (fig. 46), depicts Bute leveling the Temple of Liberty. Among the falling figures, the king has already lost his crown. Both the coach and the temple are emblems of structures designed and built by men, but what men have built, men can legitimately dismantle. The tree of liberty, however, expresses a myth of political power created independently of men, a power whose destruction by men is unnatural. The arboreal image was obviously much better suited than equally available alternatives to the rhetorical ends of Stamp Act satirists.

But how had the liberty tree come to be available to Stamp Act satirists in 1765? The answer leads us to recognize that they saw the Stamp Act Crisis not as an isolated event but rather as the latest alleged Butean attempt to destroy the rights of Britons. The tree image itself derives from such satires on the excise on cider (enacted in 1763) as *Scotch Paradice a View of the Bute{eye}full Garden of Edenborough* (see fig. 27), where Lord Bute distributes fruit labeled "Customs," "Excise," and "Stamps." The tree-of-corruption image traces back to satiric attacks on Sir Robert Walpole's unsuccessful attempt to pass an excise bill in 1733. As the verses accompanying *Scotch Paradice* make clear, in the transference of the spiritual type of the tree figure to a secular context with a political antitype, we see an example of what Paul Korshin calls abstracted typology[15]:

Like our first Parent when in Eden blest
We see you Posted higher than the rest
Laird of the Golden Pippens happy Scot
To be possesst of such a glorious Spot.

The tree of corruption's association with the tree of death becomes explicit in the lefthand design of the engraving *The Seizure, or Give the Devil His Due* (1763) (fig. 47), a print whose influence on American graphic satire has been overlooked. The verse invites us to, "With greater Joy, his L[ordship] see, / Like Judas hanging on a Tree." The devil hanging Bute from an apple tree points to Fox being hanged from the gallows tree. As one of the British farmers observes, "The Tree bears bad Fruit." Given the appearance of the tree of corruption as a secular antitype of the tree of death, it is not surprising that the British designer of *The Deplorable State of America* (see fig. 43) created the tree of liberty as a secular antitype of the tree of life.

The devil who hangs Fox on the gallows is the apparent model for the engraving of a devil on a gallows that appears in the 24 February 1766 issue of the *Boston Gazette and Country Journal;* the Judas-Bute hanging from the tree of corruption is the probable inspiration for the Judas-Huske hanging from the "Liberty Tree August 14, 1765" in Paul Revere's *View of the Year 1765* (advertised in the *Boston Gazette* of 27 January 1766). John Huske, a native of New Hampshire, had moved to England, where he was elected a member of the House of Commons and was consequently vilified in the colonies for allegedly being the Stamp Act's principal supporter. In Revere's engraving, the images of the tree of life and the tree of death are conflated into one image, the tree of liberty, that would be repeated for many years.

The Seizure needs to be added to the 1763 excise satire *A View of the Present Crisis* (BMC 4037), already identified by Clarence Brigham as a source for Revere's *View of the Year 1765*.[16] Like Copley, Revere adapts his sources for a colonial audience by, among other means, localizing the Judas figure. He asserts political as well as historical legitimacy for the colonists' cause with the addition of the figure of John Hampden, a seventeenth-century opponent of unconstitutional taxes. Two verbal substitutions that Revere makes are particularly interesting because they indicate the colonial artist's desire to be accepted as a part of the greater Anglo-American satiric and political tradition.[17] In the foreground are two bodies, one holding a

Figure 45. *The Triumph of America* (BMC 4152). Reproduced by permission of the Trustees of the British Museum.

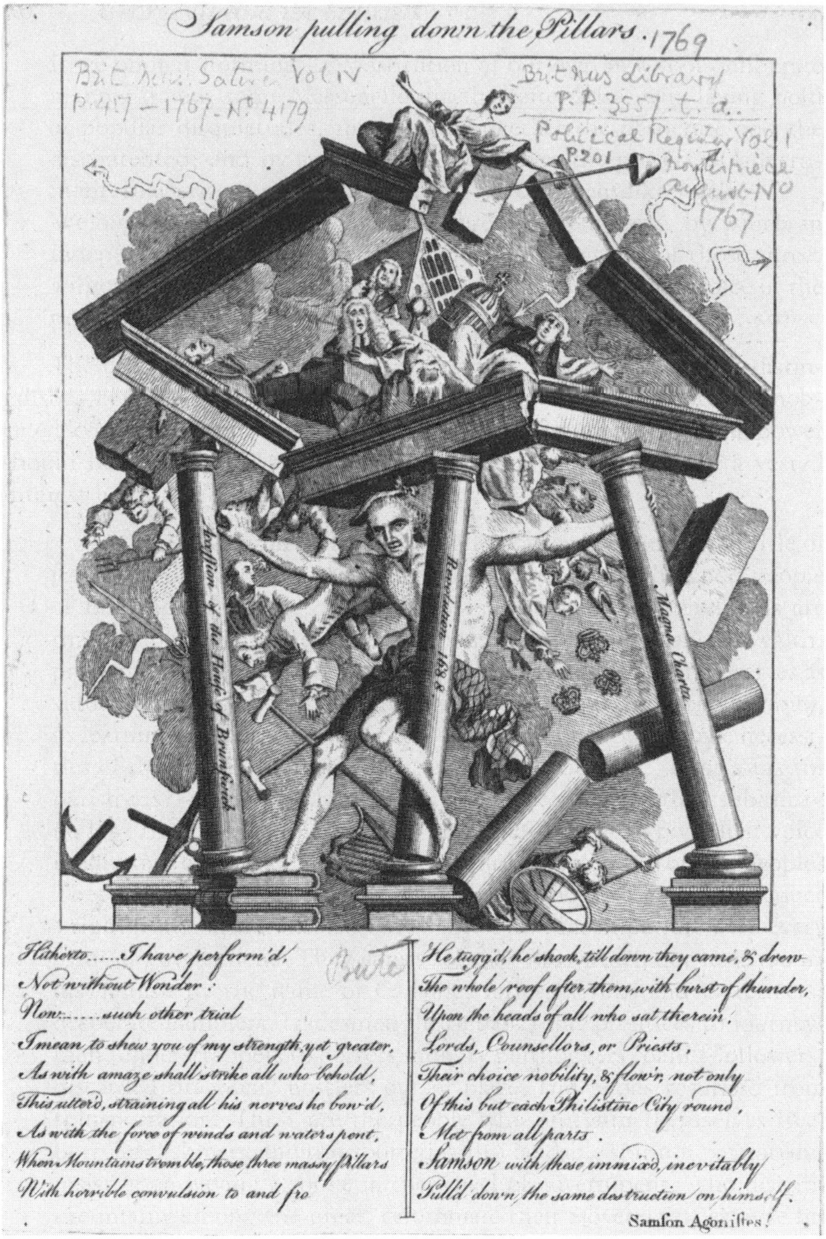

Figure 46. *Samson Pulling Down the Pillars* (BMC 4279). Reproduced by permission of the Trustees of the British Museum.

Figure 47. *The Seizure* (BMC 4026). Reproduced by permission of the Trustees of the British Museum.

scroll marked "Pym," the name of a seventeenth-century excise supporter, the other clutching a scroll marked "Anti-Sejanus," the pseudonym Dr. William Scott used to advocate the Stamp Act in the London *Public Advertiser*. Thus Revere reminds us of his Stamp Act satire's debt to recent excise prints and implies that the colonists' opposition to recurrent ministerial measures is well within the tradition of English struggles to maintain political freedom. And the appearance of Hampden is a warning of what would happen should the proponents of tyranny persist.

For a remarkably long time—until about 1775—Americans generally prided themselves on being good subjects of their king. The question Stephen Hopkins asked in 1764 was intended to be rhetorical. "Are not the people in the colonies as loyal and dutiful subjects as any age or nation ever produced; and are they not as useful to the kingdom, in this remote quarter of the world, as their fellow subjects are who dwell in Britain?" (*APW*, p. 59). And certainly most colonists during the first decade of the new reign shared Richard Bland's hope, expressed in *An Inquiry into the Rights of the British Colonies* (Williamsburg, 1776): "May the Colonies ever remain under a constitutional Subordination to Great Britain!" (*APW*, p. 86).

Given their apparently sincere belief that they were loyal British subjects, colonial engravers like Copley and Revere or colonial poets like Benjamin Church and the anonymous author of *Oppression* wanted to be received as contributors to the Anglo-American tradition, not as rebels, either artistic or political, against it. Rather than trying to hide or deny their debts, they emphasize and celebrate them. Church, for example, early in *The Times,* humbly alludes to his immediate British model—" 'Tis not great Churchill's ghost that claims your ear" (p. 3)—and then quickly adopts the pose of the virtuous Country observer independent of the corruption of the court, a pose Churchill had adapted from Alexander Pope. Even Church's assertion of an unlettered natural talent links him with the learned tradition of British political satire that Pope exemplified:

> Curs'd lack of genius, or thou soon should'st know,
> This humble cot conceals a tyrant's foe;
> By nature artless, unimprov'd by pains,
> No favour courts me, and no fear restrains,
> Wild as the soil, and as the heav'ns severe,
> All rudely rough, and wretchedly sincere;
> Whose frowning stars have thrown me God knows where,
> A wild exotic neighbour to the bear;
> One glebe supports us, brethren cubs we run,
> Shoot into form, as foster'd by the sun;
> No tutoring hand the tender sapling train'd,

Thro' walks of science, nor his growth sustain'd
Such fruit he yields, luxuriant wildings bear,
Course as the earth, and unconfin'd as air:
No Muse I court, an alien to the Nine,
Thou chaste instructress, NATURE! thou art mine;
Come, blessed parent, mistress, muse and guide,
With thee permit me wander side by side;
Smit with thy charms, my earliest joy I trace,
Fondly enamour'd of thy angel face;
Succeeding labours smother not the flame,
Still, still the dear attachment lives the same.   (pp. 4–5)

The "American" author of *Oppression* strikes a similar pose of unlettered
independence:

    I want no places at a servile [Court],
    To be the dupe of M[ini]st[eria]l sport;
    . . . .
    From such I can't expect the least, least good,
    An uncouth genius from a western wood;
    Who've neither wealth, election votes to bribe,
    Nor will, to hackney falsehood for a tribe.
    . . . .
    Such mighty nothings, from my soul I hate,
    And do despise them, as the banes of state:
    Nor would I change my happy sphere of life
    For all the folly of a c[ou]rtly strife.   (pp. 4, 5, 20)

Church and the "American" observe the conventions that the king can
do no wrong and that his ministers bear responsibility for governmental
measures. As does Church, the "American" castigates "Ye M[INI]S[TE]RS
that do surround the T[hrone]" (p. 8):

But O ye vilest vile, detested FEW!
Eager, intent, and potent to undoe;
Come out ye parricides! here take your stand.
Your solemn condemnation is at hand;
Behold your crimes, and tremblingly await
The grumbling thunder of your country's hate;
Accursed as ye are! how durst ye bring
An injur'd people to distrust their K[ing]?
Accursed as ye are, how could ye dare,
To lisp delusion in your M[onarc]h's ear?

How do I laugh, when such vain coxcombs lour,
Some grave pretence of dread, from lawless power:
To hear a scribling fry, beneath my hate,
Adopt the fraud, and sanctify deceit;
With mean importance; point regardless stings.
To aid injustice, menace mighty things;
Nay to such heights of insolence they're flown.
The knaves crave shelter underneath a throne;
A throne all-gracious, such is GEORGE'S praise,
Nor shall oppression blast his sacred bays.   (pp. 10–11)

The unnatural "parricides" are not the rebellious colonists but the ministers who mislead the king, pouring poisonous advice into his ear, and
alienate him from his people.

The Churchillian combination of precatory and monitory messages addressed to the king appears in both Church's and the "American's" poems,
though with different emphases. Church now has second thoughts about
the fulsome praise he had earlier given the new king in poems published
in *Pietas et Gratulatio* (Boston, 1761):

Not for a Monarch would I forge a lie,
To nestle in the sun-shine of his eye:
The paths of error if in youth I trod,
Dress'd a gay idol in the garb of God,
The pageant shrinks, I weep my folly past,
Heav'n frown me dead, but there I've sinn'd my last.   (p. 6)

The "American" is far more explicit in warning the king of the possible
consequences of his folly. The mixture of contempt and pity for the king
we have seen in visual satires reappears: "Th' unhappy man! I pity from
my heart, / That can't distinguish foes from friends apart" (p. 19). Bute is
held accountable for the king's loss of popularity in the first five years of
his reign:

For me, I cou'd not wish him a worse fate
Than galling conscience, and his master's hate.
The R[OYA]L ear he greatly has abus'd,
For selfish ends the R[OYA]L name has us'd;
Thus has estrang'd his subjects from their [King],
That few alas! too few, his praises sing.
Where are the shouts that wont to rend the sky,
And where the joy that gleam'd from ev'ry eye,
At sight of him, what acclamations rung,
Long live our [King], was echo'd from each tongue;

But now, unheeded may he pass along,
And scarce a wish is whisper'd by the throng.   (p. 19)

The alienation from his people that the king suffers because of his mis-education in what the "American" calls "the B[UTE]AN schools" may lead to far greater trouble:

Tho' Heaven knows! I greatly love my king,
And oft his real worth with rapture sing;
Yet if my country'd groan'd OPPRESSION'S hand,
And rose in arms, to save their sinking land;
I could not wish them harm, but wish them gain,
And to their righteous cause, must say, Amen.   (p. 20)

Like the vast majority of their compatriots on both sides of the Atlantic, Church and the "American" remain fundamentally loyal to the concept of monarchy, however disillusioned they may have become with the present king. Like Churchill, the "American," when he imagines a political reformation, offers himself as an alternative monarch, a true patriot king:

Were I a [KING]! I'd think it noble sport
To kick such mongril tyrants from my [Court].
No knavish soul, that's aggrandiz'd by wealth
Obtain'd by force, or got by meanest stealth,
Should tread the threshold of the R[oya]l dome,
But like a robber, be exil'd from home;
Or share, what best becomes a thievish wretch,
A Tyburn salutation from a Ketch.   (pp. 15–16)

Satirists of George III, particularly those in Britain, confirmed their faith in the monarchy, if not in George himself, by offering other political figures as substitute kings. Offsetting negative substitutes, Bute and the Stuart Pretender, were the king's uncle, the duke of Cumberland, who had defeated the Young Pretender in the rebellion of 1745, and John Wilkes. *The Jack-Boot Kick'd Down, or English Will Triumphant: A Dream* (fig. 48), published in 1762, is an engraved case of wishful thinking that shows Cumberland exerting regal authority. Whip in hand and standing on the steps of the throne, he has just kicked down a large jack-boot that contains Bute. Cumberland assures his nephew, Edward, duke of York, "Let me alone Ned, I know how to deal with Scotsmen;—Remember Culloden." Over Cumberland's head, the motto "In hoc Signo Vince [By that figure, conquer]" indicates that he is the country's only hope. The actual king, as the British lion, lies muzzled and asleep on the throne. To our right, through an open window, we see the results of George's alleged incompe-

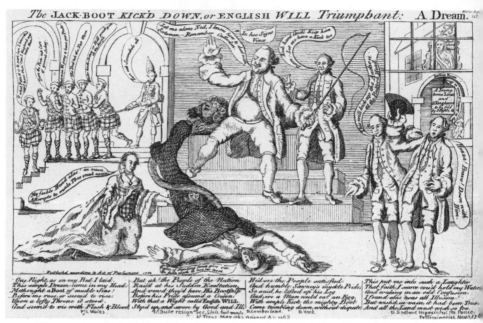

Figure 48. *The Jack-Boot Kick'd Down, or English Will Triumphant: A Dream* (BMC 3965). Reproduced by permission of the Trustees of the British Museum.

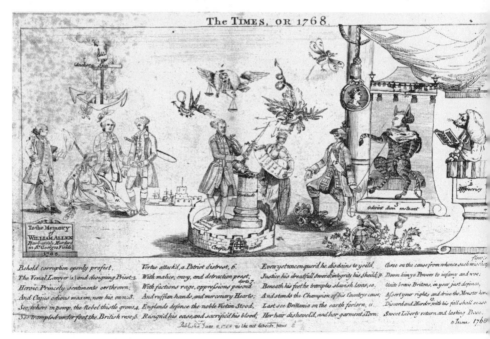

Figure 49. *The Times, or 1768* (BMC 4242). Reproduced by permission of the Trustees of the British Museum.

tence. The "Auction Room" of the "Bedford Head" offers for sale "a Young Tame Lion and 3 Kingdoms to be sold by J. Rustle Au[ctioneer]." John Russell, duke of Bedford, was the English negotiator of the Peace of Paris.

A print more subversive in its suggestion of an alternative ruler is *The Times, or 1768* (fig. 49). The subscribed verses reveal most of its meaning:

Behold corruption openly profest,
The Venal Lawyer (1) [Mansfield] and designing Priest: 2 [Henry Fox].
Heroic Princely sentiments oerthrown,
And Cajus [Caligula] odious maxim, now his own: 3.
See, where in pomp, the Rebel thistle grows, 4.
See trampled under foot the British rose; 5.
Vertue attack'd, a Patriot distrest, 6 [Wilkes].
With malice, envy, and detraction prest;
With factions rage, oppressions poison'd darts, 7.
And ruffian hands, and mercenary Hearts;
Englands defence the noble Victim Stood,
Resign'd his ease, and sacrific'd his blood;
Even yet unconquer'd he disdains to yeild [sic],
Justice his dreadfull sword 8; Integrity, his sheild [sic], 9.
Beneath his feet he tramples slavish laws, 10
And stands the Champion of his Countrys cause;
Last see Brittania on the earth forlorn, 11
Her hair dishevel'd, and her garments Torn.
Curse on the cause from whence such mischiefs flow: 12.
Doom him ye Powers to infamy and woe;
Unite brave Britons, in your just defence,
Assert your rights and drive the Monster hence;
Discord and Murder with his fall shall cease;
Sweet Liberty return and lasting Peace.

The tombstone dedicated "to the Memory of WILLIAM ALLEN" refers to "the Massacre of St. George's Fields" (10 May 1768). Allen had been killed by soldiers who mistook him for an organizer of a riotous Wilkesite crowd celebrating their hero's recent return from self-imposed exile in France to serve his prison term. The medallion portrait amidst the thistles on the right is labeled "turn Coat" to attack William Pitt for having accepted the title of earl of Chatham on 29 July 1766. Once again, the king is graphically off-center in the print, his central position taken here by Wilkes, at other times by the usurper Bute. The king is metaphorically off-center as well, depicted as a zebra, or ass, with Bute's leading-string tied to his nose. The king, as much a "Monster" as Bute with one of his goatish legs in a boot marked "Lust," is the secondary target of the satirist's call for his fellow Britons to "drive the Monster hence."

Even though George is once again shown as an inadvertent, foolish "Monster," he is nevertheless a tyrant, linked iconographically and verbally with earlier youthful tyrants. The medallion suspended near George is a portrait of Edward II, who had been the dupe of his evil favorite, Gaveston. More sinister in its implications is the "odious maxim" of Caligula, "Oderint dum metuant [Let them hate, as long as they fear]," which epitomizes the Scotch tenets Bute allegedly taught the dependent king. Despite the passion aroused by the Wilkes affair, however, Wilkes's supporters rarely intentionally posed a threat to the system of monarchy. Indeed, by offering a substitute ruler, they validated the system: "Plagiarising the distinctions employed by legitimate authority, his followers treated him as their monarch and ruler." [18] As when Jefferson, in *A Summary View of the Rights of British America* (Williamsburg, 1774), calls on George III to assume the role of Bolingbroke's "Patriot King," [19] the Wilkesites in the 1760s were calling for a proper king, not for no king at all.

But to truly radical opponents of the monarchy, like Jefferson, such calls were rhetorical ploys, rather than sincere requests, made to force the king into a politically untenable position. If the king did not assume the unrealistic role, he must bear responsibility for the consequences. Anglo-American reluctance, especially in Britain, to renounce the institution of monarchy was a force any rebel against the system had to recognize. For example, in *The Crisis* (no. 2) of 13 January 1777, addressed to Lord Howe, Paine imagines a "revolution" in England that replaced a mere king, not kingship, whereas in America he calls for the overthrow of the man and the office together: "For I, who know England and the disposition of the people well, am confident, that it is easier for us to effect a revolution there, than you a conquest here; a few thousand men landed in England with the declared design of deposing the present king, bringing his ministers to trial, and setting up the duke of Gloucester in his stead, would assuredly carry their point, while you were groveling here ignorant of the matter" (p. 92).

For Americans, particularly before the outbreak of hostilities in 1774, George III had greater significance as a symbol than as a man. He represented the ideal relationship between the parent country and its offspring. His American subjects were less familiar with his person than Englishmen, especially Londoners, who had frequent opportunity to see the man himself. Royal processions unavailable to George's colonial subjects accustomed Londoners to both the king's bodies. The king's primarily symbolic significance for Americans made the royal office at first easy to accept and ultimately easy to reject.

If we turn again to Paul Revere's satires, we note the absence, as in Revere's models, of the king. Evil measures are the ministry's responsibility; the king is the only virtual representative to whom the disfranchised colonists can appeal. A representative example of George III's symbolic status as a positive virtual representative of Americans and their cause can be seen in Revere's *View of the Obelisk Erected under Liberty-Tree in Boston on the Rejoicings for the Repeal of the ———— Stamp-Act 1766* (fig. 50). The portraits of George and Queen Charlotte are stylized, not particularized. Even more stylized is the image of George as a classical hero on the fourth side of the obelisk, labeled "And has her [America, represented as an Indian] LIBERTY restored by the Royal hand of GEORGE the Third." The lines on this column express the myth of George as the colonists' ally against the demon and Scotsmen on the other sides:

> Our FAITH approvd, our LIBERTY restor'd
> Our Hearts bend grateful to our sov'reign Lord
> That darling Monarch! by this act endeard
> Our firm affections are thy best reward
> Sh'd Britains self, against her self divide
> And hostile Armies frown on either Side
> Sh'd Hosts rebellious shake our Brunswicks Throne
> And as they dar'd thy Parent, dare the Son
> To this Asylum stretch thine happy wing
> And well contend, who best shall love our KING.

New York City manifested similar sentiments by voting to erect statues of George and Pitt to thank them for their parts in repealing the Stamp Act.

As it became clearer to everyone that measures unpopular in America had support in Parliament as well as in the ministry, the colonists clung to the belief that George was their potential, if not their actual, ally against threats to the British constitution and its guarantees of freedom. In his *Discourse at the Dedication of the Tree of Liberty* (Providence, 1768), Silas Downer stresses that Americans "live remote from the throne" and that "on this occasion we cheerfully recognize our allegiance to our sovereign Lord, *George* the third, King of *Great-Britain,* and supreme Lord of these dominions, but utterly deny any other dependence on the inhabitants of that island, than what is mutual and reciprocal between all mankind" (*APW,* p. 98). By 1774, Jefferson was espousing what Johnson, in *Taxation no Tyranny* calls "a tender tale," whereby America's only political tie with Britain is her voluntary recognition of a common sovereign, the king (10:413). "The British parliament," however, says Jefferson in *A Summary View,* "has no right to exercise authority over us."[20] By the second de-

Figure 50. Paul Revere, *A View of the Obelisk Erected under Liberty-Tree in Boston on the Rejoicings for the Repeal of the ———— Stamp-Act 1766* (Not in BMC). Courtesy of the Library of Congress.

L—d D——h | A—n B—r

L—d D—] | C—s T—d

L—d G. | S—k—e M' | D—B—t

J—n W—s—d | A C—ll

Boast foul Oppression boast thy transient Reign
While honest FREEDOM struggles in her Chair
But know the Sons of Virtue hardy brave
Disdain to lose thro' mean Disguise to save
Arouz'd in Thunder, awful they appear
With proud deliverance stalking in their Rear
While Tyrant-Foes their pallid Fears betray
Shrink from their Arms & give their Vengeance way
..e in th' unequal War OPPRESSORS fall
..he hate, Contempt and endless Curse of all

Our FAITH approv'd our LIBERTY restor'd
Our Hearts bend grateful to our sov'rign Lord
Hail darling Monarch by this act endear'd
Our firm affections are thy best reward
Sh'd Britains self, against herself divide
And hostile Armies frown on either Side
Sh'd Hosts rebellious shake our Brunswick's Throne
And as they dar'd thy Parent, dare the Son
To this Asylum stretch thine happy Wing
And well contend who best shall love our KING

Paul Revere Sculp

by her true born SONS, in BOSTON New England
..dures the Conflict for a short season (4. And has her LIBERTY restor'd by the Royal hand of GEORGE the Third

cade of George III's reign, the king's regal body, the supposed ally of the Americans, was increasingly the only political link between Britain and themselves that discontented colonists recognized.

Although in the event, as Paine recognized, the English were more firmly committed to monarchy than their colonial brethren, petitioning satires in the parent country began the assault on the king's dignity that facilitated his overthrow in America. From early in his reign, British satirists challenged the fiction that George would serve as an intermediary between the people and the ministry or Parliament. One example is the 1763 engraving *The Tenant's Complaint to David Simple, of Noodle Hall, Esqr.* (fig 51), which shows George as a country squire at the door of his estate. Holding his hand is the future Prince of Wales, and in his arms is the future duke of York. Petitioning attempts to have the Cider Act repealed occasioned the print. Their dialect identifies the apple growers of Somersetshire. The squire's tenants ask him to manage the farm himself: "An it please your Honour, we are come to beg you will lower our Rents, & Repair the Damages your Servants [the ministry] did in our Orchards"; "Humph! if you was to look more after your Affairs you would'nt be imposed upon so much"; "Zure you don't zay zo why the Esqr lives with so mutch OEconomy he cant want Money"; "But then he give greater wages to those Sawny Macboot recommended"; "Wounds Neighbours if the Esqr won't give us Zatisfaction We'll get a warrant against his Zervants at liberty Hall [Parliament]." The scene includes several spectators and their comments: "Depend upon it they'll make a great stir at Liberty Hall"; "Bribery Hall you mean"; "I'll get drunk if the late Stewart [Bute, with a pun on his family name] is sent to Jail." The familiar combination of pleading, warning, and cynicism is apparent. The simpleminded king is at least indirectly responsible for the condition of his farm: "You know good people, I don't trouble myself about my Estate, I leave the management to my Stewards & Clerks, if they supply me with mony that's sufficient."

In the course of the first decade of his reign, George's role in government was increasingly, and rightly, perceived as an active one. George's personal desire to punish Wilkes for earlier attacks on the king's mother in *North Briton* 5 was widely thought to have caused Wilkes's prosecution (considered by many to be persecution) for *North Briton* 45. The same motivation presumably explained the king's support of Parliament's power to expel Wilkes from Parliament and to nullify his reelection. Satirists interpreted as complicity in Parliament's corruption George's refusal to agree to the numerous petitions on Wilkes's behalf that Parliament be prematurely dissolved so that early elections could be held. However, the king was simply observing the principle of sovereignty Johnson sets forth in *The False Alarm* (London, 1770):

Figure 51. *The Tenant's Complaint to David Simple, of Noodle Hall, Esqr.* (BMC 4021). Reproduced by permission of the Trustees of the British Museum.

The first laws had no law to enforce them, the first authority was constituted by itself. The power exercised by the House of Commons is of this kind, a power rooted in the principles of government, and branched out by occasional practice, a power which necessity made just, and precedents have made legal.

It will occur that authority thus uncontrolable may, in times of heat and contest, be oppressively and injuriously exerted, and that he who suffers injustice, is without redress, however innocent, however miserable.

The position is true but the argument is useless. The Commons must be controlled, or be exempt from control. If they are exempt they may do injury which cannot be redressed, if they are controlled they are no longer legislative.

If the possibility of abuse be an argument against authority, no authority ever can be established; if the actual abuse destroys its legality, there is no legal government now in the world. (10:322)

Not everyone, of course, believed that George was gaining control of the government, either as tyrant or as patriot king. In *Resignation*, by imagining his reformation, Chatterton castigates George for pursuing the "trifling amusement" of button making (the subject of several earlier satires) and for allowing Bute to continue ruling from behind the scenes through his latest tool, Lord North:

His Majesty: (the buttons thrown aside)
Declard his fixd intention to preside
No longer sacrific'd to every Knave
He'd shew himself discreet as well as brave,
In evry Cabinet and Council Cause
He'd be Dictator and enforce the Laws
Whilst North sho'd in his present Office stand
As understrapper to direct his hand
  Now Expectation, now extend thy Wing
Happy the Land whose Minister's a King
Happy the King who ruling each Debate
Can peep thro' every Roguery of State.
See! Hope, array'd in Robes of virgin white
Trailing an Arch'd Variety of Light
Comes showring blessings on a ruind realm
And shews the crownd Director of the helm
Return fair Goddess till some future day
The King has seen the Error of his way
And by his smarting Shoulders seems to feel

The Wheel of State is not a Cathrine Wheel
Wise by Experience, genral Nurse of Fools
He leaves the Ministry to venal Tools
And finds his happy Talents better suit
The making of buttons for his favrite Bute
In countenancing the unlawful Views
Which North the Delegate of Bute pursues
In glossing with Authority a Train
Whose names are Infamy, and objects, Gain.   (449–76)

Similar in spirit to Chatterton's passage is the 1770 engraving *The Effects of Petitions and Remonstrances* (fig. 52). Again the king is graphically off-center to indicate his subordination to his mother and Bute, who are seated on a sofa apart from and above the king. Holding "the humble Address and Remonstrance of the C[it]y of L[ondon]," she tells the king, "This Rem[onstran]ce is T[reaso]n, but fear them not, my Lords brave Countrymen will defend you." She refers to the Scottish regiments who had fired into Wilkes's supporters in St. George's Fields and who, opponents of the ministry said, were to be the vanguard of a military takeover planned by the "King's Friends." The king replies to his mother, "I submit myself entirely to your Guidance." Under the king's foot is the petition "of the City of Westminster." Lord Bute objects, "Mun a K[ing] bear with such Language from a gang of Loons it must not be." In the background are several prominent "King's Friends": Lord Mansfield, speaker of the House of Lords, wearing a Scottish bonnet; Sir Fletcher Norton, speaker of the House of Commons, with the head of a bull; and the duke of Grafton, in the guise of an ape.

In other contemporary satires, however, George is clearly responsible for thwarting the people's will. The 1770 print *The Fate of City Rem[on-stran]ces. Engraved for the Oxford Magazine* (fig. 53) shows George III and the Prince of Wales, who tells his father, "Papa, I want some Paper to make a Kite." Pointing to several papers lying on the floor, including "the Humble Petition and Remonstrance," the king replies, "Take some of these Petitions and Remonstrances they are fit for nothing else." More sinister in its charge that the king is the source of corruption is the 1770 engraving *"To find a Man, long & in vain, Diogenes sought around, / This Citizen he meets, his Lanthorn drops, & cries I've found"* (BMC 4391), a panegyric on William Beckford, lord mayor of London, who declines George's offer of a title.

A satire that illustrates the gradual shift from depicting George as fool to depicting George as knave is the 1770 *Nero Fiddling, Rome Burning, Pompaja & Agrippina Smiling* (fig. 54), engraved for the *Oxford Magazine*. Rome, or London, burns as Nero, or George III, plays his fiddle. Beneath his foot are two books, *"Laws of Humanity"* and *"Laws of Discretion."* On one side of

Figure 52. *The Effects of Petitions and Remonstrances* (BMC 4386).
Reproduced by permission of the Trustees of the British Library.

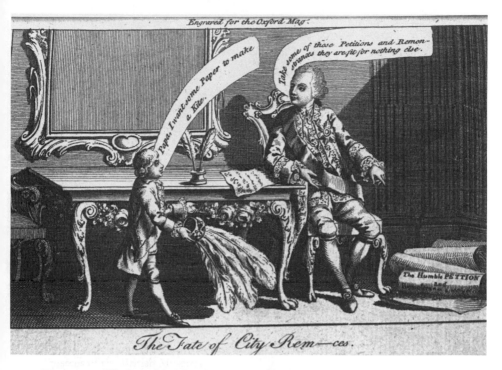

Figure 53. *The Fate of City Rem{onstran}ces* (BMC 4387). Reproduced by
permission of the Trustees of the British Library.

Figure 54. *Nero Fiddling, Rome Burning, Pompaja & Agrippina Smiling* (BMC 4381). Reproduced by permission of the Trustees of the British Museum.

the king, Pompaja (Queen Charlotte) asks, "Oh my dear play me the other little Tune"; on the other side, Agrippina (the Princess of Wales) advises, "My Son you have done well, they are all Rebels; but you should have got their Money from them first." The king exults, "What a Charming Blaze! this will let them know I am their Master."

Growing recognition of the king's active role in politics inevitably led to changes in the strategies and tactics of the government's opponents. As Edmund Burke's *Thoughts on the Cause of the Present Discontents* (1770), Junius's *Letters* (1769–71), and Paine's *Common Sense* (1776) demonstrate, important elements of the rhetorical strategy developed against Sir Robert Walpole had to be transformed. Very early in his *Thoughts*, Burke qualifies an essential premise of that strategy, the belief in uniformitarianism (the idea that human nature is always and everywhere the same), which justified the use of exemplar history to draw parallels between the past and present in order to illuminate the present and to predict the future:

> To complain of the age we live in, to murmur at the present possessors of power, to lament the past, to conceive extravagant hopes of the future, are the common dispositions of the greatest part of mankind; indeed the necessary effects of the ignorance and levity of the vulgar. Such complaints and humors have existed in all times; yet as all times have *not* been alike, true political sagacity manifests itself in distinguishing that complaint which only characterizes the general infirmity of human nature, from those which are symptoms of the particular distemperature of our own air and season. (pp. 252–53; Burke's italics)

To some extent, Burke simply reveals his recognition of recent developments in historiography (for example, David Hume's *History of England*), which challenged the easy application of the past to the present: "Every age has its own manners, and its politicks dependent upon them; and the same attempts will not be made against a constitution fully formed and matured, that were used to destroy it in the cradle, or to resist its growth during its infancy" (p. 258).[21] But, as his choice of an organic, developmental metaphor indicates, Burke's questioning of uniformitarianism and exemplar history has a rhetorical purpose as well. He implies that the creation of a system in which a double cabinet rules Britain is a factitious one. The Butean system depends upon the dual existence of a publicly acknowledged ministry who bears responsibility for measures it lacks the power to create and of a hidden ministry of "King's men" (p. 274) who have power but no responsibility.

Burke's description of systemic corruption and his challenge to received historiography anticipate Paine's more fundamental challenges to the system of monarchy and the use of the past. For Burke, the Butean system has so subtly corrupted Parliament through the influence of the Crown that legislators have been "taught by degrees" to acquiesce in the conspiracy against the constitution (p. 261). Use of the same didactic metaphor earlier satirists had employed underscores the factitiousness of what Burke later calls "that political school" (p. 267). Bute's unnatural school is built upon decay and disease in the body politic: "The power of the Crown, almost dead and rotten as Prerogative, has grown up anon, with much more strength, and far less odium, under the name of Influence. . . . It is this unnatural infusion of a *system of favoritism* into a Government which in a great part of its constitution is popular, that has raised the present ferment in the nation" (pp. 258, 276; Burke's italics). When not described as unnatural, the system appears in an architectural metaphor to stress its factitious origin: "Government may in a great measure be restored, if any considerable bodies of men have honesty and resolution enough never to accept Administration, unless this garrison of *King's men,* which is stationed, as in a citadel, to controul and enslave it, be entirely broken and disbanded, and every work they have thrown up be levelled with the ground" (p. 313; Burke's italics).

Besides the constitution and the people, the greatest victim of the Butean system, which was supposed "to prevent the King from being enslaved by a faction, and made a prisoner in his closet" (p. 287), is ironically George III. The system has squandered the good will and high hopes that had greeted the new king in 1760 (pp. 262–63). An unanticipated consequence of the Butean "political school" is diminution of the royal dignity essential to the power of the king:

> Has this system provided better for the treatment becoming his high and sacred character, and secured the King from those disgusts attached to the necessity of employing men who are not personally agreeable? This is a topic upon which for many reasons I could wish to be silent; but the pretence of securing against such causes of uneasiness, is the corner-stone of the Court-Party. It has however so happened, that if I were to fix upon any one point, in which this system has been more particularly and shamefully blamable, the effects which it has produced would justify me in choosing for that point its tendency to degrade the personal dignity of the Sovereign, and to expose him to a thousand contradictions and mortifications. (p. 289)

One result of the degradation of "the personal dignity of the Sovereign" was the production of "the most audacious libels on Royal Majesty" (pp. 297–98), some of which we have already seen.

Among Burke's motives for adapting the traditional Opposition rhetorical strategy to the current political situation was to respect the convention that the king can do no wrong. Along with his subjects, George III is the victim of the Butean school. To maintain this fiction, however, Burke must reject others: uniformitarianism, exemplar history, the undesirability of parties, and the necessity of attacking measures, not men. Among Burke's principal contributions in the *Thoughts* is his updating an inherited rhetorical strategy that had become increasingly inappropriate for satirists to apply to the current situation. As Burke says, "I have constantly observed, that the generality of people are fifty years, at least, behind-hand in their politicks. There are but very few, who are capable of comparing and digesting what passes before their eyes at different times and occasions, so as to form the whole into a distinct system" (p. 256). But George III does not come out of the *Thoughts* unscathed. No reader accustomed during the past ten years to seeing his king satirized as slumbering on the job could fail to identify one of the targets in a passage near the end of Burke's pamphlet: "Public life is a situation of power and energy; he trespasses against his duty who sleeps upon his watch, as well as he that goes over to the enemy" (p. 320).

Gradual transformation of the inherited Opposition rhetorical strategy can be traced through Junius's letters in *The Public Advertiser* from November 1768 to January 1772 and their subsequent republication with notes, preface, and "Dedication to the English Nation" in the collected Woodfall edition of 1772. Junius clearly moves toward direct attacks on the king's mortal body as he finds the traditional conventions increasingly difficult to observe. *Letter* 1 (21 January 1769) of the collected edition (Junius omitted the 21 November 1768 letter) virtually opens with an acknowledgment of the convention of the king's two bodies: "A generous nation is grateful even for the preservation of its rights and willingly extends the respect due to the office of a good prince into an affection for his person" (p. 25). Of course, Junius's rhetorical purpose is to show that he and his countrymen were predisposed to welcome monarchy and the present king: "When our gracious sovereign ascended the throne, we were a flourishing and a contented people. If the personal virtues of a king could have insured the happiness of his subjects, the scene could not have altered so entirely as it has done" (p. 26). Junius would soon alter his estimation of the value of George's private virtue.

By *Letter* 36 (14 February 1770), addressed to the duke of Grafton, the king's domestic virtues have become a diversion from real issues: "Now my lord, let us consider the situation to which you have conducted, and in which you have thought it advisable to abandon, your royal master. Whenever the people have complained, and nothing better could be said in defense of the measures of the government, it has been the fashion to

answer us, though not very fairly, with an appeal to the private virtues of
your Sovereign" (pp. 176–77). References to the king's domestic virtues
are later (*Letter* 37, 19 March 1770) seen as self-serving: "Our gracious
King, indeed, is abundantly civil to himself. Instead of an answer to petition, his majesty very graciously pronounces his own panegyric" (p. 184).
Finally, in the preface composed for the collected edition, Junius contemp-
tuously dismisses references to the king's private virtues: "And if You are,
in reality, that public Man, that King, that Magistrate, which these questions suppose You to be, is it any answer to your people, to say, that among
your domestics You are good-humored,—that to one lady You are faithful,
—that to your children You are indulgent?" (p. 23).

In the early letters (the notorious *Letter* 35, 19 December 1769, may
serve as a turning point), Junius accepts the conventions of royal innocence
and ministerial responsibility. For example, in *Letter* 8 (18 March 1769),
Junius tells Grafton,

> Before you were placed at the head of affairs, it had been a maxim
> of the English government, not unwillingly admitted by the people,
> that every ungracious or severe exertion of the prerogative should be
> placed to the account of the Minister; but, that whenever an act of
> grace or benevolence was to be performed, the whole merit of it should
> be attributed to the Sovereign himself. It was a wise doctrine, my
> Lord, and equally advantageous to the King and his subjects; for while
> it preserved that suspicious attention with which the people ought
> always to examine the conduct of ministers, it tended, at the same
> time, rather to increase than diminish their attachment to the person
> of their Sovereign. (p. 54)

Like earlier satirists, Junius at first sees George III as "the deluded
prince" at the mercy of a Butean system of miseducation that imprisons
him in his office (*Letter* 12, 30 May 1769, p. 72). Such is the charge he
makes against the duke of Bedford in *Letter* 23 (19 September 1769): "The
measures you have taken to obtain and confirm it ["absolute power"], are
too gross to escape the eyes of a discerning judicious prince. His palace is
besieged; the lines of circumvallation are drawing round him; and unless
he finds a resource in his own activity, or in the attachment of the real
friends of his family, the best of princes must submit to the confinement
of a state prisoner, until your Grace's death, or some less fortunate event,
shall raise the siege" (p. 123).

Once again we hear that the Butean system has "degraded the Royal
dignity into a base, dishonourable competition with Mr. Wilkes" (*Letter*
15, 8 July 1769, p. 83). His ministers "advise the King to hazard his dig-

nity by a positive declaration of his own sentiments. . . . As the matter stands, the minister, after placing his sovereign in the most unfavorable light to his subjects, and after attempting to fix the ridicule and odium of his own precipitate measures upon the royal character, leaves him a solitary figure upon the scene"; the system renders royal dignity "cheap and common," and the king's "sacred character is prostituted and dishonored" (*Letter* 38, 3 April 1770, pp. 189, 191).

However, the rhetorical strategy of attacking a conspiratorial Butean system that controlled the king, attractive though it was, became more difficult to maintain in light of two events: Lord North's assumption of ministerial leadership at the beginning of 1770 and the death of the Princess of Wales, the king's mother, in 1772. The accession of North, who more clearly than his predecessors cooperated with rather than controlled George III, inaugurated an administration that continued in power for the next dozen years. The death of Bute's alleged lover removed one of the supporting pillars of the conspiracy theory so usefully constructed by frustrated aspirants to power. The theory of "Scotch politics" did not disappear in 1772, but with the Princess of Wales's death, the attendant sensationalism was lost. To be sure, poets, like the author of *The Favourite* (London, 1778), would remind readers that Bute had been "PREFERR'D to quench a *Messalina's Rage,*" but Junius and others faced the choice of either tenaciously clinging to a strategy that seemed to explain events less frequently or reevaluating the king's role in politics.

Junius's reevaluation is unmistakable. George III may still be a fool, but he is now a dangerous one whose overtly personal involvement in the struggle for power undercuts his royal dignity. Junius tells the Reverend John Horne (later, Tooke) in *Letter* 52 (24 July 1771):

> You cannot but know,—nay you dare not pretend to be ignorant, that the highest gratifications of which the most detestable ———— in this nation is capable, would have been the defeat of Wilkes. I know *that man* much better than any of you. Nature intended him only for a good humoured-fool. A systematical education, with long practice, has made him a consummate hypocrite. Yet this man, to say nothing of his worthy ministers, you have most assiduously laboured to gratify. . . . What would have been the triumph of that odious hypocrite and his minions, if Wilkes had been defeated. (p. 257)[22]

By 28 September 1771, in *Letter* 57, addressed to Grafton, George III has shifted from being victim of the Butean system to being virtual director of a neo-Stuart attempt to impose tyranny on Britain. For obvious reasons of policy, Junius makes the charge indirectly:

Neither *Charles* nor his brother were qualified to support such a system of measures, as would be necessary, to change the government, and subvert the constitution of England. One of them was too much in earnest in his pleasures,—the other in his religion. But the danger to this country would cease to be problematical, if the crown should ever descend to a prince, whose apparent simplicity might throw his subjects off their guard,—who might be no libertine in behaviour,—who should have no sense of honour to restrain him, and who, with just religion enough to impose upon the multitude, might have no scruples of conscience to interfere with his morality. With these honorable qualifications, and the decisive advantage of situation, low craft and falsehood are all the abilities that are wanting to destroy the wisdom of ages, and to deface the noblest monument that human policy has erected—I know *such* a man;—My Lord, I know you both; and with the blessing of God (for I, too, am religious) the people of England shall know you as well as I do. I am not very sure that greater abilities would not in effect be an impediment to a design which seems at first sight to require a superior capacity. A better understanding might make him sensible of the wonderful beauty of that system he was endeavouring to corrupt. The danger of the attempt might alarm him. The meanness, and intrinsic worthlessness of the object (supposing he could attain it) would fill him with shame, repentance, and disgust. But these are sensations, which find no entrance into a barbarous, contracted heart. In some men, there is a malignant passion to destroy the works of genius, literature, and freedom. The *Vandal* and the *Monk* find equal gratification in it. (pp. 283–84)

Without denying George III's allegedly limited intelligence, Junius here merges George as fool with George as knave to create a figure whose mental limitations render his malevolence all the more dangerous. His domestic virtues are a consciously assumed mask of hypocrisy. In the preface, one of the last things Junius wrote, the convention that the king can do no wrong is no longer tenable. However, Junius, unlike Paine, remains a monarchist; a particular king, not kingship, is at fault:

SOME opinion may now be expected from me, upon a point of equal delicacy to the writer, and hazard to the printer. When the character of the chief magistrate is in question, more must be understood than may be safely expressed. If it be really a part of our constitution, and not a mere *dictum* of the law, *that the King can do no wrong,* it is not the only instance, in the wisest of human institutions, where theory is at variance with practice.—That the sovereign of this country is not amenable to any form of trial known to the laws, is unquestionable. But exemption from punishment is a singular privilege annexed to the royal character, and no way excludes the possibility of deserving it. How long and to what extent, a King of *England* may be protected by the forms, when he violates the spirit of the constitution, deserves to be considered. A mistake in this matter proved fatal to *Charles* and his son.—For my own part, far from thinking that the King can do no wrong, far from suffering myself to be deterred or imposed upon by the language of forms in opposition to the substantial evidence of truth, if it were my misfortune to live under the inauspicious reign of a prince, whose whole life was employed in one base, contemptible struggle with the free spirit of his people, or in the detestable endeavour to corrupt their moral principles, I would not scruple to declare to him,—"Sir, You alone are the author of the greatest wrong to your subjects and to yourself." (pp. 21–22)

In just a few years, Paine would be even less "deterred or imposed upon by the language of forms"; for him, a king, any king, could do no right and must be punished condignly. To a reformer like Junius, the fault lies in the man who corrupts the office; to a radical like Paine, the fault lies in the office, which corrupts the man.

Junius's identification of George III as the active center of court corruption was not unprecedented, but his emphasis on the king's controlling influence was an important development. Heretofore, as in the 1766(?) print *An Exact Representation of the Customs at the Court of Blunderpole in a New Discoverd Island Extracted from the Travels of Don Juan de Tell-Truth* (fig. 55), the king remained Bute's dupe. This print, an adaptation of the earlier attack on George II, *The Festival of the Golden Rump* (see fig. 10), combines images from previous attacks to show George III as the blindfolded female Fortune, with the king's profile. The subscribed allegorical key fully describes the scene. Lord Scratchum Scotchum is Bute; Prince Choplinouski (intended to represent a mock, incompetent Polish despot) is George III; Lord Cheatly Chatlum is the earl of Chatham; Lord Conjurdom is the earl of Mansfield; Bulnob Jawinton is Sir Fletcher Norton; Sekliw is Wilkes; and the Philopatrians are the Opposition.

Junius's placing George III in the central role as Britain's corrupter anticipates John Collier's depiction of the king in plate 17, entitled "Oppression," of the drawing book *Human Passions Delineated in Above 120 Figures, Droll, Satyrical, and Humorous: Design'd in the Hogarthian Style, Very Useful for Young Practitioners in Drawing. By Timothy Bobbin. . . .* (1773) (fig. 56). Collier's representation is significant because the context in which George III appears, a drawing book, which is ostensibly politically neutral, indicates

…niquitous decrees he holds a scroll of parchment coverd with necromantic Characters
…powerfully convey those he opposes to inchanted castles from whence tis hard to escape
…not Ianvinton or the Councellor an asistant to the former those who can take harangue
…ise drawn out into length for reasoning are great admirers of his abilities and infer
…ight of the argument from the heaviness of the pleading he wears a Party colourd
… on his Shoulder black & White Signifiging his eloquence can prove black white & white blac:
…(and other Blunderpolians) are represented Celebrating the festival of Charterun Crushun
…ich they dance round the Court Idol and kick about the Philopatrian records
…lin or the Patriot who laments the degeneracy of his Countrymen.

1766

Figure 56. "Oppression" (Not in BMC). Reproduced by permission of the Henry E. Huntington Library and Art Gallery, San Marino, California.

the wide range of outlets in Britain for anti-George satires in the early 1770s. The likeness of the king in the print is not a good one, but the "Explanation" for plate 15 clearly identifies the target:

So have I seen in these our modern times,
Some men rewarded for rebellious crimes;
Plaids and blue bonnets smil'd upon with grace,
Enrich'd with pensions, and adorn'd with place.
Whilst every patriot's frown'd upon with scorn,
Oppress'd with taxes, grievous to be born!
Poor England's loaden till his sinews crack,
And quite broke down with weights upon his back;
Wrinkl'd and bald, o'ercome with care and pain,
But ease expects not whilst a R——mp doth reign.
You half French-Britons can you loll at ease,
As under vines, rul'd by such ——ngs as these.

A direct connection with Junius's growing hostility to the king himself is found in two 1770 prints on press censorship. The first, *The Royal Chace* (fig. 57), shows the king following Mansfield, who shouts, "The Printer! hey! ho!" while in pursuit of three men, one of whom bears the title *London Museum*, the name of the magazine in which John Almon reproduced Junius's "Letter to the King" of 19 December 1769. (Almon, who was also Wilkes's publisher and strong supporter, was prosecuted and convicted.)[23] At the center of the landscape is the British oak, labeled "Junius," in whose upper branches sits the satirist himself. The subscribed verse reads:

To Drive the Printers [with] hound and horn,
    George and Mansfield took their Way:
The Child may rue that was unborn,
    The Hunting of that Day.
    Chevy Chace.

The second print, *Round about the Cauldron Go, / In the Tortur'd Printers Throw* (fig. 58), shows George III, enthroned and in his royal robes, directing his courtiers to toss papers marked with the names of Junius's publisher (Samuel Woodfall) and reprinters (Almon, Charles Green Say) into the cauldron. Several references to the king's use of corruption are apparent: the "Privy Purse" disgorges coins at his feet; in the foreground lie books entitled "*A List of Pensioners on the Irish Establishment*" and "*Prerogative of the Crown*." The shredded copy of "Magna Char[ta]" represents one result of George's reign. Another result is artistic corruption, a consequence of the "malignant passion to destroy the works of genius, literature, and freedom" that Junius would soon accuse George of harboring. The books

Figure 57. *The Royal Chace* (BMC 4367). Courtesy of the John Carter Brown Library at Brown University.

Figure 58. *Round about the Cauldron Go* (BMC 4392). Reproduced by permission of the Trustees of the British Library.

entitled *"Architecture"* and *"Kirby's Perspective"* refer to works by Sir William Chambers, designer of the pagoda in Kew Gardens, and Joshua Kirby, George's teacher of perspective. As in Pope's *New Dunciad,* corruption of the arts is essential to corruption of the polity.

The colonists could no longer ignore George's allegedly malevolent direction of government when, in the winter of 1775–76, within days of the appearance of Paine's *Common Sense,* the king's Royal Proclamation accused the colonies of seeking independence and defended parliamentary supremacy over them. The king's proclamation, issued months earlier in Britain, removed him as a candidate for savior of the colonists' rights just as Paine was contending that the colonists needed no such champion because they could save themselves. George's role continued to be misunderstood, perhaps willfully.[24]

Paine argued that the colonists needed no virtual representative on the throne or in Parliament; indeed, because their cause's meaning transcended the present, they became the virtual representatives, the location of political sovereignty, for future generations: "The sun never shined on a cause of greater worth. 'Tis not the affair of a city, a county, a province, or a kingdom, but of a continent—of at least one eighth part of the habitable globe. 'Tis not the concern of a day, a year, or an age; posterity are virtually involved in the contest, and will be more or less affected, even to the end of time, by the proceedings now" (p. 27).

However, to elevate the people, Paine must first dethrone the king, the primary target of his pamphlet. Paine exploits the satiric tradition of attacking the king's two bodies in order to desacralize the office. The process of desacralization begins with the epigraph from James Thomson, an earlier "Whig panegyrist": "Man knows no Master save creating Heaven, / Or those whom Choice and common Good ordain."[25] At first glance, this epigraph seems compatible in theory with Burke's concept of the relationship between Britain's government and the divine order: "The King is the representative of the people; so are the Lords; so are the Judges. They are all trustees for the people, as well as the Commons; because no power is given for the sole sake of the holder; and although Government certainly is an institution of Divine authority, yet its forms, and the persons who administer it, all originate from the people" (*Thoughts,* p. 292). In practice, however, Burke and Paine differ profoundly because of their respective views on the value of history. For Burke, the longevity of monarchy as a system of government gives it value by virtue of prescriptive right. This argument, to Paine, is based on pride and prejudice: "The prejudice of Englishmen in favour of their own government by king, lords and commons, arises as much or more from national pride than reason" (p. 18). Prescriptive right implies that the basis of the present system is the divinely ordained popular contract Burke and Paine agreed was the only means to legitimate government. But Paine goes much further than Burke in challenging the applicability of the past to the present: just because something has been wrong for centuries does not make it right now. He substitutes the absolute standard of natural rights for the relative standard of prescriptive rights and finds monarchy illegitimate.

Paine rejects two of the most important historiographic tenets of Whig political orthodoxy—the notion of the immemorial Anglo-Saxon constitution and the belief that William of Normandy was not a conqueror who irrevocably altered that constitution.[26] The anonymous *An English Patriot's Creed, Anno Domini, 1775* (Boston, 1776) expresses the orthodox view: "I believe the claim of the Norman Invader to the crown was not conquest but testamentary succession; that he renounced his conquest by a coronation oath; and before he commenced tyrant, confirmed the use of the Saxon laws" (*APW,* p. 319). Paine disagrees completely: "As to usurpation, no man will be so hardy as to defend it; and that William the Conqueror was an usurper is a fact not to be contradicted. The plain truth is, that the antiquity of English monarchy will not bear looking into" (p. 24). Paine is most explicit about the significance of whether or not William was a conqueror in *Rights of Man: Being an Answer to Mr. Burke's Attack on the French Revolution* (1791): "Mr. Burke will not, I presume, deny the position I have already advanced; namely, that governments arise, either *out* of the people, or *over* the people. The English government is one of those which arose out of a conquest, and not out of society, and consequently it arose over the people; and though it has been much modified from the opportunity of circumstances since the time of William the Conqueror, the country has never yet regenerated itself, and is therefore without a constitution" (p. 94).

Paine's revisionist history would be more aptly called demythologizing than desacralizing were it not buttressed by his attack on the claims for divine sanction of monarchy. Kingship, for Paine, is one of the punishments for the Fall: "Government, like dress, is the badge of lost innocence; the palaces of kings are built on the ruins of the bowers of paradise" (p. 13). Paine's recurrent use of biblical phrasing and analogy is aimed in part at swaying an audience steeped in religious values; he uses such references in part to undercut the claims, made by advocates of the present king, that George is a very devout man. Religion, Paine argues, is actually a republican virtue. Paine avoids the issue of George's personal virtue by avoiding him by name. As he had promised in his introduction, dated 14 February 1776, Paine apparently eschews personal attacks because he is concerned with measures, not men: "In the following sheets, the author hath studiously avoided every thing which is personal among ourselves. Compliments as well as censure to individuals make no part thereof" (p. 11). Because "the Object for Attention is the *Doctrine itself*" (p. 12), Paine supposedly does not want his readers to be distracted from the subject of kingship by an argument about the virtues and vices of a particular ruler. He can, however, take the low road of personal attack when it suits his rhetorical purposes. Paine can take either road because he quickly divides the two bodies in order to more easily undercut both: "Neither do the characters of the few good kings which have lived . . . either sanctify the title, or blot the sinfulness of the origin; the high encomium given of David takes no notice of him *officially as a king,* but only as a *man* after God's own heart" (pp. 21–22). The bodies divided, Paine employs the traditional satiric tactic of dehumanizing his target.

Paine's desacralization of the king's royal body is direct in its assault on the origin of the institution: "Government by kings was first introduced into the world by the Heathens, from whom the children of Israel copied the custom. It was the most prosperous invention the Devil ever set on foot for the promotion of idolatry. The Heathens paid divine honors to their deceased kings, and the Christian world hath improved on the plan, by doing the same to their living ones. How impious is the title of sacred majesty applied to a worm, who in the midst of his splendor is crumbling into dust!" (p. 19).

Paine displaces responsibility for creating kingship from the people to the Devil, thereby denying its origin any political legitimacy. That step taken, the next steps are easy and obvious. A satanic creation must be opposed because he is a perversion of nature. A king becomes "the monster" (p. 29), "the Royal Brute of Britain" (p. 41), and "the hardened, sullen tempered Pharoah of England . . . with the pretended title of FATHER OF HIS PEOPLE" (p. 36). Finally, "He, who hunts the woods for prey, the naked and untutored Indian, is less a Savage than the King of Britain" (p. 54). Anyone who embraces perversity dehumanizes himself: "And he who can calmly hear, and digest such doctrine, hath forfeited his claim to rationality—an apostate from the order of manhood; and ought to be considered—as one, who hath not only given up the proper dignity of man, but sunk himself beneath the rank of animals, and contemptibly crawls through the world like a worm" (p. 54).

Behind Paine's words one can hear his fear of Adam Smith's observation, in *The Theory of Moral Sentiments* (1759), that even when events have brought "the bulk of the people" to the point of rebellion, "they are apt to relent every moment, and easily relapse into their habitual state of deference to those whom they have been accustomed to look upon as their natural superiors. They cannot stand the mortification of their monarch. Compassion takes the place of resentment, they forget all past provocations, their old principles of loyalty revive, and they run to re-establish the ruined authority of their old masters, with the same violence with which they had opposed it" (1:53). Paine responds to seventeenth-century patriarchalist arguments, like that of Sir Robert Filmer, who traced kingship back to Adam, by accepting the Garden of Eden as the place of origin: "A family of kings forever, hath no parallel in or out of scripture but the doctrine of original sin, which supposes the free will of all men lost in Adam; and from such comparison, and it will admit of no other, hereditary succession can derive no glory" (p. 24).

Colonists were quick to follow Paine's argument to its logical conclusion. The symbol of kingship they had cherished turns out to be a satanic delusion, a perversion of political values. Consequently, as Samuel West maintains in *On the Right to Rebel against Governors* (Boston, 1776), the present king should be opposed for religious as well as political reasons:

> For any one from hence to infer that the apostle [Paul] enjoins in this text unlimited obedience to the worst of tyrants, and that he pronounces damnation upon those that resist the arbitrary measures of such pests of society, is just as good sense as if one should affirm, that because the Scripture enjoins us obedience to the laws of God, therefore we may not oppose the power of darkness; or because we are commanded to submit to the ordinance of God, therefore we may not resist the ministers of Satan. Such wild work must be made with the apostle before he can be brought to speak the language of oppression. It is as plain, I think, as words can make it, that, according to this text, no tyrant can be a ruler; for the apostle's definition of a ruler is, that he is not a terror to good works, but to the evil; and that he is one who is to praise and encourage those that do well. Whenever, then, the ruler encourages them that do evil, and is a terror to those that do well,—*i.e.*, as soon as he becomes a tyrant,—he forfeits his authority to govern, and becomes the minister of Satan, and, as such, ought to be opposed. (*APW*, p. 428)

West makes the conventional distinction between monarchs and tyrants, whereas Paine equates the two. West proceeds from hypothesis to example in a way that helps to explain the satirists' attraction to Nero as an analogue to George III. "Nero, that monster of tyranny," is a type of the good leader perverted by evil. West argues that the apostle Paul, "by enjoining submission to the powers that then were, does [not] require unlimited obedience to be yielded to the worst of tyrants." West suggests "that this epistle was written most probably about the beginning of Nero's reign, at which time he was a very humane and merciful prince, did everything that was generous and benevolent to the public, and showed every act of mercy and tenderness to particulars, and therefore might at that time justly deserve the character of the minister of God for good to the people." Only later did Nero become "a monster of tyranny and wickedness" and Paul, consequently, a satirist: "Nero, so far forth as he was a tyrant, could not be the minister of God, nor have a right to claim submission from the people; so that this [epistle] ought, perhaps, rather to be viewed as a severe satire upon Nero, than as enjoining any submission to him" (*APW*, pp. 428–29). Just as George was alleged to have done, Nero had betrayed the trust of his people.

This sense that George had betrayed his reign's opening promise does much to explain the sudden and complete reversal of his symbolic value in many of his subjects' eyes. Thus he becomes the false father figure in Paine's tract, just as he had increasingly become the object of attack in Churchill's verse. At one point, Paine is remarkably explicit about the tenor and vehicle of the metaphor he chooses to describe monarchy's perverse betrayal of expectations: "One of the strongest *natural* proofs of the folly of hereditary right in kings, is, that nature disapproves it, otherwise she would not so frequently turn it into ridicule by giving mankind an *Ass for a Lion*" (p. 22). Having dehumanized the regal body, Paine cleverly taps the satiric tradition of depicting George III as a zebra, or ass, we saw illustrated in *The Times, or 1768* (see fig. 49) to mock the king's mortal body as well. The specific reference in *The Times* is to a zebra given to Queen Charlotte in 1762 that became the vehicle for attacks on the king in several satires, including *The Queen's Ass* (fig. 59).

Closely akin, if not equivalent, to the unnatural in Paine's system of values is the unreasonable, and he again taps the satiric tradition when he reminds his readers of George's boyishness when he came to the throne: "In point of right and good order, there is something very ridiculous, that a youth of twenty-one (which hath often happened) shall say to several millions of people, older and wiser than himself, I forbid this or that act of yours to be law" (p. 37).[27] Paradoxically, monarchy should be opposed because, while the institution depends upon age (prescriptive right), one of its greatest dangers is youth (hereditary right). Paine also exploits the paradox found frequently in the satires that the British monarchy is at once too weak—"In countries where he [the king] is neither a judge nor a general, as in England, a man would be puzzled to know what is his business"—and too strong—"The corrupt influence of the crown, by having all the places in its disposal, hath so effectually swallowed up the power, and eaten out the virtue of the house of commons . . . that the government of England is nearly as monarchical as that of France or Spain" (p. 26). The paradox, for Paine, is explained by Britain's lack of a written constitution to limit the

The QUEEN's ASS.

A

NEW HUMOROUS ALLEGORICAL SONG.

Honi soit qui mal y pensé.

By H. HOWARD.

To the Tune of, *Stick a Pin there.*

I.

YE Bucks and ye Jemmies who amble the Park,
    Whose Hearts and whose Heads are as lightsome as Cork,
Through *Buckingham-Gate*, as to *Chelsea* you pass,
Without Fee or Reward, you may see the Q———'s A———.
    See the Q———'s A—: See the Q———'s A---,
                Without Fee or Reward, &c.

II.

A Sight such as this surely never was seen;
Who the Deuce would not gaze at the A--- of a Q———n?
What Prospect so charming !—What Scene can surpass
The delicate Sight of her M———'s A--- ?

III.

Though squeamish old Prudes with Invective and Spleen,
May turn up their Noses, and censure the Q———n;
Crying out,—" 'Tis a Shame, that her Q———ship, alas,
" Should take such a Pride—in exposing her A---."

IV.

Let them rail if they will; yet I'll bett Ten to One,
Not a Prude of them all but would alter her Tone,
Provided that Fortune, so kind to each Lass,
Had bestow'd *such* an A--- as her M———'s A----,

V.

The Fribbles cry out, " 'Tis a Sin and a Shame
" To suffer a Sight with so *filthy* a Name :"
Though they rail, yet will each take a Peep thro' his Glass,
For who wou'd not peep at her M———'s A--- ?

VI.

From *Macklinburgh Strelitz*, a Place of Renown,
This good-natur'd P--n--ss came here for a Crown ;
And now in Return to the Folks as they pass,
She kindly repays them—by shewing her A---.

Ye Gods ! I with Pleasure cou'd gaze Day and Night,
At so charming, so pretty, so curious a Sight :
In truth, I must own—nay, I swear by the Mass,
I could kiss (if no Treason)---her M———'s A---,

VII.

But this for a Subject, though loyal, I fear
Would be look'd on by some Folks as coming *too* near ;
Then in Prudence my Passion I'll stifle, alas !
Content but to gaze on her M———'s A---.

VIII.

Resign'd to my Fate, thus to gaze and no more,
In vain for Possession I sigh and implore ;
But Scripture informs us that all Flesh is Grass,
And *such*, I presume, is her M———'s A---.

IX.

Since then there is no mighty Diff'rence between
The A--- of a Subject, and that of a Q---n,
Let each Lad full of Glee take his Bottle and Glass,
And drink the Q———'s Health----not forgetting her A---,
    Not forgetting her A---: Not forgetting her A---,
                And drink the Q———'s Health, &c.

Sold by the AUTHOR, opposite the Union Coffee-House, in the Strand, near Temple-Bar; and by all the Print and Pamphlet-sellers.
(PRICE SIXPENCE.)
N. B. In a few Days will be published, *A Song on the CHEROKEES*, with a Head-Piece.

Figure 59. *The Queen's Ass* (BMC 3870). Reproduced by permission of the Trustees of the British Museum.

competing sources of power in her government. In theory the monarchy is very weak; in practice (through corruption) it is very strong.

The imagery of unnaturalness that Paine associates with the unreasonable institution of monarchy contrasts with the organic imagery he uses to describe republicanism. Again, Paine offers us a paradox: republicanism is both old and young because it restores man to a kind of Blakean Beulah-realm, a higher innocence of government based on reason. Hence, Paine's vision of the mythical origin of government takes place in a land very like the America that the colonists first discovered. Republicanism is older than monarchy and yet by its nature eternally young because natural rights are inherently nurturing and reproductive of energy, life, and growth. Thus we find in *Common Sense* metaphors like that of a rival to the royal oak of British monarchy: "Now is the seed-time of continental union, faith and honor. The least fracture now will be like a name engraved with the point of a pin on the tender rind of a young oak; the wound will enlarge with the tree, and posterity read it in full grown characters" (pp. 27–28). The colonies are "ripe" for independence (p. 43), and "the birthday of a new world is at hand" (p. 59). America will literally be renewed by replicating the mythical origin of government.

Complementing Paine's attack on kings as false father figures who betray their children is his use of the image of human psychological and physiological development to represent America's relationship to Britain. In a passage that anticipates Blake's depiction of George III as a monstrous pope, Paine asserts that Britain is a false parent who perverts a familial relationship:

> But Britain is the parent country, say some. Then the more shame upon her conduct. Even brutes do not devour their young, nor savages make war upon their families; wherefore the assertion, if true, turns to her reproach; but it happens not to be true, or only partly so, and the phrase *parent* or *mother country* hath been jesuitically adopted by the king and his parasites, with a low papistical design of gaining an unfair bias on the credulous weakness of our minds. Europe, and not England, is the parent country of America. . . . Hither have they fled not from the tender embraces of the mother, but from the cruelty of the monster. (p. 29)[28]

The identity of America's true parent notwithstanding, the time for "childishness" (p. 34) is over: the colonies have "come of age" (p. 37), having passed the point "like that of a youth, who is nearly out of his time" (p. 38). The implications of America's maturation, like the validity of natural rights, can be neither ignored nor resisted by appeals to a prescriptive and factitious British constitution of supposedly immemorial origin.

Loyalists like Samuel Johnson, in *Taxation no Tyranny*, were not about to concede natural imagery to the radicals without at least a counterclaim: "These antipatriotic prejudices are the abortions of Folly impregnated by Faction, which being produced against the standing order of Nature, have not strength sufficient for long life. They are born only to scream and perish, and leave those to contempt or detestation, whose kindness was employed to nurse them into mischief" (10:412). Johnson's prediction of stillbirth was mistaken. For Paine, and soon for many others, the Declaration of Independence was inevitable. The image of a monstrous, unnatural tyrant we have seen develop in the satires finds its way into Jefferson's draft, where he accuses George III of having "waged cruel war against human nature itself, violating it's [*sic*] most sacred rights of life and liberty." And behind John Hancock's insolent comment—that his signature was large enough for even George III to read—lay the king's satiric persona as a shortsighted ignorer of petitions.

Chapter 4

"Monarchy Is the Popery of Government"

O what have Kings to answer for . . . !
—Blake, "Gwin, King of Norway"

The attacks by Paine and Jefferson on the regal rather than the mortal body of the king in the 1770s anticipated the strategy of radicals like Paine in *Rights of Man* (1791–92), William Godwin in *An Enquiry concerning Political Justice* (1793), and William Blake in his pre-*Milton* or Lambeth prophecies of 1783–95. Paine, divorcing the king's two bodies, argues that the problem with monarchy is structural and not necessarily personal:

> It was not against Louis the XVIth, but against the despotic principles of the government that the nation revolted. . . . Perhaps no man bred up in the style of an absolute King, ever possessed a heart so little disposed to the exercise of that species of power as the present King of France. . . . The Monarch and the Monarchy were distinct and separate things; and it was against the established despotism of the latter, and not against the person or principles of the former, that the revolt commenced, and the revolution has been carried. (*ROM*, p. 69)

Godwin agrees on the need to distinguish between private virtue and public office: "If there have been kings, as there have been other men, in the forming of whom particular have outweighed general causes, the recollection of such exceptions has little to do with the question whether monarchy be, generally speaking, a benefit or an evil. . . . We are not to fix our minds upon prodigies, but to think of the species as it is usually found." [1]

As Blake's case illustrates, particular attacks on George III become more and more difficult to identify in paradigmatic satires on monarchy as an institution. Any satire on monarchy in general during George III's reign is to some extent an implicit satire on George III in particular, but, as the development of the first ten years of William Blake's poetical career demonstrates, Blake increasingly transcends particular historical contexts as his vision becomes more universal in application.[2] His development parallels Pope's movement from the more particular Horatian *Imitations* to the prophetic *Dunciad*'s wider implications. Both poets draw increasingly larger deductions from particular, inductively received evidence. In Blake's instance, the poet's historical experience with George III leads directly, and perhaps ineluctably, to his metaphysical vision of Urizen and Nobodaddy. Blake's grand revision and subversion of received, orthodox Judeo-Christian mythology may be traced back to his earliest revisions and subversions of received political orthodoxy.

Among Blake's *Political Sketches* (1783) are his first political poems, and in them George III appears as a target in his regal but not his mortal body.[3] In "Gwin, King of Norway," an allegory about rebellion against tyranny, George is certainly among those addressed at the poem's opening:

> Come, Kings, and listen to my song,
>   When Gwin the son of Nore,
> Over the nations of the North
>   His cruel sceptre bore.

The moral of this allegory, conceived in a rather conventional eighteenth-century example of exemplar history or of mythology, has an obvious application to George III in the wake of his American defeat:

> O what have Kings to answer for,
>   Before that awful throne!
> When thousand deaths for vengeance cry,
>   And ghosts accusing groan!

But to acknowledge George III as one target of this general attack on regal tyranny does little to illuminate the poem. Very different is the case with "King Edward the Third," a fragment of dramatic poetry also published in the *Poetical Sketches* of 1783. Increasingly accepted as an ironic satire rather than an uncharacteristically jingoistic piece, "Edward" may be approached from the perspective of the tradition of regal satire and seen as ironically subverting traditional regal iconography and exemplar history.[4] Blake chooses as his protagonist the supposedly exemplary king that Samuel Johnson, in *London: A Poem* (1738), had called "Illustrious Edward" (6:53). Blake wrote his poem within the satiric tradition that compared present rulers with this past model of kingly behavior. We have seen George III measured against Edward III and found wanting. The continued high prestige of Edward III was reflected in George III's commissioning Benjamin West to paint scenes of Edward's exploits for the royal palace, thereby expressing George's own identification with his regal ancestor.[5] Blake implies that George III, *qua* king, is necessarily like Edward III, not in the positive sense depicted in the 1768 print *Edward the Third Seizing Mortimer* (fig. 60) but ironically. In the wishful 1768 print, the young George III (as Edward III) finally comes to his senses and arrests the traitor Mortimer, shown in the likeness of Bute, despite the protests of the king's mother. The subscribed lines from Ben Jonson's *Mortimer His Fall* refer to one of the most frequent charges made against regal favorites—that they rise mushroomlike to glory and title solely at the king's whim:

> Mortimer
> Is a great Lord of late, and a new;
> A Prince, an Earl, and Cousin to the King.

Blake relies on recognition of the traditional satiric (and historical) representation of Mortimer to undercut with irony King Edward's opening speech to his son, the Black Prince:

> And thou, my son, be strong: thou fightest for a crown
> That death can never ravish from thy brow,
> A crown of glory: but from thy very dust
> Shall beam a radiance, to fire the breasts
> Of youth unborn! Our names are written equal
> In fame's wide trophied hall: 'tis ours to gild
> The letters, and to make them shine with gold
> That never tarnishes: whether Third Edward,
> Or the Prince of Wales, or Montacute, or Mortimer,
> Or ev'n the least by birth, shall gain the brightest fame,
> Is in his hand to whom all men are equal.   (sc. [1], lines 21–31)

The inclusion and especially the placement of Mortimer's name implicitly mock the catalog of heroes; the "crown" he has achieved is that of infamy; and the hand that sees men as equal becomes not God's impartial judgment but a king's undiscriminating favoritism.

Others have demonstrated the parallels between Blake's "King Edward" and contemporary events and have shown how Blake ironically undercuts orthodox political positions on commerce, chartered rights, the role of the church, and right by conquest. The traditional justifications of English monarchy are all subverted in this early fragment offering us a paradigm of kingship, complete with its conventional iconography of oak and sun imagery and concern with royal dignity, here expressed by Lord Percy to Lionel, duke of Clarence:

> But keep a proper dignity, for now
> You represent the sacred person of
> Your father; 'tis with princes as with the sun,

Edward the Third Seizing Mortimer

Mortimer

Is a great Lord of late, and a new thing;
A Prince, an Earl, and Cousin to the King.

Ben Johnson.

Figure 60. *Edward the Third Seizing Mortimer* (BMC 4150). Courtesy of the John Carter Brown Library at Brown University.

If not sometimes o'er-clouded, we grow weary
Of his officious glory.   (sc. [2], lines 50–54)

The irony of "King Edward," however, is often difficult to detect because Blake seems to accept without question the iconography of kingship while he rejects its substance. This manner of proceeding would soon
change. For example, by 1792, the probable date of "A Song of Liberty,"
which concludes *The Marriage of Heaven and Hell,* the sunlike quality of
royalty has been satirically diminished to the image of "the starry king,"
associated with minimal light and heat; the icon of the sun, with its illu-
mination and warmth, has been transferred to the revolutionary opponents
of monarchy.

Transformations or, better, transcendences of the minute particulars of
occasional political contexts increasingly mark Blake's satires of the 1790s.
In a brief but famous autobiographical poem sent to John Flaxman on
12 September 1800, Blake attributes his initial political awareness to the
outbreak of the American Revolution:

Terrors appeard in the Heavens above
And in Hell beneath & a mighty & awful change threatend the
Earth
The American War began[.] All its dark horror passed before my face
Across the Atlantic to France.   (pp. 707–8)

In other words, Blake responded to the radical premise of power found in
Common Sense and the Declaration of Independence: the true problem with
monarchy is not corruption but perfection. Unfortunately, the radicals con-
tended, Blackstone was right when he said that in the 1670s the British
constitution had been "perfected," that is, restored to its pre-Norman
condition. Blackstone meant, of course, in theory only, not in practice.[6]
Radicals in effect equated theory and practice to argue that abuse of power
was legal use of power under the "perfected" constitution; hence, that
constitution must be rejected. King and Parliament acted as one should
expect because the British constitution institutionalized tyranny. In light
of this point of origin, we find, not surprisingly, that the sources of much
of Blake's political imagery are in the satiric and nonsatiric words and pictures, albeit transformed and transcended, of his radical predecessors on
both sides of the Atlantic as well as in those of his radical contemporaries.
In considering the verbal and visual iconography Blake shared with other
satirists, we shall see that he usually transmutes that iconography by either
imploding or exploding it into a larger vision.

Blake implodes, or expands inward, iconography by rendering the
historical psychological. A good example of this process of implosion is

seen in the textual history of the second stanza of "London" in *Songs of Experience* (1794)[7]:

> In every cry of every Man,
> In every Infants cry of fear,
> In every voice: in every ban,
> The mind-forg'd manacles I hear.

The manuscript reading of "mind-forg'd manacles" is "german forged links." Our concern for the moment is not with the happy substitution of "manacles," more appropriately suggesting isolation, for the earlier "links," less fittingly implying association. The earlier choice, "german forged," explodes outward from a thinly veiled reference to George III to a reference to despotism in general. In the narrowest sense, Blake reclaims the traditional objection against the Hanoverian monarchs—that they are foreign-born—a complaint Paine makes in *Rights of Man:* "This ought to be a caution to every country, how it imports foreign families to be kings. It is somewhat curious to observe, that although the people of England have been in the habit of talking about kings, it is always a Foreign House of kings; hating Foreigners, yet governed by them—It is now the House of Brunswick, one of the petty tribes of Germany" (pp. 141–42). But, like Paine, Blake uses the national reference to reach beyond the man to a principle, the "German despotism" found in, though not limited to, a small European principality: "This species of Government comes from Germany. . . . God help that country, thought I, be it England or elsewhere, whose liberties are to be protected by German principles of government, and Princes of Brunswick!" (*ROM,* pp. 174, 143). Charles Pigott, in *The Jockey Club: or A Sketch of the Manners of the Age* (London, 1793), observes that "the tyrannical maxim, 'Divide et impera' [Divide and conquer], has been played off with admirable effect, and the sanguinary plans that have been long in embryo, and which are now laboring to annihilate the only free government in Europe, originated in the cabinet of German Despots" (p. 178). John Butler makes explicit the link between George III and "German despotism" in *The Political Fugitive: Being a Brief Disquisition into the Modern System of British Politics . . . Written during a Voyage from London to New York* (New York, 1794): "Reason, and common sense, will alone delineate the purport of his [George III's] mission, which is the establishment of German principles, by which the interest of Britain is sacrificed to that of the electorate [Hanover]" (p. 24).

The "manacles" in Blake's phrase, like the substitution of "chartered" for the manuscript's "dirty" earlier in the poem, also tap a fund of traditional iconography that other satirists had used to attack oppression and its unresisting victims. The anonymous author of the 1775 pamphlet *The*

Present Crisis, with Respect to America, Considered. Number 1, published first in London and reprinted several times in New England, expresses a common radical view of the colonial situation:

> [Ministerial apologists] tell the world, what was tyranny in the time of Charles the first, is not tyranny in the reign of George the third, and to this they add a long catalogue of virtues which he never possessed; they say he is pious; that his chief aim is to render his subjects, a happy, great, and free people; (and indeed he has more than once said so himself) these and many other falsehoods, equally wicked and absurd, they endeavour to instill into the minds of the too easily deluded English. These, and such like artifices, have ever been made use of in the reign of arbitrary Kings, to deceive the people, and make them with more ease, and to chains well polished, submit their necks, and even reverence and adore the hand that rivets them. Thus do tyrants succeed, and the galling yoke of slavery, so much complained of by almost every nation in the world, becomes a crime of the first magnitude, in the people through their own credulity and vile submission. (p. 5)

Blake expands inward, or implodes, the image of victims sharing responsibility for their oppression by internalizing what George Richards, in *The Declaration of Independence: A Poem* (Boston, 1793), calls the "iron nets of law" (p. 7), a phrase that echoes Pope's couplet in *An Essay on Man:* "In vain thy Reason finer webs shall draw, / Entangle Justice in her net of Law" (3:191–92). Hence the "german forged links" become "mind-forg'd manacles" in a process to be repeated many times in Blake's iconography. This process of imploding from external oppression to internal repression, whereby the victim is in part also the villain, is the central theme of *Visions of the Daughters of Albion* (1793). Blake universalizes his theme by moving from an opening that, analogous to "german forged," suggests an external, historical context, to a concern with the timeless, psychologically based sources of oppression and repression that are manifestations of "mind-forg'd manacles." Plate 1 of the poem (fig. 61) is a rehearsal for the preludium of *America: A Prophecy* (1793), which is considered below. Blake's fondness for tantalizing his audience with seemingly incomplete allegories is evident in the initial relationship among Oothoon, Theotormon, and Bromion.

Blake's expanding vision demanded a larger, newer mythology and iconography as Blake rendered poetic Paine's notion that the French Revolution (and for Blake particularly the American Revolution) presented "a scene so new, and so transcendentally unequalled by anything in the European world, that the name of a Revolution is diminutive of its character, and it rises into a regeneration of man" (*ROM*, p. 136). One of the most

Figure 61. William Blake, *Visions of the Daughters of Albion*, Plate 1 (Not in BMC). Reproduced by permission of the Yale Center for British Art, Paul Mellon Collection.

important figures who undergoes radical transformation in Blake's Lambeth prophecies is George III. The nature of Blake's transcendent image making is such that the creating of a simple, one-to-one equivalency between an allusion in his verse and a historical person would diminish his poetic purpose. Fear of such diminution was probably at least a contributing cause in Blake's decision to cancel a plate in *America* that contains an explicit reference to George III.[8] Like "german forged" in "London," the canceled "George the third" of *America* would have restricted the referentiality of Blake's target. It would also have separated the figures of the king and "Albions Angel." The minute historical particular of George III, however, frequently and importantly makes its way into Blake's political satire.

An early example is the *finis* illustration of the mad King Nebuchadnezzar crawling on all fours, which concludes *The Marriage of Heaven and Hell*, completed around 1790 (fig. 62). Nebuchadnezzar was a traditional archetype of the regal oppressor, of course, but a depiction of him in his madness could hardly fail to strike viewers, had there been any, as an attack on George III, the most celebrated lunatic of the times. Contemporary satirists must have enjoyed the opportunity to identify the king with those "*idiots* and *lunatics*" who were, according to the constitution, under his particular care (Blackstone, 3:427).[9] Paine slyly uses the chance to develop the association between the king and those who should be in his custody: "When it is laid down as a maxim, that *a King can do no wrong,* it places him in a state of similar security with that of idiots and persons insane, and responsibility is out of the question with respect to himself" (*ROM,* p. 163). In the fall of 1788, George had suddenly lapsed into porphyria-induced madness, which lasted until early spring 1789.[10] The press exhaustively reported the progress and treatment of the king's madness. From this point on, the slightest or subtlest hint of George's allegedly precarious mental state was telling. In light of recent history, the archetype of Nebuchadnezzar gave radical satirists an effective vehicle for attacking the present king: both madness and oppression were individually both cause and effect of George III's actions; the image of Nebuchadnezzar was at once explanatory and monitory.

Prior to George's illness, allusions to Nebuchadnezzar were usually only implicitly monitory, as in the 1780 print *The Invisible Junto, Dedicated to the Truly Honorable Lord G. Gordon* (fig. 63).[11] This engraving shows George III weighed and found wanting by a pair of scales held by a hand coming from the clouds. The hand and the eye on the cloud inscribed "He that formed the Eye shall he not see" represent the divine judgment overlooking the king on the left scale, who stands uncrowned, hands on hips, his ears projecting at right angles to his head. He is "K. Menassah,"

Figure 62. Blake, *The Marriage of Heaven and Hell, Finis* Plate (Not in BMC). Courtesy of the Library of Congress.

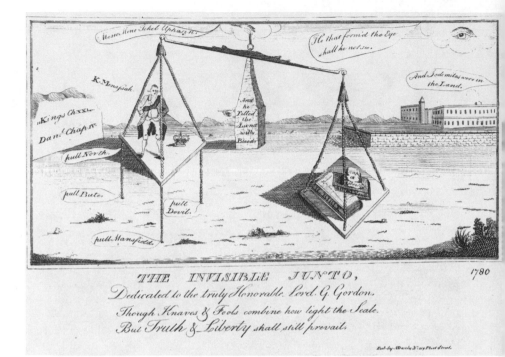

Figure 63. *The Invisible Junto* (BMC 5671). Reproduced by permission of the Trustees of the British Museum.

who reigned during the worst period of apostasy in Judah's history. A rock on the left reads, "II Kings Ch. xxi [the account of Menassah's wicked reign], Dan. Chap. IV [the account of Nebuchadnezzar's madness]." The label over the scale, "Mene Mene Tekel Uphasin (Numbered, Numbered, Weighed, Divided)," refers to the divine warning given to King Belshazzar at his feast in Daniel, chapter 5. Four ropes labeled "pull North, pull Bute, pull Mansfield, pull Devil" indicate that the king's support comes from evil secret influence. But this influence is easily outweighed by two books, "H[oly] Bible" and "*Sidney on G{overnment}*," in the scale on the right, surmounted by the "cap of Liberty." Behind the scales is a pinnacle inscribed "And he filled the Land with Blood." From its side, a hand points to the king. The inscription "And Sodomites were in the Land" on a palace in the background indicates Britain's present condition. Beneath the engraving's title we read, "Though Knaves & Fools combine how light the scale, / But Truth & Liberty shall still prevail."

Biblical allusions were especially appropriate to the anti-Catholic Gordon Riots, which this print defends, but satirists felt quite comfortable applying biblical types in more completely secular political contexts. Such is the case in the 1784 engraving *The Golden Image That Nebuchadnezzar the King Had Set Up* (BMC 6445), which refers to George III's establishing William Pitt, son of William Pitt, earl of Chatham, as the new idol, that is, the new prime minister, after the king's overthrow of the short-lived North-Fox ministry, which Burke had actively supported. The king, seated on a balloon representing transience and marked "Prerogative," points to a column inscribed "Family Presumption" and surmounted by an image of Pitt as a naked child. The king addresses North, Fox, and Burke: "I command you O Shadrach Mesech & Abednego!" But the heroes of the piece respond, "Know O King we will not worship ye Golden Image." The dilapidated "St. Stephens" on the left represents George III and Pitt's victory over Parliament, and the subscribed verses express the artist's hope that the victory will be as short-lived as the balloon and clouds of popularity that support it:

A Gilded Image—& before it—
A Mob on Marrow-bones adore it
That immemorial time have sold
All Conscience to his God-ship Gold:
Look ere you leap & scan the PIT,
You sapient worships may be bit
Not all that glitter's Gold, alass,
Your baby's but a thing of Brass.

Typically, before the king's actual madness in 1788–89, allusions to Nebuchadnezzar stress his actions as a tyrant and his appropriateness as an exemplum of divine retribution condignly administered. But after George's attack, attention shifted toward the way divine retribution was exercised on Nebuchadnezzar, as in the Blake illustration and in the definition that Charles Pigott gives for Nebuchadnezzar in *A Political Dictionary* (New York, 1796): "He was a hirsute king, and like other brute beasts, ate grass and potatoes, whence the name of the potentate (*vide* Lemon). It is thought by physiologists, that it would greatly conduce to the welfare of his people, if the king of *Georgia* was turned out to grass before the meeting of every session of Parliament" (pp. 97–98).

Fear of provoking sympathy for the king and his ministers perhaps helps to explain why satirists like Blake tended to be suggestive rather than explicit about allusions to George's madness. For example, only in the preface to the French edition of *Rights of Man* do we find George referred to as "the Elector of Hanover, sometimes styled King of England, a feeble and crazy personage." For his British audience, Paine is a bit more circumspect. James Gillray's 1791 *Wierd-Sisters; Ministers of Darkness; Minions of the Moon* (fig. 64) is a superb example of a more direct, and less common, allusion to the king's madness.[12] In this parody of Henry Fuseli's famous illustration of *Macbeth*, act 1, scene 3, the witches Dundas, Pitt, and Thurlow contemplate a two-faced moon. Illuminated on one side is the allegedly ascendant Queen Charlotte; darkened on the other is the old moon, George, with closed eyes. The moon serves here as a powerful, economical image: a reference to the king's illness through the etymology of lunacy and an assertion of the diminution of his political power by substituting the lesser moon for the normal solar emblem of kingship.

At times, satirists reminded their audience of the king's lunacy with the tactic of madness by association or infection. The anonymous creator of *St. Stephen's Mad-House; or, The Inauguration of King William the Fourth* (1789) (fig. 65) uses this tactic to satirize the ministry during the Regency Crisis. Beneath the title, we are told that the engraving is "Designed by Margaret Nicholson, Etched by Mr. Stone." Nicholson, to whom Pitt is compared in the print, was the madwoman who had attacked George III with a knife on 2 August 1786. Stone was a lunatic who sought to marry the Princess Royal. The scene suggests that George's madness has infected Parliament. Burke observes that "Benevento's Devils were nothing to this" as five members of the Opposition, including Fox, escape from the asylum Pitt rules. The straw in his crown and the hearth brush that serves as his scepter indicate Pitt's madness. He says, "Nelly Rogers shall be Queen! hear it ye winds and bear it on your rosey wings to Heaven!" Additional figures and comments satirize both the many addresses to Pitt thanking him for preserving Parliament and the many peerages created during his ministry.

Figure 65. *St. Stephen's Mad-House; or, The Inauguration of King William the Fourth* (BMC 7495). Reproduced by permission of the Trustees of the British Museum.

Burke would soon see the political implications of the French Revolution as "such a plague, that the precautions of the most severe quarantine ought to be established against it" (*Reflections*, p. 185). Others, like Wollstonecraft, anticipated Blake in seeing the illness at court and its political effects as a metaphor for the condition of the nation because "it is madness to make the fate of thousands depend on the caprice of a weak fellow-creature, whose very station sinks him *necessarily* below the meanest of his subjects. . . . The indolent puppet of a court . . . makes the contagion which his unnatural state spread, the instrument of tyranny." [13]

For Blake, recent events must have given added bite to his print of Nebuchadnezzar, in itself an entirely apposite close to a Menippean satire on the abuse of reason. The appropriateness of the illustration to the theme of the poem is independent of any possible allusion to George III, but I think it highly probable that Blake, like others of his political persuasion, saw the affliction of the present king as evidence of the archetypicality of the Babylonian tyrant. Nobody was immune from the madness of reason abused.

George III was the most salient example of "mind-forg'd manacles" available, and I think that Blake aims at the king in *Visions of the Daughters of Albion*, Blake's first revision of the American Revolution. The image of the fiery sky-god (itself a revision of the traditional sun-king emblem) on the title-page, I believe, alludes to George III (see fig. 61). I take the sky-god to be Theotormon and the scene to be an illustration of the following lines:

And thus I turn my face to where my whole soul seeks.
Over the waves she went in wing'd exulting swift delight:
And over Theotormon's reign, took her impetuous course.   (1:13–15)

In the scene and the verse, Oothoon, "the soft soul of America" (1:3), is about to enter unwillingly the arms of Bromion, an amoral if not immoral ur-Orc, a force of revolutionary violence that will cause her divorce from Theotormon, within whose "reign" Oothoon is initially placed. The parallelism of the opening allegory, given the identification of Oothoon with America, suggests that Theotormon is at least an analogue of Britain, or Albion. And the self-enclosed isolation of Theotormon, the "mind-forg'd manacles" that separate him from Oothoon, is expressed in the posture of a lunatic in a straitjacket, or straitwaistcoat, his arms wrapped around himself. [14] An even more likely allusion to the self-limitation of George III identified with Britain as a whole appears on plate 7 (fig. 66), where the upraised face of one of the daughters of Albion has George III's likeness. Compare her head to that of the king in the Gaetano Testolini engraving (ca. 1785) after the painting by Thomas Stothard, a friend of Blake, who also engraved many pictures after Stothard in 1780–86 (fig. 67). [15] In

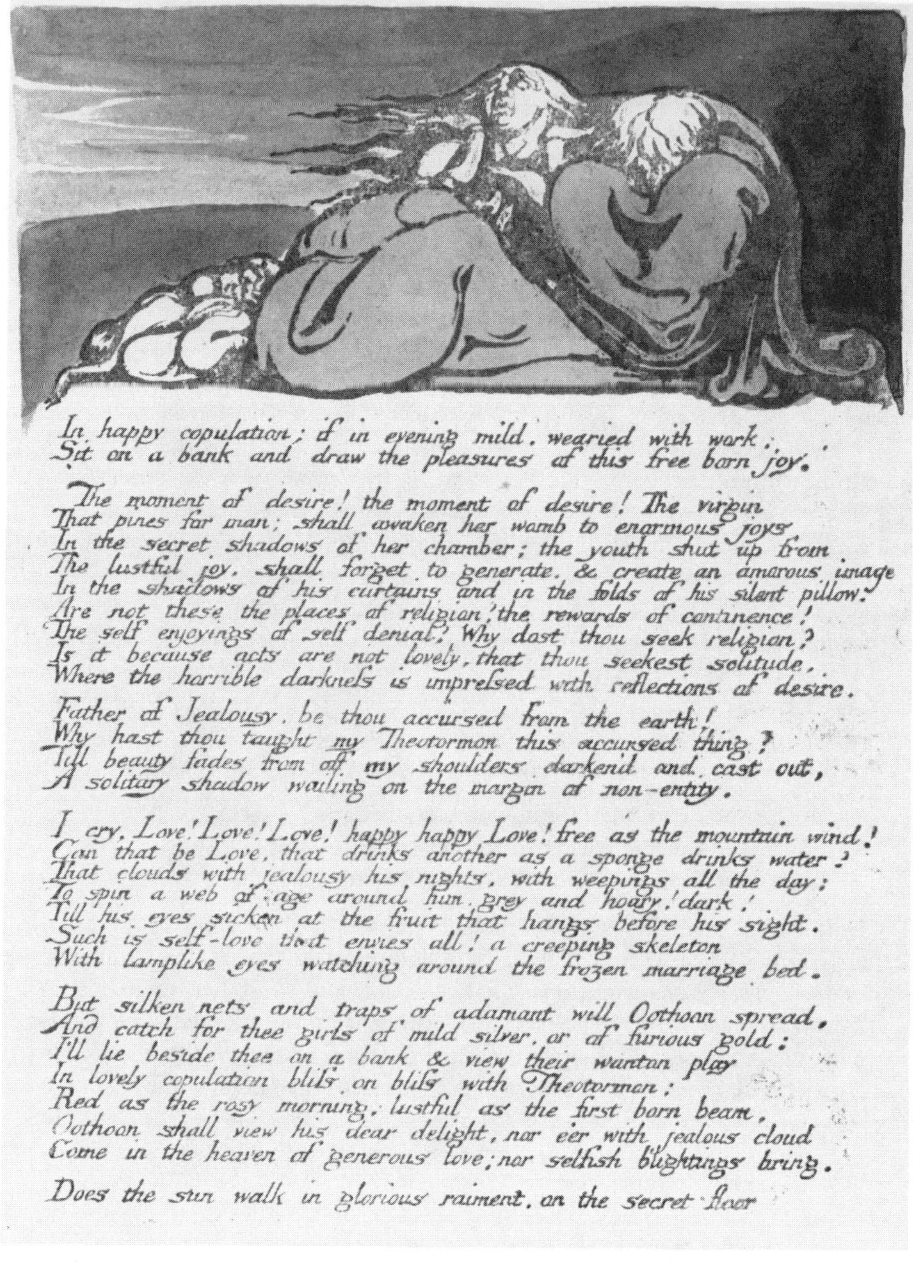

In happy copulation; if in evening mild. wearied with work;
Sit on a bank and draw the pleasures of this free born joy.

The moment of desire! the moment of desire! The virgin
That pines for man; shall awaken her womb to enormous joys
In the secret shadows of her chamber; the youth shut up from
The lustful joy. shall forget to generate. & create an amorous image
In the shadows of his curtains and in the folds of his silent pillow.
Are not these the places of religion? the rewards of continence?
The self enjoyings of self denial? Why dost thou seek religion?
Is it because acts are not lovely, that thou seekest solitude,
Where the horrible darkness is impressed with reflections of desire.

Father of Jealousy. be thou accursed from the earth!
Why hast thou taught my Theotormon this accursed thing?
Till beauty fades from off my shoulders. darkend and cast out,
A solitary shadow wailing on the margin of non-entity.

I cry, Love! Love! Love! happy happy Love! free as the mountain wind!
Can that be Love. that drinks another as a sponge drinks water?
That clouds with jealousy his nights, with weepings all the day:
To spin a web of age around him. grey and hoary! dark!
Till his eyes sicken at the fruit that hangs before his sight.
Such is self-love that envies all! a creeping skeleton
With lamplike eyes watching around the frozen marriage bed.

But silken nets and traps of adamant will Oothoon spread,
And catch for thee girls of mild silver. or of furious gold:
I'll lie beside thee on a bank & view their wanton play
In lovely copulation bliss on bliss with Theotormon:
Red as the rosy morning. lustful as the first born beam,
Oothoon shall view his dear delight. nor eer with jealous cloud
Come in the heaven of generous love; nor selfish blightings bring.

Does the sun walk in glorious raiment. on the secret floor

Figure 66. Blake, *Visions*, Plate 7 (Not in BMC). Reproduced by permission of the Yale Center for British Art, Paul Mellon Collection.

Painted by T. Stothard Esqr R.A   Pub.^d by G. Testolini, Cornhill   Engraved by G. Testolini

His Most Gracious Majesty
(*GEORGE*) *THE* (*THIRD*)

Figure 67. Gaetano Testolini, *His Most Gracious Majesty George the Third* (Not in BMC). Courtesy of the John Carter Brown Library at Brown University.

what is probably something of an inside joke, Blake indicates that for him George III is a type of all those who are "ENSLAV'D" by their own passive acceptance of oppression, whether its source be external or reason misused.

Besides the sun-king tradition of iconography, Blake had a more particular reason to satirically translate George III into a sky-god. We looked earlier at how Blake applies the tactic of satiric diminution to the icon of the regal sun by reducing it to "the starry king" in "A Song of Liberty," which he added to *The Marriage of Heaven and Hell* around 1792. The inspiration for such diminution may have come from events in the preceding decade, events that would have given Blake the opportunity to subvert intended praise into satire.

On 31 March 1781, Sir William Herschel had discovered the planet we now know as Uranus, though at first he believed it to be a comet. As discoverer, he had the right to name the new planet, which he called *Georgium sidus* (the star of George) in honor of his royal patron. To satirists, George's sidereal translation, especially at the hands of a Hanoverian in his service, was an apt emblem of regal pretence and of British imperialism.[16] In David Williams's satiric *Royal Recollections* (London, 1788), George confesses, "I love fame," and he admits that he acted as Herschel's patron because he wanted to have the new planet named after himself.[17] In reality, George was an ardent student of astronomy. In sum, the historical George III seems a very likely inspiration for Blake's mythical "starry king."

Blake's juxtaposition in the final version of *The Marriage* of the mad Nebuchadnezzar and "the starry king" of "A Song of Liberty" is similar to William Dent's contemporary design, *The Terrifying Comet; or, Modern Planetary System* (BMC 8115), a 1792 print satirizing the Royal Proclamation of 21 May 1792 "for the preventing of tumultuous meetings and seditious writing," aimed mainly against Paine's influence. The satire's second object was the new system of military maneuvers conducted on Bagshot Heath during July and August under the duke of Richmond's command. The comet's head contains the heads, joined at the neck, of George III and the duke of Richmond. George's wig slips forward to reveal his bald head, thereby suggesting insanity.[18] Close to the comet, "Venus" contains Queen Charlotte's profile, "Jupiter," Pitt's head, and "Georgium Sidus," Burke's. Military figures appear in the comet's tail. In the lower left corner, a rising (or falling?) sun encompasses the Prince of Wales's ostrich feathers. Six small stars enclose Opposition heads.

The subversion of traditional iconography in *Poetical Sketches, The Marriage of Heaven and Hell,* and *Visions of the Daughters of Albion* prepared the way for the regeneration of traditional iconography in *America: A Prophecy* (1793) and the later prophecies, as Blake shifted his attention from external, political revolution to internal, spiritual regeneration, a process of increasing implosion. Blake's shift may well express his growing recognition that his radical cause was a lost one, at least in the near future; the American and French revolutions were not about to be replicated in Britain unless his compatriots altered their fundamental political beliefs first. Blake's early optimism quickly faded.

Strikingly original though it remains, *America* owes much of its power to the iconic conventions Blake inherited and transformed, including, of course, images of the king. Although Blake changed his mind about naming George specifically in *America,* his presence is unavoidably pervasive in this poem whose historical impetus was the American Revolution. By not naming George, Blake emphasizes his attack on the king's regal body so that he can more easily translate the historical king into another antitype of the tyrant. George III himself is no less a target for that, but now he serves as an exemplum of the paradigm of tyranny. Blake does not intend to create a historically consistent allegory; his is internally, mythically consistent, though inspired, as a close look at its content will show, by external, factual events. In the poem, George III's mortal body is insignificant: Blake's point is that any king, by the nature of his office, is evil. The problem is not *who* George is but *what* George is. The primary opposition in the poem is between the type of revolutionary regeneration, Orc, and the various types of tyranny that subsume George III, be they called "the Guardian Prince of Albion," "the King of England," "Albion's Angel," or "Urizen." As David V. Erdman perceptively notes, "in *America* George III has modulated to a higher spiritual form." [19]

George is but one of many inherited icons and conventions Blake modulates to higher spiritual forms in *America.* Two of the most common found in contemporary discourse about the American conflict are the image of vegetation and the concept of the war as civil rather than revolutionary. Blake visually frames *America* with an illustrated equivalent of Paine's famous conclusion to *Rights of Man:*

> It is now towards the middle of February. Were I to take a turn into the country, the trees would present a leafless winterly appearance. As people are apt to pluck twigs as they walk along, I perhaps might do the same, and by chance might observe, that a *single bud* on that twig had begun to swell. I should reason very unnaturally, or rather not reason at all, to suppose *this* was the *only* bud in England which had this appearance. Instead of deciding thus, I should instantly conclude, that the same appearance was beginning, or about to begin, everywhere; and though the vegetable sleep will continue longer on some trees and plants than on others, and though some of them may not *blossom* for two or three years, all will be in leaf in the

summer, except those which are *rotten*. What a pace the political summer may keep with the natural, no human foresight can determine. It is, however, not difficult to perceive that the spring is begun. (pp. 294–95)

In *America,* Orc's potential power is shown in the lower left-hand corner of the "Preludium," as a human seed about to germinate and burst through the ground in the next plate (fig. 68). Counterbalancing the generating Orc of the opening, Urizen, "the ultimate proponent of royalism," in the *finis* plate is returning to a passive, vegetative state, curled up into an *in posse* condition, his flowing hair rerooting him to the ground (fig. 69).[20] The middle plates of the poem reiterate Blake's paradoxical mirroring of the opposing icons of energy and order. The clothed Urizen in the clouds of plate 8 strikes essentially the same pose, only reversed, as the naked Orc in the flames of plate 10 (figs. 70, 71). Blake further underscores the interrelationship between Orc and Urizen by having Urizen's image illustrate the plate on which Orc verbally describes himself. The implication of Blake's Orc-Urizen images reflecting one another may indicate that, like so many others, Blake was disillusioned by the measures of the French revolutionaries, who after 1793 seemed to betray their original principles as energy led increasingly to oppression, as their *revolution* became one in the strict sense of coming full circle to the point of origin. Another likely explanation for why Blake chose to organize *America* by wit—an emphasis on the essential similarity between two apparently dissimilar objects— lies in recognizing the pervasive British perception of the American conflict as a civil war between parent and child, king and subject, Britain and America, George III and George Washington. Of the hundreds of pamphlets about the war produced in Britain during the war, almost all refer to the conflict as a civil rebellion.[21] Blake's acknowledgment of this view is reflected most directly in plate 9, line 20, when Albion's Angel accuses Orc of being "Devourer of thy parent."

American colonists and their English brethren readily accepted the familial metaphor.[22] Richard Bland, in *An Inquiry into the Rights of the British Colonies* (Williamsburg, Va., 1766), acknowledges the "King as Father of his People" (*APW,* p. 85). Nathaniel Niles, in *Two Discourses on Liberty* (Newburyport, Mass., 1774), uses the familial metaphor to identify the king with the state, an identification implicit in the transformation George III undergoes in *America:* "We have sought in vain for relief from our parent state—from our King" (*APW,* p. 273). Blake's radical predecessors, like Silas Downer in *A Discourse at the Dedication of the Tree of Liberty* (Providence, R.I., 1768), realized that the familial metaphor, particularly in its feminine form, was a rhetorical impediment to political action:

The shadowy daughter of Urthona stood before red Orc.
When fourteen suns had faintly journey'd o'er his dark abode;
His food she brought in iron baskets, his drink in cups of iron.
Crown'd with a helmet & dark hair the nameless female stood;
A quiver with its burning stores, a bow like that of night,
When pestilence is shot from heaven; no other arms she need:
Invulnerable tho' naked, save where clouds roll round her loins,
Their awful folds in the dark air; silent she stood as night:
For never from her iron tongue could voice or sound arise;
But dumb till that dread day when Orc assay'd his fierce embrace.

Dark virgin; said the hairy youth, thy father stern abhorr'd;
Rivets my tenfold chains while still on high my spirit soars;
Sometimes an eagle screaming in the sky, sometimes a lion,
Stalking upon the mountains, & sometimes a whale I lash
The raging fathomless abyss, anon a serpent folding
Around the pillars of Urthona, and round thy dark limbs,
On the Canadian wilds I fold, feeble my spirit folds,
For chain'd beneath I rend these caverns; when thou bringest food
I howl my joy, and my red eyes seek to behold thy face
In vain! these clouds roll to & fro, & hide thee from my sight.

Figure 68. Blake, *America: A Prophecy*, "Preludium" (Not in BMC). Reproduced by permission from the Collection of Mr. and Mrs. Paul Mellon, Upperville, Virginia.

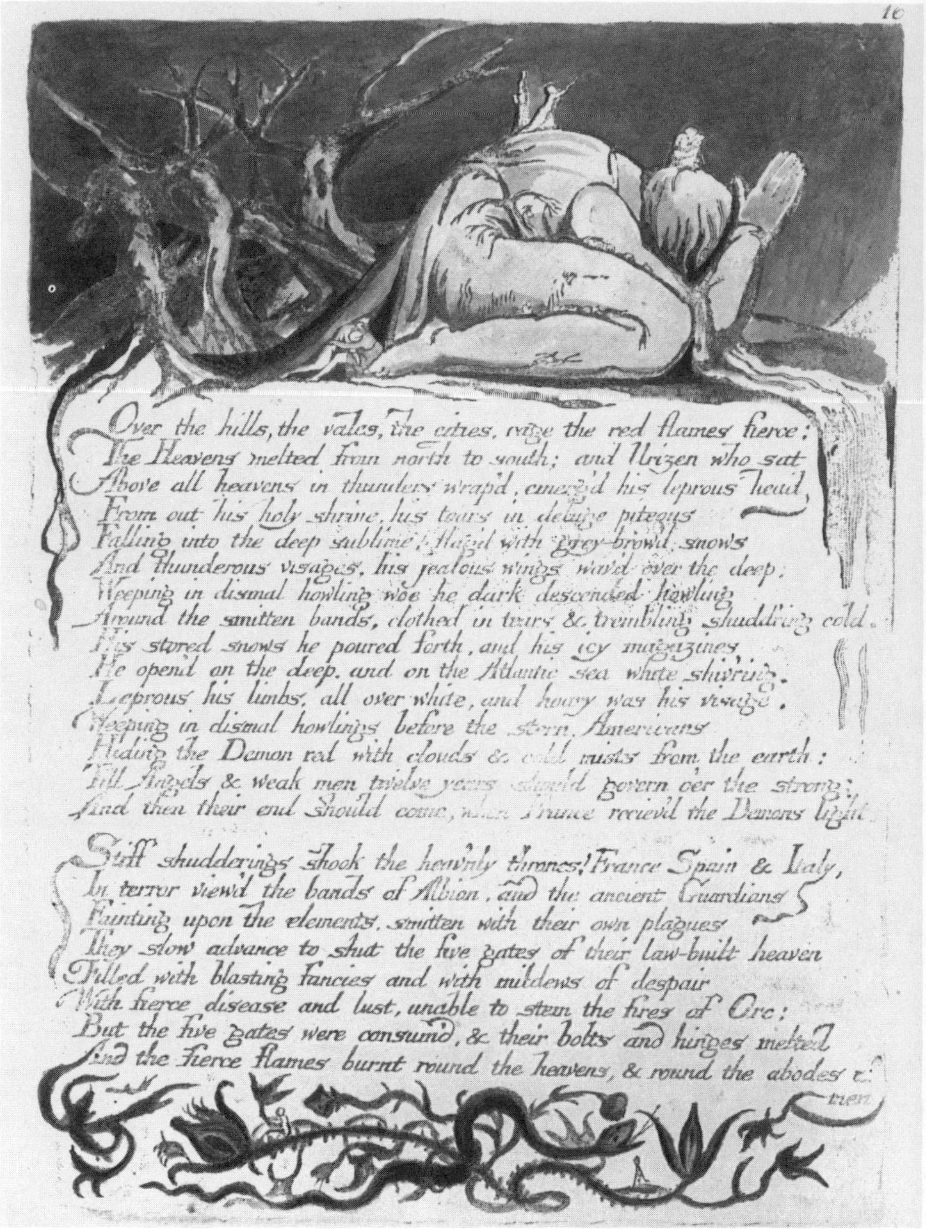

Figure 69. Blake, *America, Finis* Plate (Not in BMC). Reproduced by permission from the Collection of Mr. and Mrs. Paul Mellon, Upperville, Virginia.

8

Figure 70. Blake, *America*, Plate 8 (Not in BMC). Reproduced by permission from the Collection of Mr. and Mrs. Paul Mellon, Upperville, Virginia.

Thus wept the Angel voice & as he wept the terrible blasts
Of trumpets, blew a loud alarm across the Atlantic deep.
No trumpets answer; no reply of clarions or of fifes,
Silent the Colonies remain and refuse the loud alarm.

On those vast shady hills between America & Albions shore;
Now barr'd out by the Atlantic sea: call'd Atlantean hills;
Because from their bright summits you may pass to the Golden world
An ancient palace, archetype of mighty Emperies.
Rears its immortal pinnacles, built in the forest of God
By Ariston the king of beauty for his stolen bride.

Here on their magic seats the thirteen Angels sat perturb'd
For clouds from the Atlantic hover o'er the solemn roof.

Figure 71. Blake, *America*, Plate 10 (Not in BMC). Courtesy of the Library of Congress.

This claim of the commons to a sovereignty over us, is founded by them on their being the *Mother Country*. It is true that the first emigrations were from *England;* but upon the whole, more settlers have come from *Ireland, Germany,* and other parts of *Europe,* than from *England*. But if every soul came from *England,* it would not give them any title to sovereignty or even to superiority. . . . It is to be hoped that in future the words *Mother Country* will not be so frequently in our mouths, as they are only sounds without meaning. (*APW,* pp. 104–5)

Blake is careful to visually identify England with the patriarchal dimension of the familial relationship, despite Albion's Angel's rhetorical attempts to cast Orc as the villain in a sentimental tragedy who attacks children and his own mother: "Art thou not Orc: who serpent-form'd / Stands at the gate of Enitharmon to devour her children?" (7:3–4).

Devourer of thy parent, now thy unutterable torment renews.
Sound! sound! my loud war trumpets & alarm my thirteen Angels!
Ah terrible birth! a young one bursting! where is the weeping
    mouth?
And where the mother's milk? Instead those ever-hissing jaws
And parched lips drop with fresh gore; now roll thou in the clouds.
Thy mother lays her length outstretch'd upon the shore beneath.
                                                                    (9:20–25)

Offsetting the obviously self-interested sentimental rhetoric of Albion's Angel are the implicitly more objective visual expressions of the familial relationship, which frame the words. Blake depicts the tyrannical oppressor, one of whose antitypes in the poem is George III, in a serious transformation of the comic patriarchal ogre who appears in *Poor Old England Endeavoring to Reclaim His Wicked American Children,* published in 1777 (fig. 72). Blake reserves for America the image of the victimized female, daughter of a wicked father.

However, as is often the case, Blake transforms in order to transcend his inherited iconography. The *action* of the "Preludium," the rape of "the shadowy daughter of Urthona," is dated "when fourteen suns had faintly journey'd o'er his dark abode" (1:1–2). Fourteen years before Parliament punished Boston with the Coercive Acts of March–June 1774, the poem's precipitating historical event, George III had ascended Britain's throne. Radicals frequently cited his accession as the date from which could be traced a new system of tyranny in Britain and British America, and 1774 was a commonly accepted date for the commencement of hostilities, were one disposed to see Britain as forcing the colonies into rebellion. Various models for the "shadowy daughter" have been suggested, including

Figure 72. *Poor Old England Endeavoring to Reclaim His Wicked American Children* (BMC 5397). Reproduced by permission of the Trustees of the British Museum.

Diana, Athena, and a Valkyrie.[23] Blake's polysemous imagination invites wide-ranging source investigation and interpretation, but this case needs Occam's razor. Given the subject (and title) of the poem, as well as the iconographic traditions investing it, this female is an adaptation of the female Indian warrior that Blake's predecessors so frequently used as an emblem of America:

> Crown'd with a helmet & dark hair the nameless female stood;
> A quiver with its burning stores, a bow like that of night,
> When pestilence is shot from heaven; no other arms she need:
> Invulnerable tho' naked, save where clouds roll round her loins,
> Their awful folds in the dark air.   (1:4–8)

She is not, however, simply either the American Indian or Oothoon transposed from *Visions of the Daughters of Albion,* though she is genetically related to both. She is both her precedent figures transformed by prophetic revision. Nor is she restrictedly identified with the thirteen formerly British colonies. She describes herself as encompassing all of the Americas, North and South (during the eighteenth century "the South-sea" usually meant the Pacific coast of South America, the intended trading domain of the South Sea Company):

> On my American plains I feel the struggling afflictions
> Endur'd by roots that writhe their arms into the nether deep:
> I see a serpent in Canada, who courts me to his love;
> In Mexico an Eagle, and a Lion in Peru;
> I see a Whale in the South-sea, drinking my soul away.   (2:10–14)

The female remains nameless probably because Orc's complete revolutionary embrace is here prophesied, not effected. Her future identity is not yet clear and hence is unnameable. Blake's not naming her is also similar to his not naming George III in the final version of the poem; in both cases he seeks to expand the referentiality of his figure.

Once we recognize Blake's complex relationship to the satiric tradition, we begin to better appreciate some of his iconography's possible implications. Blake's "Preludium" is similar in conception to Paine's prophecy of European political reformation: "The insulted German and the enslaved Spaniard, the Russ and the Pole, are beginning to think. The present age will hereafter merit to be called the Age of reason, and the present generation will appear to the future as the Adam of a new world" (*ROM,* p. 290). Blake's version of "the Adam of a new world" is Orc, repeatedly associated visually in the poem with a regenerated Garden of Eden. Opposed to Orc is the "father stern" (George III, England) of "the nameless female" (America) (1:11, 1:4). But Blake sees the historical conflict between America and

England as a momentary manifestation, limited by time and space, of a universal and atemporal process of opposition, best represented in terms of various received myths transformed, all exemplified in the same poem. Orc, to the extent that he is a new Adam, is the old Adam regenerated. He becomes a kind of George III, or Albion's Angel, or Urizen redeemed and reborn.

Another way Blake expresses this idea of rebirth is through the phoenix image of Orc in the flames, which reverses the image of Urizen on the clouds that precedes it. Representing the process that occurs from the Urizen to the Orc plates is the intervening plate 9, where ripening wheat shelters an infant (fig. 73). Behind the Orc phoenix plate lies the tradition represented by the anonymous poet of *Bedlam, a Ball, and Dr. Price's Observations on the Nature of Civil Liberty. A Poetical Medley* (London, 1776):

> Vainly shall Britain spill her blood,
> So Heav'n ordains for Britain's good,
> 'Till, like a phoenix in her nest
> Consum'd, she rises in the West.   (p. 17)

Blake was not the first to express the American conflict in terms of a phoenix revolting against a god. The anonymous author of *The Remonstrance. A Poem* (London, 1770) had anticipated him:

> The patriot soars, in urging his great cause,
> Above all civil, and all sacred laws.
> Should freedom's weal and hardy deed require,
> 'Tis his to set the trembling globe on fire:
> Then, Phoenix-like, he'd from his ashes rise,
> Grasp all his honours, and assert the skies;
> O'erturn the adamantine throne above,
> And reign the better substitute of JOVE.   (p. 12)

Blake's conception of Orc and of his mirrored counterpart Urizen is indebted, moreover, to a continuous tradition of the *translatio* of England's Genius or Freedom from Britain to America. In 1775, the unidentified poet of *The Genius of Britain. An Ode. In Allusion to the Present Times* (London) asks,

> WHERE roams the Genius of the British Isle,
> The awful spirit of the ancient times?
> Sun-born, the child of fire, what distant climes
> Lure thy lorn steps from this thy native soil?   (st. 1)

The "Genius" is nowhere to be found in a Europe described in Blakean imagery:

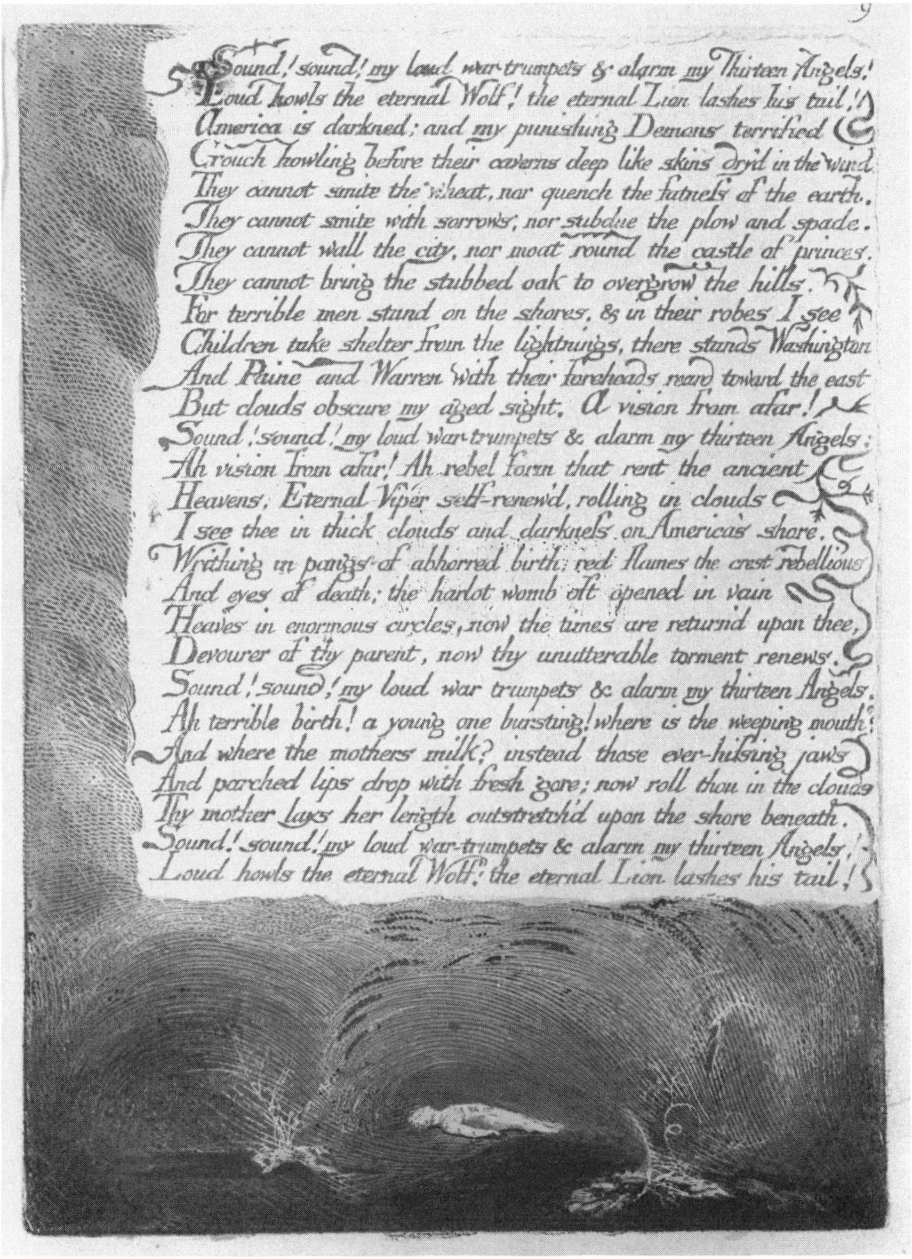

9

Sound! sound! my loud war-trumpets & alarm my Thirteen Angels!
Loud howls the eternal Wolf! the eternal Lion lashes his tail!
America is darkned; and my punishing Demons terrified
Crouch howling before their caverns deep like skins dry'd in the wind
They cannot smite the wheat, nor quench the fatness of the earth.
They cannot smite with sorrows, nor subdue the plow and spade.
They cannot wall the city, nor moat round the castle of princes.
They cannot bring the stubbed oak to overgrow the hills.
For terrible men stand on the shores, & in their robes I see
Children take shelter from the lightnings, there stands Washington
And Paine and Warren with their foreheads reard toward the east
But clouds obscure my aged sight. A vision from afar!
Sound! sound! my loud war-trumpets & alarm my thirteen Angels:
Ah vision from afar! Ah rebel form that rent the ancient
Heavens; Eternal Viper self-renew'd, rolling in clouds
I see thee in thick clouds and darkness on America's shore.
Writhing in pangs of abhorred birth; red flames the crest rebellious
And eyes of death; the harlot womb oft opened in vain
Heaves in enormous circles, now the times are returnd upon thee,
Devourer of thy parent, now thy unutterable torment renews.
Sound! sound! my loud war trumpets & alarm my thirteen Angels!
Ah terrible birth! a young one bursting! where is the weeping mouth?
And where the mothers milk? instead those ever-hissing jaws
And parched lips drop with fresh gore; now roll thou in the clouds
Thy mother lays her length outstretchd upon the shore beneath.
Sound! sound! my loud war-trumpets & alarm my thirteen Angels!
Loud howls the eternal Wolf! the eternal Lion lashes his tail!

Figure 73. Blake, *America*, Plate 9 (Not in BMC). Reproduced by permission from the Collection of Mr. and Mrs. Paul Mellon, Upperville, Virginia.

O lands, rever'd of old, the gaze of all
How vast your zenith's height, how deep your fall!
Here the mooned Prophet raves
Midst a dark'ned land of slaves;
There the spotted dragon flings
Woes, desolations, deaths, from his terrifick wings.   (st. 6)

The "Genius of Britain" has fled to America, where William Mason also locates him in *An Epistle to Dr. Shebbeare* (London, 1777):

Old England's genius turns with scorn away,
Ascends his sacred bark, the sails unfurl'd,
And steers his state to the wide western world:
High on the helm majestic Freedom stands,
In act of cold contempt she waves her hands.
Take, slaves, she cries, the realms that I disown,
Renounce your birth-right, and destroy my throne.   (p. 18)

Renamed, the figure appears again in John Adams's *Answer to Pain's* [sic] *Rights of Man* (London, 1793).[24] The similarity to Blake's Orc is obvious, and Adams's renaming, like Blake's, enables the author to expand the application of the figure beyond America or France: "The friends of liberty and of man have seen with pleasure the temples of despotism levelled with the ground, and the Genius of Freedom rising suddenly in his collected and irresistible strength, and snapping in an instant all the cords with which, for centuries, he had been bound" (p. 1).

Probably a direct influence on Blake was James Barry's *The Phoenix or The Resurrection of Freedom,* published in 1776 and reissued around 1790 (fig. 74).[25] In Barry's etching, we see several men, Milton and Locke among them, on the near shore mourning Britain's lost Freedom, whose spirit is reborn across the water atop America's Temple of Liberty. Directly beneath her, a phoenix sits amidst flames. The phoenix was a traditional emblem for the perpetuity of a king's royal body, as it is in Dryden's funeral tribute to Charles II, *Threnodia Augustalis* (London, 1685):

As when the New-born Phoenix takes his way,
His rich Paternal Regions to Survey,
Of airy Choristers a numerous Train
Attend his wondrous Progress o're the Plain;
    So, rising from his Father's Urn,
    So Glorious did our *Charles* return.   (364–69)

Once again, the radicals appropriated royalist iconography in their attempt to alter the body politic.

Figure 74. James Barry, *The Phoenix or The Resurrection of Freedom* (Not in BMC). Reproduced by permission of the Yale Center for British Art, Paul Mellon Collection.

The allegory of the Genius of Britain or Freedom translated from England to America derives from the nature of civil war—the division of a former unity. Blake refers to this unity in a number of ways other than the reflecting images we have considered. One of the most pervasive is the metaphor of the body politic rent asunder by war and disease. William Mason's observation that Britain committed a kind of political suicide when she crossed the Atlantic, "Herself to vanquish in America" (*An Epistle to Dr. Shebbeare*), was shared by many because, in the words that appeared in *Reflections on the Rise and Progress of the American Rebellion* (London, 1780), attributed to Wesley, "the politic, like the natural body, is liable to disorders, which often terminate in death. To know the cause of the disease in either system, is necessary to a radical cure. The American rebellion is an event which has struck deep into the health of the British state, enfeebled its powers, and may bring on convulsions, the consequences of which are not within the reach of human foresight" (p. 3). Earlier, Adam Smith had warned in *Wealth of Nations* that "the monopoly of the colony trade" by Britain threatened "the most dangerous disorders upon the whole body politick" because "in her present condition, Great Britain resembles one of those unwholesome bodies in which some of the vital parts are overgrown" (2:604–5).

In Blake's *America*, George III in his various guises causes the disease, and the plagues that recoil upon England symbolize the unforeseen consequences. George should have heeded the author of *The Triumph of Liberty, and Peace with America: A Poem. Inscribed to General Conway* (London, 1782):

> Kings are but men; nature will ever reign,
> Rouse all the husband, father, in his heart,
> Paint war before him with its horrid train,
> Brunswick shall willing drop the hostile dart.
>
> . . . .
>
> England can ne'er be conquer'd but at home,
> Let princes keep in mind the aweful sound;
> Her strength, her safety from herself must come,
> And if she falls, herself first gave the wound.   (pp. 22, 25)

In "A Song of Liberty," Blake expresses the view that if England is diseased, America displays the symptoms: "Albion's coast is sick, silent; The American meadows faint!" (1:2). He repeats this central idea in *America:* "Albion is sick. America Faints!" (4:4), and the opening of the poem points to the shared fire, blood, and familial ties uniting the body politic that George is about to sunder:

> The Guardian Prince of Albion burns in his nightly tent.
> Sullen fires across the Atlantic glow to America's shore:

Piercing the souls of warlike men, who rise in silent night.
Washington, Franklin, Paine & Warren, Gates, Hancock & Green
Meet on the coast glowing with blood from Albion's fiery Prince.
Washington spoke: "Friends of America, look over the Atlantic sea;
A bended bow is lifted in heaven, & a heavy iron chain
Descends link by link from Albion's cliffs across the sea to bind
Brothers & sons of America."   (3:1–9)

Blake alludes to and merges the complementary metaphors of body
and family in the illustration of the eagle attacking the supine woman in
the upper section of plate 13, one of the pictures never directly referred
to in the verbal text (fig. 75). But recollection of visual traditions allows
us to recognize the synoptic implications of Blake's visual statement. The
eagle is another dehumanized version of George III in his "Dragon form,"
shown on plate 4 to underscore his unnatural role in fomenting the civil
war (fig. 76). The eagle icon's ideal function is as the nurturing, parental
emblem of kingship that Paul Revere shows on the third side of *A View
of the Obelisk Erected under Liberty-Tree in Boston on the Rejoicing for the Repeal
of the* ———— *Stamp-Act, 1766* (see fig. 50). Thomas, Baron Lyttelton ar-
ticulates the eagle icon's significance in his posthumously published "The
State of England, in the Year 2199," dated 21 March 1771 (*Poems* [Lon-
don, 1780]). An American visiting England long past her prime encounters
another version of "Albion's Guardian," who asks,

Know ye not me? ye knew me once, and hail'd
My sovereign pow'r, when forth from Britain sent
My fleets and armies hover'd o'er your coasts.
When like an eagle o'er her new-fledg'd brood,
I watch'd your infant colonies, and spread
My parent wings over your growing state,
Then rising towards maturity.   (p. 8)

On the oval medallion at the bottom center of the print, the anonymous artist of *The Parricide. A Sketch of Modern Patriotism* (fig. 77), engraved
for the *Westminster Magazine* (May 1776), ingeniously conflates the icon of
the paternal, protecting eagle with that of the maternal, nurturing pelican vulning its young. The pelican, an emblem of Christ and Christ-like
self-sacrifice because it was thought to feed its young with blood from its
own breast, had earlier been conscripted for political service. For example,
the 1771 print *Advice to a Great K{in}g* (BMC 4424) includes a picture,
entitled "The Patriot King," of a pelican vulning its offspring. In *The Parricide,* the female emblem of Discord or Faction prompts America, an Indian
woman armed with tomahawk and dagger, to attack her mother Britannia,
whom members of the "patriotic" Opposition restrain. America tramples

What time the thirteen Governers that England sent con-
In Bernards house; the flames coverd the land, they rouze they
      cry
Shaking their mental chains they rush in fury to the sea,
To quench their anguish; at the feet of Washington down falln
They grovel on the sand and writhing lie: while all
The British soldiers thro' the thirteen states sent up a howl
Of anguish: threw their swords & muskets to the earth & run
From their encampments and dark castles seeking where to hide
From the grim flames; and from the visions of Orc; in sight
Of Albions Angel; who enrag'd his secret clouds opend
From north to south, and burnt outstretchd on wings of wrath cov'ring
The eastern sky, spreading his awful wings across the heavens;
Beneath him rolld his numrous hosts, all Albions Angels camp'd
Darkend the Atlantic mountains & their trumpets shook the valleys
Arm'd with diseases of the earth to cast upon the Abyss,
Their numbers forty millions, mustring in the eastern sky.

Figure 75. Blake, *America*, Plate 13 (Not in BMC). Reproduced by permission
from the Collection of Mr. and Mrs. Paul Mellon, Upperville, Virginia.

Appear to the Americans upon the cloudy night.

Solemn heave the Atlantic waves between the gloomy nations,
Swelling, belching from its deeps red clouds & raging fires.
Albion is sick. America faints! enrag'd the Zenith grew.
As human blood shooting its veins all round the orbed heaven
Red rose the clouds from the Atlantic in vast wheels of blood
And in the red clouds rose a Wonder o'er the Atlantic sea;
Intense! naked! a Human fire fierce glowing, as the wedge
Of iron heated in the furnace; his terrible limbs were fire
With myriads of cloudy terrors banners dark & towers
Surrounded; heat but not light went thro' the murky atmo-
                                                    -sphere

The King of England looking westward trembles at the
                                                    Vision

Figure 76. Blake, *America*, Plate 4 (Not in BMC). Reproduced by permission from the Collection of Mr. and Mrs. Paul Mellon, Upperville, Virginia.

The Parricide.
A Sketch of Modern Patriotism.

Figure 77. *The Parricide* (BMC 5334). Courtesy of the John Carter Brown
Library at Brown University.

Britannia's shield and broken spear as the British lion futilely tries to break its leash to aid Britannia. This print portrays visually the verbal accusations of cannibalism and parricide that Albion's Angel levels against Orc in *America*.

Blake's visual counterstatement on plate 13 is akin to the theme of the 1780 engraving *The Allies.—Par Nobile Fratrum!* (Equally noble brothers) (fig. 78), which charges George III with eating his children. George III, wearing the Order of the Garter's ribbon and star, sits at the center of the print, sharing an Indian chief's unnatural feast. Above him fly the tattered remains of a flag reading, "GEO——GE the T[hird] by the Grace of —— —— of —————— King [Def]ender of the Faith &c." Next to the flagpole stands an upended Holy Bible paralleled by the grisly coronal pun in the king's hand. The remnant of the flag suggests that George, the sworn "Defender of the Faith," has, through his actions, become the "ender of the Faith" and has thus lost "the Grace of [God]" as well as his proper identity, which is also torn from the flag. An obese bishop, hypocritically holding "Form of Prayer 4th Febry General Fast," approaches and says, "That thy Ways may be known upon Earth, thy saving Health among all Nations." Behind him is a sailor who says, "D——n my dear Eyes, but we are hellish good Christians," and brings "Scalping Knives, Crucifixes, Tomahawks, Presents to Indians 96,000." The upper right corner of the print contains a quotation from *The Remembrancer* (vol. 8, p. 77), which, like the engraving itself, was published by John Almon: "The Party of Savages went out with Orders not to spare Man, Woman, or Child. To this cruel Mandate even some of the Savages made an Objection, respecting the butchering the Women & Children, but they were told the Children would make Soldiers, & the Women would keep up the Stock." In the foreground, a dog, the traditional emblem of natural fidelity, comments on these perverse actions and values by vomiting.

Blake's reversal of the nurturing eagle icon places him with those who, like the designer of *The Allies,* accused George III of being the "ender of the Faith" by betraying his paternal trust, by devouring rather than protecting his own children. One of the justifications for the American Declaration of Independence was the charge that the king "endeavoured to bring on the inhabitants of our frontiers the merciless Indian savages," a charge to which Benjamin Franklin attempted to lend substance in his fictitious *Supplement to the Boston Independent Chronicle* (Passy, 1782). Franklin invented letters from Indians and British officers seeking payment from George III for the scalps of men, women, and children. The fullest treatment of the cannibalistic eagle appears in a belated attack on Bute entitled *The Favourite; A Character from the Life* (London, 1778):

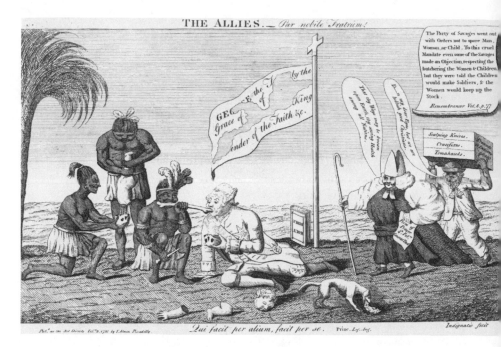

Figure 78. *The Allies* (BMC 5631). Courtesy of the John Carter Brown Library at Brown University.

Thus finish'd for the *Cabinet,* this *Laird*
Of *Britain* his own Conscience declar'd;
Preferr'd *himself* to rule no *little State,*
Made by *one Woman's Lust* supremely great;
Proud as a new-fledg'd *Eagle,* stretch'd his Wing,
And under it receiv'd a *passive* [king];
Taught him that *royal Birds* shou'd spurn at *Forms,*
And look on *Subjects* as *Pride* looks on *Worms.*
Why shou'd *Jove's* fav'rite Bird his *Thunder* bear,
But as *Viceregent-Tyrant* of the Air?
With *Drops* of Blood he scorns to stain his Bill;
Floods only give his *royal Thirst* its *Fill.*
Before his awful Eye *whole Flights* must fall,
Nor *struggle* whilst *their King* ingulphs'em *all.*
Thus half the *Species* is *one Despot's* Food,
Whose happiest Meals are crown'd with Tides of *Blood.*   (pp. 31–32)

Blake's subversion of the eagle image is just one of several icon re-
versals in the poem. For example, Orc's coming will replace the regal sun
icon: " 'The Sun has left his blackness, & has found a fresher morning' "
(6:13). Moreover, Orc is repeatedly associated with the image of the vine,
opposing the royal oak. The identification of America with the vine blessed
by God had become a commonplace, as in Cotton Mather's *The Wonders of
the Invisible World* (Boston, 1692), in Jacob Duche's sermon *The American
Vine* (Philadelphia, 1775), or in Benjamin Young Prime's *Columbia's Glory,
or British Pride Humbled* (New York, 1791). Blake acknowledges the regal
associations with the oak in *Ahania* (1795), where Urizen sits "on his dark
rooted Oak" (3:16). And in the complaint by Albion's Angel in *America,*
George III's spokesman regrets that "my punishing Demons . . . cannot
bring the stubbed oak to overgrow the hills" (9:3–8)—that is, royalism
has failed to take root in America. Blake agrees with the anonymous poet
of *The Triumph of Liberty, and Peace with America* (London, 1782): when
Peace resided in Britain, "the stately oak that guards its sacred coast" (p. 2)
flourished, but during the war "no more the spreading oak bestow'd its
shade" (p. 3). In Blake's *America,* the warning of *England's Glory, a Poem to
the King* (London, 1777) has become reality:

As a tall Oak with tow'ring Branches spread,
Whose perish'd Root can scarce support its head.
Without Resistence to each Blast gives way,
And owes its downfall to its own Decay;
That Country's Safety sinks where Honor fails;
Where Vice predominates, and Spite prevails.   (pp. 23–24)

Blake in effect seeks to demonstrate the validity of the Aesopian analogy Johnson alludes to in *Taxation no Tyranny* (London, 1775), though Blake disputes the traditional conclusion:

> A colony is to the mother-country as a member to the body, deriving its action and its strength from the general principle of vitality; receiving from the body, and communicating to it, all the benefits and evils of health and disease; liable in dangerous maladies to sharp applications, of which the body however must partake the pain; and exposed, if incurably tainted, to amputation, by which the body likewise will be mutilated.
>
> The mother-country always considers the colonies thus connected, as parts of itself; the prosperity or unhappiness of either is the prosperity or unhappiness of both; not perhaps of both in the same degree, for the body may subsist, though less commodiously, without a limb, but the limb must perish if it be parted from the body. (10:425)

Blake agrees, rather, with Wollstonecraft's conclusion that "the gangrene, which the vices engendered by oppression have produced, is not confined to the morbid part, but pervades society at large."[26]

The catalog of dishonors, vices, and spite that "Boston's Angel" gives in *America* lists George III's alleged hypocrisies, which for more than thirty years had supposedly been weakening England's royal oak:

> Who commanded this? what God? what Angel!
> To keep the gen'rous from experience till the ungenerous
> Are unrestraind performers of the energies of nature,
> Till pity is become a trade, and generosity a science
> That men get rich by, & the sandy desart is giv'n to the strong
> What God is he, writes laws of peace, & clothes him in a tempest
> What pitying Angel lusts for tears, and fans himself with sighs
> What crawling villain preaches abstinence & wraps himself
> In fat of lambs?   (11:7–15)

The plagues that recoil upon Albion as a logical result of a political body's attacking itself in a civil war include the madness visited upon "Albion's Guardian," both symbolically and actually, as recent history had demonstrated when George III lapsed into madness from November 1788 until February 1789. Blake suggests that George's recent lunacy was unintentionally self-inflicted, yet condign, given his political and personal vices. Blake's George suffers Churchill's "lep'rous plague" (*The Author*, 81) of power abused:

> The red fires rag'd! the plagues recoil'd! then roll'd they back with
>   fury

On Albion's Angels: then the Pestilence began in streaks of red
Across the limbs of Albions Guardian.
. . . .
Albions Guardian writhed in torment on the eastern sky,
Pale, quivring toward the brain his glimmering eyes, teeth
    chattering,
Howling and shuddering his legs quivering; convuls'd each muscle &
    Sinew.   (14:20–15:8)

The verbal description of George's madness, providentially visited upon
him, recalls the visual images of incipient madmen holding their heads in
attempts to contain reason on plates 4 and 5 of *America* (figs. 76, 79).[27]

The cure for reason, however, lies in Orc's redemptive, regenerative
powers. Turn again to plate 8 (see fig. 70). At the top we find the un-
redeemed image of royal tyranny visualized; at the bottom we find the
mad tyrant Nebuchadnezzar's dream regenerated verbally; in between we
find many of the reclaimed and transformed image patterns we have been
discussing:

The terror answerd: I am Orc, wreath'd round the accursed tree;
The times are ended; shadows pass the morning gins to break;
The fiery joy, that Urizen perverted to ten commands,
What night he led the starry hosts thro' the wide wilderness:
That stony law I stamp to dust: and scatter religion abroad
To the four winds as a torn book, & none shall gather the leaves.
But they shall rot on desart sands, & consume in bottomless deeps;
To make the desarts blossom, & the deeps shrink to their fountains,
And to renew the fiery joy, and burst the stony roof.
That pale religious letchery, seeking Virginity,
May find it in a harlot, and in coarse-clad honesty
The undefil'd tho' ravish'd in her cradle night and morn:
For every thing that lives is holy, life delights in life;
Because the soul of sweet delight can never be defil'd.
Fires inwrap the earthly globe, yet man is not consumd;
Amidst the lustful fires he walks; his feet become like brass,
His knees and thighs like silver, & his breast and head like gold.

This passage contains one of the most important icons we have yet to
consider: the book. Blake's own canon suggests that for him the icon of
the book in the most general sense represents rigidity, containment, and
death. He may have published so little and revised so frequently because
he sought to avoid ever completing a static book, unchanging and therefore lifeless. Such seems to be the message of the "Memorable Fancy" of
the "Printing house in Hell" in *The Marriage of Heaven and Hell,* where vital

Figure 79. Blake, *America*, Plate 5 (Not in BMC). Reproduced by permission from the Collection of Mr. and Mrs. Paul Mellon, Upperville, Virginia.

knowledge is ultimately incarcerated: "There they were reciev'd by Men who occupied the sixth chamber, and took the forms of books & were arranged in libraries" (plate 15). The grave door on plate 12 of *America* takes the form of a bound volume on a bookshelf (fig. 80). *The Marriage* concludes with Blake's promise to engage in a new "battle of the books": "I have also: The Bible of Hell, which the world shall have whether they will or no" (plate 24).

Investigation of the book icon in *America,* one of the earliest constituents of Blake's "Bible of Hell," leads to larger constellations of allusions, including Scottish policy, systems making, political mysteries, papal despotism, antiepiscopalianism, and usurpation. The wider implications of Blake's icon are not apparent until we recollect the image of the book in other components of Blake's "Bible." The icon achieves its most general, abstract illustration on the title page of *The Book of Urizen* (1794), versified in *Urizen* 4:24–40:

  6. Here alone I in books formd of metals
     Have written the secrets of wisdom
     The secrets of dark contemplation
     By fightings and conflicts dire,
     With terrible monsters Sin-bred:
     Which the bosoms of all inhabit;
     Seven deadly Sins of the soul.
  7. Lo! I unfold my darkness: and on
     This rock, place with strong hand the Book
     Of eternal brass, written in my solitude.
  8. Laws of peace, of love, of unity:
     Of pity, compassion, forgiveness.
     Let each chuse one habitation:
     His ancient infinite mansion:
     One command, one joy, one desire,
     One curse, one weight, one measure
     One King, one God, one Law.

The political effects of Urizen's book making are more explicit in Blake's *Europe: A Prophecy* (1794), plate 11:

Ablions Angel rose upon the Stone of Night.
He saw Urizen on the Atlantic;
And his brazen Book
That Kings & Priests had copied on Earth
Expanded from North to South.

To appreciate fully Blake's achievement in his more abstract and general representations of the book icon, we should inspect closely the image in

So cried he, rending off his robe & throwing down his scepter.
In sight of Albions Guardian. and all the thirteen Angels
Rent off their robes to the hungry wind, & threw their golden scep
     -ters
Down on the land of America, indignant they descended
Headlong from out their heavenly heights, descending swift as
     fires
Over the land: naked & flaming are their lineaments seen
In the deep gloom, by Washington & Paine & Warren they stood
And the flame folded roaring fierce within the pitchy night
Before the Demon red, who burnt towards America,
In black smoke thunders and loud winds rejoicing in its
     terror
Breaking in smoky wreaths from the wild deep, & gathering thick
In flames as of a furnace on the land from North to South

Figure 80. Blake, *America*, Plate 12 (Not in BMC). Reproduced by permission from the Collection of Mr. and Mrs. Paul Mellon, Upperville, Virginia.

the more particular, historically allusive *America* and the tradition of the book that informs its reappearance in Blake's canon. By so doing we shall recognize that George III, in a variety of guises, is associated with the book icon and that, paradoxically, Blake's most explicit visualization of the historical king appears on plate 11 of *Europe,* amidst one of his more abstract treatments of the icon.

In relation to Blake's later use of the image, the icon appears in relatively embryonic form in *America,* but already with a strong tradition behind it. Urizen premises regal tyranny upon the issuance of stony tablets that Orc likens to a book he will tear up and scatter to the winds. Plate 4 (see fig. 76) illustrates this book on the back of George III's manifestation, shown here wielding a scepter with a French fleur-de-lis to signify tyranny. He is identified at the bottom of the plate as "the King of England" (4:12) and on the preceding plate as "Albion's wrathful Prince" (3:14). Commentators have rightly linked Urizen's book of stony law with the restrictive Decalogue of the Old Testament.[28] But I think that Blake also makes a more contemporary allusion to the thirty-year-old tradition of identifying George's allegedly tyrannical inclinations with rule by prescriptive law and tyrannical book. The upended Holy Bible in the 1780 engraving *The Allies* (see fig. 78) briefly alludes to repeated charges that George III has perverted the Bible, as does Urizen in Blake's eyes, to establish a book-based tyranny.

Charles Churchill had earlier linked abuse of books with abuse of power. In *The Ghost* (1763), he refers to "Pow'r's dread book" (4:865), and in *Gotham* (1764), he accuses Bute of betraying George into political theory so that George abandons the law's living spirit for the "weak, dead letter" (3:473, 607–8). In *The Conference* (1763), Churchill acknowledges that only the king can assure that the law does not become an instrument of tyranny:

'Tis not on Law, a System great and good,
By Wisdom penn'd, and bought by noblest Blood,
My Faith relies: By wicked Men and vain,
Law, once abus'd, may be abus'd again.—
No, on our great Law-giver I depend,
Who knows and guides them to their proper End;
Whose Royalty of Nature blazes out
So fierce, 'twere Sin to entertain a doubt.   (325–32)

Churchill's recognition that law abused could be the basis of absolutist monarchy and his tying political doubts to theological sin clearly anticipate Blake's Urizenic vision in *America* of George III's claims to power. Churchill and his fellow satirists, as we have seen, quickly labeled this alleged system of law abused as "Scotch politics," a satiric target still very much available to Blake when he composed *America*. As is usually the case with Blake, he acknowledges the traditions to which he is indebted even as he moves beyond them. The satiric targets of the book and "Scotch politics" were intermingled when he received them, and they remain so in *America*.

Blake's use of the thistle image, identified by Blake commentators as his general emblem for tyranny, is, I think, his acknowledgment of the continuous satiric emphasis on the Scottish system of tyranny that George III allegedly practices and that Urizen justifies in *America*. Plate 6, replete with verbal images of rebirth, release, resurrection, and regeneration, is surmounted by the visual image of a nude young man representing the liberated power of the American Revolution (fig. 81). Directly beneath him, at the bottom of the plate, a thistle bends toward the ground, symbolically subdued by the figure above it. The thistle undergoes transformation in plate 9 (see fig. 73), and the rose image replaces it at the poem's conclusion (see fig. 69). Given the subject of the poem, Blake's choice of thistle (emblem of Scotland) and rose (emblem of England) icons is not likely to be idiosyncratic.

Blake's use of the thistle and rose as opposed framing icons is similar to their use in the 1768 engraving *The Many Headed Monster of Sumatra, or Liberty's Efforts against Ministerial Oppression: A Vision* (fig. 82), a print supporting John Wilkes (holding the liberty staff) against the duke of Grafton's ministry during the 1768 election, while Wilkes was still in prison.[29] The rose appears on Wilkes's side of the frame as well as on Wilkes's coat; the thistle appears next to an androgynous devil, who wears Scottish plaid and waves another thistle. Wilkes triumphs over a monster labeled "Arbitrary Power," one of whose heads is "On Law" and another the earl of Mansfield, then Lord Mansfield, lord chief justice. Mansfield threatens, "I'll Claw ye Sirrah and Law ye too, you shall see I am Judge of the Laws not You." Among the monster's other heads is that of Lord Bute, who refers to *North Briton* 45 and his own alleged liaison with the king's mother: "I wish I was under my Lassies Petticoat, for I dont like that damned 45."

Unlike the languishing thistle at the bottom center of *America,* plate 6 (see fig. 81), the corresponding thistle in the 1775 engraving *The Scotch Butchery. Boston. 1775* (fig. 83) flourishes, signifying the apparent triumph of "Scotch politics" over Boston. Blake, from the vantage of historical hindsight, sees the same events as the beginning, not the end, of freedom's fight against the thistle's power. In *The Scotch Butchery,* the "Scotch Butchers" wear plaids and are directed by Bute, dressed as a Highland chief, and Mansfield, in judicial wig and robe. "The English Fleet with Scotch Commanders," so identified in the subscribed key, flies flags emblazoned with thistles.

The morning comes, the night decays, the watchmen leave
    their stations;
The grave is burst, the spices shed, the linen wrapped up;
The bones of death, the covring clay, the sinews shrunk & dry'd.
Reviving shake, inspiring move, breathing! awakening!
Spring like redeemed captives when their bonds & bars are burst;
Let the slave grinding at the mill, run out into the field:
Let him look up into the heavens & laugh in the bright air;
Let the inchained soul shut up in darkness and in sighing,
Whose face has never seen a smile in thirty weary years;
Rise and look out, his chains are loose, his dungeon doors are open.
And let his wife and children return from the opressors scourge;
They look behind at every step & believe it is a dream.
Singing. The Sun has left his blackness, & has found a fresher morning
And the fair Moon rejoices in the clear & cloudless night;
For Empire is no more, and now the Lion & Wolf shall cease.

Figure 81. Blake, *America*, Plate 6 (Not in BMC). Reproduced by permission from the Collection of Mr. and Mrs. Paul Mellon, Upperville, Virginia.

Figure 82. *The Many Headed Monster of Sumatra, or Liberty's Efforts against Ministerial Oppression: A Vision* (BMC 4231). Courtesy of the John Carter Brown Library at Brown University.

...BERTY'S EFFORTS *against*

A VISION.

Again she at the Land arrives,
And in a favourite Son revives,
Whose friends pursue with Joy each Plan,
To kill the Monster, if they can
The fight was fierce, each did his best
And the noise wak'd me from my rest
When surely every one must Laugh
I found myself in England safe.

Publish'd according to Act of Parliam.t June 10.th 1768. Price 6.d

The SCOTCH B

1 B——— } Super Intendants of the Butche
2 ——M——— from the two great Slaughter Ho
3 Col·F·———
4 W——— } Deputies to the above

Figure 83. *The Scotch Butchery* (BMC 5287). Courtesy of the
John Carter Brown Library at Brown University.

5 ---- Scotch Butchers.
6 ---- English Soldiers struck with Horror, & dropping their Arm
7 ---- The English Fleet with Scotch Commanders
8 ---- Boston.

In the 1783 engraving *The Blessings of Peace* (fig. 84), George III is a fool, not the Urizenic tyrant of *America,* but he is still the instrument of "Scotch politics," signified here by the healthy thistle on the English side of the Atlantic as well as by the king's conspicuous boots (with the inevitable pun on Bute), one of which lies on the ground. Figures of the law frame George: Thurlow in wig and robe on his right, Mansfield in wig and kilt on his left. The subscribed key identifies all the figures. The bewildered king faces Mansfield while asking, "My Lords and Gentlemen, what shall I do." In the upper right we see "England's Sun Setting," and on the left, across the Atlantic, Benjamin Franklin holds a crown of laurel over the head of America, an Indian woman, seated between the kings of Spain and France. She holds the hand of each.

The malevolent influence and effects of "Scotch politics," be they directed by Bute or by Mansfield, the "Scotch Chief Justice, the glorious advocate for despotic sway," as *The Present Crisis* calls him (p. 2), are also attacked repeatedly in the verbal satires that precede Blake's *America.* At times, as in William Scott's *O Tempora! O Mores! or, The Best New-Year's Gift for a Prime Minister* (London, 1775), George is directly implicated: Scott tells North, "To the ROYAL (i.e. the SCOTCH) FAVOUR, *My Lord,* you owe what You are—What You *should* be" (p. iii). Elsewhere, as in William Mason's *Congratulatory Poem* (London, 1776), we find the charge that Britain seeks to pervert America into another Scotland, where man will turn against master so that the king can commemorate tyrannical actions and erase the effects of satirists:

> Exalted heroes! that the deep explore
> To find *new Scotlands* on the western shore
> Behold, a *Scotia* spreads her friendly plains,
> Where cold and hunger purify the brains
> With skill to scent advantage from afar,
> With arts of peace, and stratagems of war:
> There learn to send your missionary band,
> Your ministers of peace with sword in hand,
> Lead conquering foes by second-sighted charms
> To trust your promises before their arms,
> With suppliant voice the savage tribes implore,
> To dip the tomahawk in *British* gore,
> And rouse the negro slave with prosp'rous art,
> To plant the ponyard in his master's heart:
> Your tapst'ried deeds in *Kew* shall be displayed
> And bloom when Churchill's and young Ammon's [Alexander the
>   Great's] fade! (p. 8)

Figure 84. *The Blessings of Peace* (BMC 6212). Courtesy of the John Carter Brown Library at Brown University.

Bute's imagined political ambitions remained topical through the 1770s. Thus, upon the death of Chatham, the author of *The Favourite* writes, lest

B{ute} may return to *reign,* unaw'd by *Pitt,*
To dry-nurse G{eorge}, and patronize *Mauduit* [30];
Give Hints to *Johnson,* Spirits to *Shebbeare,*
And once again our *shatter'd Vessel* steer.   (p. 38)

In David Williams's *Royal Recollections* (London, 1788), George III finally recognizes that from the beginning of his reign "the Scots, like hungry locusts, surrounded me. The sources of venality were drained, and the Scots were unsatisfied. The oppression of America was proposed, under the idea of concentrating power; but with the view of obtaining appointments of Scotsmen. I was deluded by the idea" (p. 6). At a time when Charles Pigott defines "*Scots* [as] The name of North-Britons, who are celebrated for fair promises and non-performances, fair faces and black hearts. They are whited sepulchres; and God Almighty has placed them in a country as barren of the fruits of nature, as their souls are barren of virtue and honesty" (*A Political Dictionary,* p. 147), and given the thistle icon's satiric tradition, Blake must have known the implications of the image in *America.*

Although George III is frequently almost as much a victim of "Scotch politics" and the system of tyranny it promulgates as any of his subjects, his importance as the essential tool of the conspirators against liberty earns him the central position in prints like *The Blessings of Peace* or the far more artistic 1779 engraving *The Botching Taylor Cutting His Cloth to Cover a Button* (fig. 85), which combines a number of familiar satiric tactics. At the direction of Bute, dressed as a Highland Scot, George is about to sever Ireland and Great Britain, leaving only Hanover still attached to the mother country. To the king's right, Lord North holds the cloth marked "North-America"; at his feet lie "West Indies" and "Africa." Behind North stand two men, one of whom, holding "a Scheme for ruining the Navy," is Sandwich; the other is probably Germain. [31] Between North and George III stands Mansfield in judicial wig and robe. Embracing each other in the background on our right are the pope, with his triple crown, and Charles Edward, the Stuart Pretender to the British throne. They observe the scene with great interest. The composition of the print is virtually Hogarthian in its skillfulness. The shared interest of the representatives of papal and Stuart tyrannies, signified by their mutual embrace, is reflected by the circle of hands tightening around the unwitting king. From North's hand on the piece of cloth inscribed "Ireland," through Mansfield's hand on North's shoulder, to Mansfield and Bute's handclasp, the circle will be complete as soon as Bute's hand or the king's scissors close on the bond between "Ire-

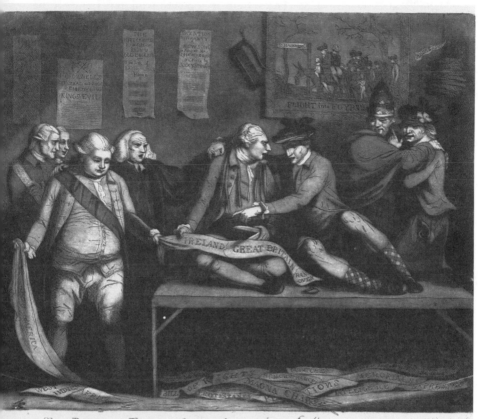

Figure 85. *The Botching Taylor Cutting His Cloth to Cover a Button* (BMC 5573).
Courtesy of the John Carter Brown Library at Brown University.

land" and "Great Britain." The system is about to triumph. Beneath the
table lie torn, frayed, or discarded pieces of cloth marked "Bill of Rights,"
"Magna Charta," "Memorials," "Pe[ti]tions," "Intelligence," "Expresses,"
"Remonstrances," "Dispatches," "Petition from Jamaica," "Account of the
distress'd situation of Ireland," all losers in this battle of the books between
liberty and tyranny. The Hogarthian quality of the print is maintained in
the symbolic figures on the wall that gloss the action in the foreground.
From left to right these images include four broadsides, a tailor's goose, a
painting, and a pile of spiked papers labeled "Addresses." The broadsides
are entitled "The Highland Laddie, a favourite Court Air, proper to be
sung in all Churches," "Dr. Cromwell's effectual and only remedy for the
Kings-evil,"[32] "The Button-Maker's Downfall or Ruin to Old England to
the tune of Britons strike Home," and "Taxation No Tyranny A New Song
as Sung at the Theatre Royal the Words by Jockey Stewart," a title that
renders Samuel Johnson a Scottish coconspirator. In lieu of a crown, the
goose hangs over George's head, punning visually on the role he plays.
The painting, entitled "Flight into Egypt," predicts the king's fate. In it,
the king and queen sit astride an ass headed "to Hanover."

The overall theme of *The Botching Taylor* is articulated by Lord Paramount (Bute) in John Leacock's(?) *The Fall of British Tyranny, or American Liberty Triumphant. The First Campaign. A Tragi-Comedy of Five Acts, as
Lately Planned at the Royal Theatrum Pandemonium, at St. James's. The Principal Place of Action in America* (Philadelphia, 1776). This closet drama opens
with Paramount soliloquizing about how he rules through corruption and
royal proclamation instead of the constitution and laws. His goal is to use
"Scotch politics" to create so much discord that a weakened Britain will fall
prey to Rome, France, and Spain, who will then be able to install Stuart
tyranny directly. Blake's tipping the king's scepter with the fleur-de-lis on
plate 4 in *America* (see fig. 76) may be an allusion to the argument that as a
tool of Scotch politics George was also a tool of Continental tyranny in his
disastrous American policy.

The result of the tensions between Britannia and her daughter prophesied in 1767 in the *Companion* to *The Colonies Reduced* (fig. 86) has been
realized. Bute, lifting Britannia's petticoat, stabs her as Spain defiles her
with his sword. A man with a Maltese cross on his coat prepares to flog
her bared buttocks. Bute exults, "Now I show you her Weakness you may
strike Home." All three stand on Britannia's shield. Britannia aims her
spear at America, whom she holds by a feather. America rushes into the
arms of France, who says, while stabbing Britannia in the eye, "Now me
will be de grande Monarque indeed! me will be King of de whole World
begar." Representing Britannia's loss of trade, a smirking Dutchman carries

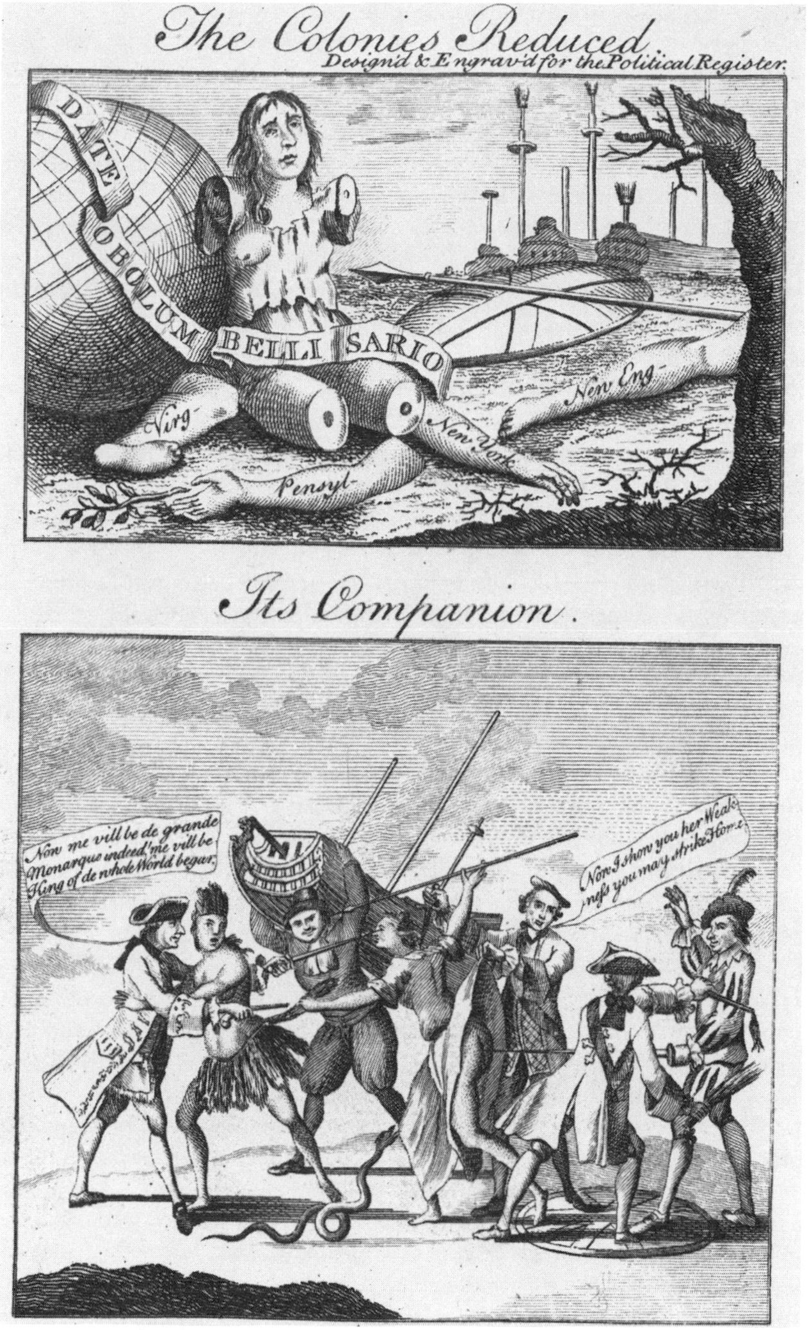

The Colonies Reduced.

Design'd & Engrav'd for the Political Register.

Its Companion.

Figure 86. *Companion* to *The Colonies Reduced* (BMC 4183). Courtesy of the John Carter Brown Library at Brown University.

off one of her ships. In the foreground, a serpent attacks the beleaguered Britannia.

In James Gillray's 1770 engraving *Argus* (fig. 87), Blake's "Guardian Prince of Albion" sleeps on his throne while he is stripped of his symbols of authority. The tassels on his girdle are thistles, and the cross and chain around his neck represent popish influence. Bute, in Highland dress and holding the royal scepter, asks of the robed Mansfield, "What shall be done with it?" Mansfield replies, "Wear it Your sel my Leard." But the object of their concern, the crown, is already in the grasp of a Scotch Jacobite, who settles the question: "No troth I'se carry it to Charly & hel not part with it again Mon!" Behind the throne, an Indian notes, "We in America have no Crown to fight for or Loose." Harp in hand, an Irishman takes advantage of the confusion by leaving, commenting, "I'le take Care of Myself & Family." A Dutchman takes his advantage in another way—by stealing the beehive of British industry. Lamenting figures frame the central scene: on the left, a John Bull–like figure says, "I have let them quietly strip me of every thing"; on the right, a sleeping and chained British lion lies next to despairing Britannia. Before her, a torn map of "Great Britain" partially covers one of "America." Here, again, George is not the villain he plays in *America,* but his inactivity, his failure to act the watchman that Burke, in *Thoughts on the Cause of the Present Discontents,* admonished him to be, has equally calamitous effects.

The "Scotch politics" that Churchill explicitly and Blake implicitly satirize was from the beginning of its satiric tradition associated with books, as we have briefly noted. In the 1765 print *The Tomb-Stone* (fig. 88), which commemorates the death of William, duke of Cumberland, the Scotch Devil who calls the tune stands on a large book entitled "*Jemmy Twitcher's* [i.e., Sandwich's] *Laws for the Gang.*" [33] By 1768, when *The Pillars of the State* (fig. 89) appeared in *The Political Register,* the literary basis of Scotch tyranny had increased fourfold. Two alleged Buteans support a beam inscribed "English or Irish here shall freely swing, / No Scot while Sawney rules, shall grace ye String." On the left is Thomas Harley, lord mayor of London and member of Parliament. He holds emblems of Bute and the Princess of Wales—a hack-boot and a petticoat—as he stands on three pedestals marked "Harley E[arl]. of Oxford's Trial for High Treason," "ambition of Court favor," and "Pride & Hypocrisy." Opposite him is Justice of the Peace Samuel Gillam, pointing to a Wilkesite street riot. Four books support Gillam: "*New Art of Enforcing Ye Law,*" "*Gillam's Trial for Murder,*" "*Ministerial Protection,*" and "*Killing no Murder.*" [34] Above the beam, from which hangs a halter, the British ship of state crashes on the rocks as its lone survivor, perhaps the king, curses, "Oh Da——n that Scottish Pilot! he has run us on Rocks & is now fled to ye Enemy." In *The*

ARGUS.

Figure 87. Gillray, *Argus* (BMC 5667). Courtesy of the John Carter Brown Library at Brown University.

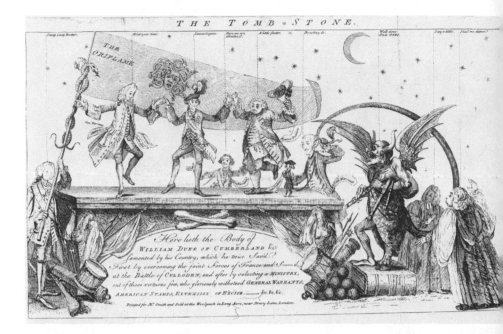

Figure 88. *The Tomb-Stone* (BMC 4224). Courtesy of the John Carter Brown Library at Brown University.

Figure 89. *The Pillars of the State* (BMC 4235). Courtesy of the John Carter Brown Library at Brown University.

North Star of 1768 (fig. 90), an open volume entitled *"The Laws of England"* supports Bute and his system. Symbolically, his feet both trample the true laws and depend upon the perverse laws advocated by "Scotch" politicians like the duke of Grafton and the earl of Chatham, who frame Bute on the clouds that blot the face of the sun, or regal authority. In a mingling of theological and political book imagery that anticipates Blake's usage of the icon in *America* and *Europe,* Mansfield sacrifices, on "the Altar of Baal," books that include *"Rights of the Subject"* and *"Habeas Corpus."* He steps on *"Liberty of the Press."* We have already seen the book of law in the hands of the Devil in *Remarkable Characters* (see fig. 36). The theological-political image of the book is rendered verbal in *The Watch, an Ode, Suggested to the Author by a Late Present of a Superb Watch from the King of France to His Majesty of Great-Britain* (London, 1778), where the author ironically says, "M[an]s[fiel]d is my Law-Bible" (p. 16). The "Law-Bible" appears under Mansfield's arm in *The Scotch Butchery* (see fig. 83) and in another 1775 print, *Bunkers Hill, or The Blessed Effects of Family Quarrels* (fig. 91), where the demonic inspiration for the "Law-Bible" of Scotch politics is clearly identified. Mansfield and North flank Bute in the clouds, overseeing the fight between America and Britannia. Spain pierces the shield of the latter while France stabs her. Behind all of these verbal and visual satires may lie Churchill's lines on the Law and the Book in *The Duellist* (1764):

> OPPRESSION, willing to appear
> An object of our love, not fear,
> Or at the most a rev'rend awe
> To breed, usurp'd the garb of LAW.
> A Book she held, on which her eyes
> Were deeply fix'd, whence seem'd to rise
> Joy in her breast; a Book of might
> Most wonderful, which black to white
> Could turn, and without help of laws,
> Could make the worse the better cause.
> She read, by flatt'ring hopes deceiv'd,
> She wish'd, and what She wish'd, believ'd,
> To make that Book for ever stand
> The rule of wrong through all the land;
> On the back, fair and worthy note,
> At large was MAGNA CHARTA wrote,
> But turn your eye within, and read,
> A bitter lesson, N[ORTON]'S CREED.   (3:625–42)

And surely in back of Churchill's lines lies Pope's observation in *An Essay on Man* that after an implicit Fall, "Force first made Conquest, and that conquest, Law" (3:245), and hence Nature warns Man,

Figure 90. *The North Star* (BMC 4229). Courtesy of the John Carter Brown Library at Brown University.

Bunkers hill, or the blessed effects of Family quarrels.

Figure 91. *Bunkers Hill, or The Blessed Effects of Family Quarrels* (BMC 5289). Courtesy of the John Carter Brown Library at Brown University.

"In vain thy Reason finer webs shall draw,
Entangle Justice in her net of Law,
And right, too rigid, harden into wrong;
Still for the strong too weak, the weak too strong."   (3:191–94)

The anti-Scot tradition and the "Law-Bible" concept may, moreover, direct us to an inspiration for another central Blakean image in *America*, "the Stone of Night," which "Albion's Angel stood beside" (5:1, 7:2) and which reappears in *Europe* (10:26, 11:1) with more directly Druidic or Celtic associations.[35] Besides the religious suggestions of the stones of the Decalogue or the stone of Matthew 16:18 from which the pope claimed his authority, "the Stone of Night" may be intended to convey the political suggestion of the Stone of Scone or Stone of Destiny of Scotland. Until 1296, when Edward I removed it and placed it in Westminster Abbey, where it became known as the Chair of St. Edward, the Stone of Destiny had been the coronation site of the Scottish kings. Blake's apprentice work with the monuments of Westminster Abbey surely made him familiar with the story of the Chair of St. Edward:

> It has ever since {1296} remained in the Abbey of Westminster, and has been the Royal Chair in which the succeeding Kings and Queens of this Realm have been inaugurated. . . . Between the seat and this board is enclosed a stone, commonly called Jacob's or the Fatal Marble Stone. . . . History relates, that it is the stone whereon the Patriarch Jacob laid his head in the plain of Luz. It is also added that it was brought to Brigantia, in the kingdom of Gallicia, in Spain, in which place Gathol, King of Scots, sat on it as his Throne. Thence it was conveyed into Ireland by Simon Breech, who was the King of Scots, about seven hundred years before Christ's time; from thence into Scotland by King Fergus, about three hundred and seventy years afterwards; and in the year 850, it was placed in the Abbey of Scone, in the Sheriffdom of Perth, by King Kenneth, who caused it to be enclosed in this wooden chair, and a prophetical verse to be engraved, of which the following is a translation—Should Fate not fail, wher'er this stone is found, / The Scots shall Monarchs of that Realm be crown'd.[36]

The Stone of Destiny had appeared in at least one earlier political satire. In James Ogden's *The Contest, a Poem, in Two Parts* (Newcastle-upon-Tyne, 1776), Scotsmen proudly admit that their object in manipulating George III is the British throne:

> "We who were born to do unheard of things,
> Kings from our house descend, not we from kings
> Nor will we, while the fatal stone lies there,
> Confine our views to aught save Edward's chair."   (p. 5)[37]

As a source, the Stone of Destiny offers Blake an apt portmanteau icon for *America* and *Europe:* a symbol of England's claim to right by conquest; a reminder of "Scotch politics"; an image of the perversion of religious values in support of British tyranny.

Blake's vision of the perversely religious-political foundation for British tyranny finds its most richly complex expression in plate 11 of *Europe: A Prophecy* (fig. 92), which reflects the confluence of satiric traditions ready for Blake's imaginative powers. *Europe* is Blake's revision of Pope's *Dunciad* 4, whose close reveals the satiric heritage and context of Blake's own female tyrant dominating a nocturnal world:

> In vain, in vain,—the all-composing Hour
> Resistless falls: The Muse obeys the Pow'r.
> She comes! she comes! the sable Throne behold
> Of *Night* Primaeval, and of *Chaos* old!
>
> . . . .
>
> Thus at her felt approach, and secret might,
> *Art* after *Art* goes out, and all is Night.
>
> . . . .
>
> *Religion* blushing veils her sacred fires,
> And unawares *Morality* expires,
> Nor *public* Flame, nor *private,* dares to shine;
> Nor *human* Spark is left, nor Glimpse *divine*!
> Lo! thy dread Empire, CHAOS! is restor'd;
> Light dies before thy uncreating word;
> Thy hand, great Anarch! lets the curtain fall;
> And Universal Darkness buries All.   (4:627–56)[38]

Europe is Blake's view of the world after the fall of darkness. Pope's Dulness has become Enitharmon triumphant during "the night of Enitharmons joy" (5:1). Blake shifts Pope's emphasis on the effects of Dulness-Enitharmon's deadening powers from art and intellect to politics and religion, but his desire to be seen as a son of Scriblerus is apparent. Like Dulness, Enitharmon is "the Mighty Mother" (*Dunciad* 1:1) who rules a nightmarish world of unnatural births and thwarted or misdirected energy. Blake hints at his debts to the *Dunciad* and mock-epic tradition with such details as "She call'd her sons & daughters / To the sports of night" (13:12). Central to both Pope's and Blake's vision (verbally in the *Dunciad,* visually in *Europe*) is the coronation of a dunce—for Pope the model is Colley Cibber, for Blake, George III. A far less certain Scriblerian debt may explain Blake's choice of the pope as an image of madness, a figure he could have borrowed from the text and illustrations of Swift's *A Tale of a Tub* (composed 1696–97, published 1704, first illustrated in fifth edition, 1710).

Figure 92. Blake, *Europe: A Prophecy*, Plate 11 (Not in BMC). Reproduced by permission from the Collection of Mr. and Mrs. Paul Mellon, Upperville, Virginia.

David V. Erdman is surely correct in identifying George III as the historical model for the enthroned satanic dunce of plate 11, but he overlooks the ambiguous quality of the reference in the accompanying verse:

> Albion's Angel rose upon the Stone of Night.
> He saw Urizen on the Atlantic;
> And his brazen Book,
> That Kings & Priests had copied on Earth
> Expanded from North to South.

By leaving unclear the question of whether the figure above the lines is the seer or the seen, Albion's Angel or Urizen, Blake encourages us even more directly here than in *America* to conflate George III, Albion's Angel, and Urizen. The systematic tyranny authorized in the "brazen Book" may expand "from North to South" not only because the North is traditionally the home of Satan but also because, in a more narrowly political sense, the North is where "Scotch politics" comes from. Satirists, like John Trumbull in *McFingal: A Modern Epic Poem. Canto First* (Philadelphia, 1775), repeatedly remind their audience that

> Rebellion from the northern regions
> With Bute and Mansfield swore allegiance;
> And all combin'd to raze as nuisance,
> Of church and state, the constitutions;
> Pull down the empire, on whose ruins
> They meant to edify their new ones;
> Enslave th' American wildernesses,
> And tear the provinces in pieces.   (pp. 2–3)

As head of the church as well as the state of England, George III is the perfect symbol of Urizenic "Kings & Priests," and his appearance on plate 11 is similar to his earlier appearance in "dragon form" as the crowned defender of the faith illustrating plate 5 (fig. 93), when Enitharmon calls forth Rintrah and Palamabron, explicit archetypes, respectively, of "Kings & Priests."[39] A passage from Wollstonecraft's *Vindication of the Rights of Woman* can serve as a gloss on Blake's image of a ruler on a cloud (a traditional sign of insubstantiality): "Power, in fact, is ever true to its vital principle, for in every shape it would reign without control of inquiry. Its throne is built across a dark abyss, which no eye must dare to explore, lest the baseless fabric should totter under investigation."[40] Wearing the papal crown and holding the "Law-Bible" of what Paine calls "Law-religions, or religions established by law" (*ROM*, p. 109), Blake's George III is the visualization of Paine's verbal image of "Monarchy . . . the popery of government": "It can only be by blinding the understanding of man, and

Figure 93. Blake, *Europe*, Plate 5 (Not in BMC). Reproduced by permission from the Collection of Mr. and Mrs. Paul Mellon, Upperville, Virginia.

making him believe that government is some wonderful mysterious thing, that excessive revenues are obtained. Monarchy is well calculated to ensure this end. It is the popery of government; a thing kept up to amuse the ignorant, and quiet them into taxes" (*ROM*, p. 206).[41] Paine sees the sanctification of a popish monarchy as akin to misusing historical precedent to justify present tyrannies:

> Since the Revolution of America, and more so since that of France, this preaching up the doctrine of precedents, drawn from times and circumstances antecedent to those events, has been the studied practice of the English government. The generality of those precedents are founded on principles and opinions, the reverse of what they ought; and the greater distance of time they are drawn from, the more they are to be suspected. But by associating those precedents with a superstitious reverence for ancient things, as monks show relics and call them holy, the generality of mankind are deceived into the design. Governments now act as if they were afraid to awaken a single reflection in man. They are softly leading him to the sepulchre of precedents, to deaden his faculties and call his attention from the scene of revolutions. They feel that he is arriving at knowledge faster than they wish, and their policy of precedents is the barometer of their fears. (*ROM*, p. 218)

Historical precedent is Enitharmon's essential tool, dulling the mind so that it will readily accept what has been as what should be. The argument from authority, which Urizen uses in *America* to justify regal tyranny, is supplemented in *Europe* by Rintrah's use of precedent to create a "political popery," under which the finite and infinite are confused and God is indistinguishable from the tyrant:

> In thoughts perturb'd, they rose from the bright ruins silent
>   following
> The fiery King, who sought his ancient temple serpent-form'd
> That stretches out its shady length along the Island white.
> Round him roll'd his clouds of war; silent the Angel went,
> Along the infinite shores of Thames to golden Verulam.
> There stand the venerable porches that high-towering rear
> Their oak-surrounded pillars, form'd of massy stones, uncut
> With tool, stones precious; such eternal in the heavens,
> Of colours twelve, few known on earth, give light in the opake,
> Plac'd in the order of the stars, when the five senses whelmd
> In deluge o'er the earth-born man; then turn'd the fluxile eyes
> Into two stationary orbs, concentrating all things.

The ever-varying spiral ascents to the heavens of heavens
Were bended downward; and the nostrils golden gates shut
Turn'd outward barr'd and petrify'd against the infinite.
Thought chang'd the infinite to a serpent; that which pitieth:
To a devouring flame; and man fled from its face and hid
In forests of night; then all the eternal forests were divided
Into earths rolling in circles of space, that like an ocean rush'd
And overwhelmed all except this finite wall of flesh.
Then was the serpent temple form'd, image of infinite
Shut up in finite revolutions, and man became an Angel;
Heaven a mighty circle turning; God a tyrant crown'd.   (10:1–23)

By reducing God to a tyrant and inflating a tyrant into a God, the British practice, in the words of Jonathan Mayhew and the icon of William Blake, "Popish Idolatry": "Idolatry consists in general in the service of idols, or false, imaginary deities. . . . The worship of a creature under the formal notion of its being the true God, exclusively of him, is the grossest kind of idolatry" (*Popish Idolatry: A Discourse Delivered in the Chapel of Harvard College* [Boston, 1765], p. 6). Blake's semiotics of clothing and nakedness underscores the idolatrous nature of George's papal status in *Europe.* Would-be oppressors, remarks Vicesimus Knox in *The Spirit of Despotism* (London, 1795), "consider the church . . . as an engine to keep down the people: upon the head of their despot, they would put a triple covering, the crown, the mitre, and the helmet" (pp. 101–2). In other words, they become popes. Knox's observations on the semiotics of kings and popes serve as a gloss on Blake's iconic practice in *Europe:*

> Politicians, observing this effect of finery and parade on the minds of the unthinking, take care to dress up the idol, which they themselves pretend to worship, and which they wish the people really to adore, in all the tawdry glitter of the lady of Loretto: They find this kind of vulgar superstition extremely favorable to their interested views. Accordingly, in all despotic countries, great pains are taken to amuse and delude the people with the trappings of royalty. Popery prevailed more by the gaudiness of its priests and altars, and the pomp of its processions, than from the progress of conviction. . . . Princes and priests dressed themselves in grotesque garbs, in a kind of masquerade habit, to carry on the delusion. But the reign of great wigs, fur gowns, hoods, and cloaks, is nearly at its close. (pp. 173–74, 178)

In *America,* Urizen is clothed to symbolize his enclosure by false values, while Orc is naked to symbolize the naturalness of his values. To move from allegiance to Albion's guardian to that of America's, the thirteen guiding angels must divest themselves of "the trappings of royalty," their robes and scepters. Blake's practice demonstrates the validity of Burke's repeated association in the *Reflections* of radicals and nakedness. In *Europe*, however, George is satirized, clothed or not. His clothing serves to masquerade the madness of his person and position, which is revealed when the idol is undressed, as he is on plates 1 and 2. Blake in effect denies Burke's assertion that "art is man's nature" (*An Appeal from the New to the Old Whigs*, 1791). The figure Blake leaves us with is that of "a poor, bare, forked animal," identifiable by his bat wings on plate 1 (fig. 94) and the similar figure on plate 11. His bat wings recall the long-standing satirical tactic of showing him as suffering "mental blindness" (*The New Foundling Hospital for Wit* [London, 1771], p. 61), which Blake had seen become actual madness in 1788–89. The wings also act to link him with the more overtly satanic figure of plate 11. Hence, he is at once blindly foolish and satanically evil in serving Enitharmon. Next to the bat-winged, straitjacketed George III is another Blakean icon of madness, a figure whose head is upside down. George's madness is again alluded to, I think, on plate 2 (fig. 95), whose naked, bareheaded figures may have been influenced by Hogarth's depiction of the mad rake in the closing scene of *The Rake's Progress* (1735) (BMC 2246), which displays the "Tyranny of Fancy's Reign." Blake's subject is probably the lunacy of contemporary British political struggles for power, in which the outcome does not affect the system's tyranny. Stripped down to the essence of the conflict, the fight's craziness is clearly revealed. Blake's scene may be an allusion to an earlier print showing George victorious in wrestling a monster with the heads of Fox, North, and Burke: *The Royal Hercules Destroying the Dragon Python* (1784) (fig. 96), which celebrates George's ouster of the Fox-North coalition.[42]

Blake's images of George III, clothing, and madness reconverge on plate 12, in one of the poem's passages that most directly alludes to contemporary history:

> They heard the voice of Albions Angel howling in flames of Orc,
> Seeking the trump of the last doom
> Above the rest the howl was heard from Westminster louder &
>   louder:
> The Guardian of the secret codes forsook his ancient mansion,
> Driven out by the flames of Orc; his furr'd robes & false locks
> Adhered and grew one with his flesh, and nerves & veins shot thro'
>   them
> With dismal torment sick, hanging upon the wind: he fled
> Groveling along Great George Street thro' the Park gate; all the
>   soldiers

Figure 94. Blake, *Europe*, Plate 1 (Not in BMC). Reproduced by permission from the Collection of Mr. and Mrs. Paul Mellon, Upperville, Virginia.

Unwilling I look up to heaven! unwilling count the stars!
Sitting in fathomless abyss of my immortal shrine.
I seize their burning power
And bring forth howling terrors, all devouring fiery kings.

Devouring & devoured roaming on dark and desolate mountains
In forests of eternal death, shrieking in hollow trees.
Ah mother Enitharmon!
Stamp not with solid form this vigrous progeny of fires.

I bring forth from my teeming bosom myriads of flames.
And thou dost stamp them with a signet, then they roam abroad
And leave me void as death:
Ah! I am drown'd in shady woe, and visionary joy.

And who shall bind the infinite with an eternal band?
To compass it with swaddling bands? and who shall cherish it
With milk and honey?
I see it smile & I roll inward & my voice is past.

So ceast & rolld her shady clouds
Into the secret place.

Figure 95. Blake, *Europe*, Plate 2 (Not in BMC). Reproduced by permission from the Collection of Mr. and Mrs. Paul Mellon, Upperville, Virginia.

Figure 96. *The Royal Hercules Destroying the Dragon Python* (Not in BMC). Courtesy of the Library of Congress.

>Fled from his sight; he drag'd his torments to the wilderness.
>   (12:12–20)

Blake's treatment of plague imagery in *America* is relevant here. Earlier in *Europe*, Blake refers to a fleeing "Albions Angel smitten with his own plagues" (9:8). On plate 12 the "trapping of royalty," the "furr'd robes & false locks," now become the condign entrappings of royalty; the false coverings masquerading madness become the man, advertising his lunacy for all to see. His soldiers no longer flee *with* him, as they do on plate 9; now they flee *from* his sight. Indeed, Blake puns on the word *bands*, retrospectively, in the line "Till Albions Angel smitten with his own plagues fled with his bands" (9:8). The earlier *bands*, or obedient soldiers, become on plate 12 the restraints of robes and locks. The restraining *bands* flee with him, the *bands* of soldiers from him. This notion that George's office, symbolized by his dress, is also his punishment may explain why in copy C of plate 11 his silver necklace looks "like a choking manacle." [43]

George III is "Above the rest" because as king he is the supreme magistrate of Britain, keeper of the "Law-Bible," "Guardian of the secret codes" punningly referred to earlier on plate 12 as the "Rolling volumes of grey mist [that] involve Churches, Palaces, [and] Towers" when "Urizen unclasp'd his Book" (12:3–4). Secrecy and mystery had long been associated with both political and religious despotism. "Those laws which prescribe the rights of prerogative, and the rights of the people," observes Daniel Shute in *An Election Sermon* (Boston, 1768), "should be founded on such principles as tend to promote the great end of civil institution, and as they are to be held sacred by both, it may be supposed, ought to be as plain as the nature of the thing will admit: Mysteries in civil government relative to the rights of the people, like mysteries in the laws of religion, may be pretended, and to the like purpose of slavery, *this* of the souls, and *that* of the bodies of men" (*APW,* p. 117). John Tucker, in *An Election Sermon* (Boston, 1771), points out that "mysteries in the governing plan" enable what Blake would call Urizenic rulers to practice "tyrannical oppression, under colour of lawful authority" (*APW,* p. 164). In *Rights of Man,* Paine repeatedly inveighs against the "mystery and secrecy" (p. 256) underlying tyranny. Although Urizenic oppressors "represent government as a thing made up of mysteries, which only themselves" understand, Paine is optimistic that "the trade of courts is beginning to be understood, and the affectation of mystery, with all the artificial sorcery by which they imposed upon mankind, is on the decline" (pp. 189, 230–31). Decline they had better, because, as John Butler complains in apologizing for his satire, "things wear a dismal aspect, when mysteries and secrecy become the fundamentals of government, or when discussion is stifled to screen deformity" (*The*

Political Fugitive, p. 111). Isaac Cruikshank's 1795 engraving *Shakespeare's Prophecy: The Last Act but One in the Tempest, or The Jack Daws in Borrowed Feathers* (fig. 97) celebrates the mysterious and secret powers of the king, who appears here as Prospero expelling Caliban, Trinculo, and Stephano (Thurlow, Fox, and Sheridan), who bear the stolen trappings of power. The bearded king wears a hunting cap and belted robe and stands beside the "Treasurey" door commanding Ariel (Pitt), "Go. Go. Go. charge my goblins that they grind their joints with dry convultions; shorten up their sinews with aged cramps; & more pinch-spotted make them than pard. or cat o mountain, cat o mountain." Ariel responds, "Hey, Mountain. Hey! Silver! there it goes Silver! Fury, Fury! there Tyrant, there! hark, hark!"

No symbol better expresses the concept of a religious-political power dependent upon mystery and "secret codes" than the image of papacy with which Blake damns George III in *Europe,* plate 11 (see fig. 92). Moreover, Blake's icon of Pope George enables him to exploit a healthy satiric tradition linking George and Roman Catholicism. Once again Blake succeeds in assailing the king on both the general and the particular levels simultaneously. The American Revolution, as Erdman reminds us, is the central historical event *Europe* alludes to, and in that context the accusation that George III was in league with the pope was especially relevant and telling. The colonists, here represented by Jonathan Mayhew, were prone to view the Roman Catholic influence in Britain as increasing: "Popery is now making great strides in England; as great perhaps, as it did in the reign either of Charles or James the second. I pray God, things may not at length be brought to as bad a pass! Thousands of weak and wicked Protestants are annually perverted to an impious, horrid system of tyranny over the bodies and souls of men" (*Popish Idolatry,* p. 50).

With the passage of the Quebec Act in 1774, whereby Britain granted her recently conquered Canadian subjects the continuation of French civil law and limited toleration for the practice of Roman Catholicism, the colonists' worst fears seemed to be realized. As Samuel Johnson acknowledges in the ironically entitled *The Patriot* (1774), the Opposition quickly seized upon the act as evidence "that the king is grasping at arbitrary power; and that because the French in the new conquests enjoy their own laws, there is a design at court of abolishing in England the trial by juries" (10:392). He returns to the subject in *Taxation no Tyranny* (1775). The Quebec Act was immediately perceived on both sides of the Atlantic as part of an even grander scheme against liberty. *The Present Crisis, with Respect to America, Considered, Number 1* (London, 1775) was reprinted at least six times in Hartford, Connecticut, and other American towns: "The Altar of despotism is erected in America, and we shall be the next victims to lawless power; all the horrors of slavery now stare us in the face; our religion sub-

Figure 97. Isaac Cruikshank, *Shakespeare's Prophecy* (BMC 8618). Reproduced by permission of the Trustees of the British Museum.

verted, freedom, law, and right artfully undermined, the Roman Catholic religion not tolerated but established, a majority of the House of Commons and the House of Lords mere creatures of the king; in short every engine of oppression and arbitrary power is at work to accomplish our ruin" (pp. 6–7).

The Catholic Relief Act of 1778 seemed to be yet more evidence of the alleged conspiracy against British liberty and prompted several direct attacks on the king. One of the most violent (and relevant to Blake's iconography) is Peter Powers's *Tyranny and Toryism Exposed: Being the Substance of Two Sermons* (Westminster, 1781), in which George III, "the bloody Nero of England" (p. 8), is likened to Antiochus, who "aimed to be more than a Nebuchadnezzar and Alexander both" (p. 4). The underlying typology of Blake's Satan-George is revealed: "We learn that a Tyrant and a Traitor is abandoned of God, a Friend of Hell, a Companion of Satan, and an Enemy to the human Species. Satan the Chief, the old Tyrant and first Traitor, and these his Seconds" (pp. 12–13). George's diabolical intentions are identified: "The Tyrant of England [has] begun his Persecutions in this Land, by his notorious Quebec Bill, by which he established Popery in the extended Province of Canada; and also by establishing the Popish Religion in England last year by Act of Parliament" (p. 6). The anonymous author of *An Heroic Epistle to an Unfortunate Monarch* (London, 1779) accuses George III of breaking his coronation oath as defender of the faith:

> Proceed, great Sir! and, breaking all restraint,
> Embrace the scarlet whore, and be a Saint.
> Sworn to maintain the establish'd Church advance
> The cross of Rome, the miracles of France.   (195–98)

Royal perfidy is one of the charges in the 1779 emblematic engraving *Sawney's Defence against the Beast, Whore, Pope, and Devil &. &.* (fig. 98), occasioned by the unsuccessful attempt to extend the Catholic Relief Act of 1778 to Scotland. The Scottish setting on the left of the River "Tweed" is indicated by the mountains in the background and the foregrounded Sawney, dressed as a Highland soldier with drawn sword and a shield inscribed "Begone Judas." From his spear flies a Union flag, which reads, "See Articles Union Claim of Rights Protestant Succession." Sawney exclaims, "A Protestant Church & King I'll defend," and, addressing the supine figure of John Bull across the river, "For shame Brother John arise." "The Church as in Rev. XII" appears above him as a winged woman from behind a radiant sun. Sawney resists the temptations of two men: one— promising, "It's quite harmless now Sawney"—offers a "Popesh Bill"; the other, a Roman bishop, proffers a money bag of "140,000" and assures him, "No Faith keep with Heritick." On the English side of the Tweed,

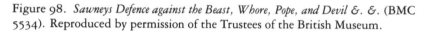

Figure 98. *Sawneys Defence against the Beast, Whore, Pope, and Devil &. &.* (BMC 5534). Reproduced by permission of the Trustees of the British Museum.

the Seven-Headed Beast of Rome, ridden by the Whore of Babylon, has subdued the shackled J[oh]n Bull, who warns, "Take care brother Sawney he took the advantage of me." George III, wearing a ribbon and star, leads the beast. The king tramples the Union flag as he offers Sawney shackles to match those of John Bull. The king complains, "That hot headed Scot will spoil my Plot." Pointing to George from above, a demon says, "Haman was but a Fool to Him." The pope, in his triple crown, tells George III, "I absolve the [*sic*] from the breach of thy Oath."

The anti-Catholic Gordon Riots of 1780 and the atmosphere surrounding them spurred several prints accusing George III of being a fellow traveler of Roman Catholicism, and the Scots resumed their usual villainous role. In *The Royal Ass* (fig. 99), George is the title character, led toward "Rome" by a devilish Bute, who brags, "This is my Ass & I'll lead it where I please." Markham, archbishop of York, in miter and gown, threatens the king's hindquarters with a birch rod (an allusion to his previous headmastership at Westminster School). He tells Bute, "Lead on my Lord I'll drive the beast along." Beside Markham stand two little boys, representing the Prince of Wales and his brother, to whom Markham had been preceptor. One of the boys asks, "Where are they driving Papa too [*sic*]?" In *Father Peters Leading His Mangy Whelp to Be Touched for the Evil* (fig. 100), George III is again led to Rome, this time as a crowned dog. Saying, "He cocks his Tail yet," "Father Peters" (i.e., Edmund Petre, James II's confessor) brings the king to the pope, seated on the rocks, who promises them, "Hold out my Sons to the End & I'll give you a Crown of Glory."

George III is more actively Roman Catholic in the 1780 engraving *A Priest at His Private Devotion* (fig. 101), where, as a tonsured monk, he kneels in prayer before an altar whose altar-cloth reads "The Holy Catholic Faith." On the wall, behind the altar's crucifix, is "*Ecce Homo* [Behold the Man]" within a halo. On the wall on both sides of the crucifix are bust-portraits: on the left, "Twitcher" (the earl of Sandwich); on the right, "Boreas" (Lord North). An open door, over which is a bust-portrait of a pope with his triple crown, reveals a water closet, its floor strewn with papers: "Protestant Petitions for Necessary Uses," "Middles[ex] Petitio[n]," "Surry Petition." The mingling of Protestant and county petitions indicates that George has sullied both church and state. A print of "Martin Luther," torn and unframed, is on the wall, next to the door.

For Blake and his fellow radicals, the more abstractly popish qualities of George III loomed larger than his historical association with the fortunes of Roman Catholicism in contemporary England. Satan and the pope are archetypes of would-be usurpers of the highest thrones, those of God the Father and of God the Son. By conflating George's image with theirs in *Europe* 11 and again in his contemporary engraving *Lucifer and the Pope in*

Figure 99. *The Royal Ass* (BMC 5669). Reproduced by permission of the Trustees of the British Museum.

Figure 100. *Father Peters Leading His Mangy Whelp to Be Touched for the Evil* (BMC 5670). Reproduced by permission of the Trustees of the British Museum.

Figure 101. *A Priest at His Private Devotion* (BMC 5680). Reproduced by permission of the Trustees of the British Museum.

Hell, Blake visually elevates the present king of Britain to mythical, archetypal status, just as he does so verbally on plate 12, where he alludes to his Scriblerian predecessor Jonathan Swift's description of the king of Laputa using his island of flying rock to suppress rebellions (*Gulliver's Travels,* pt. 3, ch. 3):

> The youth of England hid in gloom curse the paind heavens; compell'd
> Into the deadly night to see the form of Albions Angel
> Their parents brought them forth & aged ignorance preaches canting,
> On a vast rock, percieved by those senses that are clos'd from thought:
> Bleak, dark, abrupt, it stands & overshadows London city
> They saw his boney feet on the rock, the flesh consum'd in flames:
> They saw the Serpent temple lifted above, shadowing the Island white:
> They heard the voice of Albions Angel howling in flames of Orc,
> Seeking the trump of the last doom.   (12:5–13)

Blake's view of George III and kings generally as impious, oppressive usurpers was long-lived. Near the end of his life, in his marginalia on Robert John Thornton's *The Lord's Prayer, Newly Translated* (1827), he employs the satiric form of parodying the Lord's Prayer, a form closely akin to the parodies of the Athanasian Creed we saw aimed at George II. Kings claim even the power to mandate "a Lawful Heaven," and the Scottish language is once again linked with mystery and oppression:

> This is Saying the Lord's Prayer Backwards, which they say Raises the Devil.
> Doctor Thornton's Tory Translation, Translated out of its disguise in the Classical & Scotch languages into the vulgar English:
> Our Father, Augustus Caesar who are in these thy Substantial Astronomical Telescopic Heavens Holiness to thy Name or Title & reverence to thy Shadow Thy Kingship come upon Earth first & thence in Heaven Give us day by day our Real Taxed Substantial Money-bought Bread deliver from the Holy Ghost so we call Nature whatever cannot be Taxed for all is debts & Taxes between Caesar & us & one another lead us not to read the Bible but let our Bible be Virgil & Shakespeare & deliver us from Poverty in Jesus that Evil One For thine is the Kingship or Allegoric Godship & the Power or War & the Glory or Law Ages after Ages in thy Descendants for God is only an Allegory of Kings & nothing Else Amen. (p. 669)

Behind the mythic, reason-abusing Urizen with his "secret codes" and the failed paternal figure Nobodaddy, "Father of Jealousy," lies the minute historical particular of the usurper George III, "for God is only an Allegory of Kings & nothing Else Amen."

Blake was not alone in calling the king of Britain a usurper. With the coming of the American Revolution, the image of Bute as the usurper of the throne gradually began to be replaced by the image of George III as the usurper first of English rights and then of all men's rights. The charge achieves its most famous expression in the Declaration of Independence: "The history of the present king of Great Britain is a history of repeated injuries and usurpations all having in direct object the establishment of an absolute tyranny over these states." Benjamin Young Prime's *Columbia's Glory, or British Pride Humbled: A Poem on the American Revolution* (New York, 1791) may serve as a summary of typological attacks on George III as a usurper. He is warned to beware the ends of Rehoboam, Charles I, and James II because he has become an antitype of Lucifer:

> O *George,* thou MONSTER! how transform'd thou art!
> Thou didst at first act so sublime a part,—
> In thee there seem'd such saintly signs of grace,
> Such mildness, such integrity of heart,
> Humility and goodness, that thy face
> Shone like a SERAPH's when thy reign began;
> But, if a *seraph,* from thy furrow'd brow,
> Deep mark'd with guilt, thou canst not disavow,
> 'Tis plain thou art a fallen angel now:
> Not in a *Serpent's* but the shape of *man.*
>
> . . . .
> *How art thou fallen, proud offspring of the morn!*   (p. 32)

Blake's more radical view is that of Paine, who sees George III and all kings as usurpers by birth and inheritance. George's claim to power is based on the brutal conquest of William I, who lost "the name of Robber in that of Monarch; and hence the origin of Monarchy and Kings": "The original character of monarchy . . . was ruffian torturing ruffian. The conqueror considered the conquered, not as his prisoner, but his property. . . . As time obliterated the history of their beginning, their successors assumed new appearance, to cut off the entail of their disgrace, but their principle and objects remained the same. What at first was plunder, assumed the softer name of revenue; and the power originally usurped, they affected to inherit" (*ROM,* pp. 190–91). Blake, in *Jerusalem,* plate 73, gives an even more sinister genealogy (like that offered by Peter Powers), though he later canceled the bracketed line:

Satan Cain Tubal Nimrod Pharoh Priam Bladud Belin
Arthur Alfred the Norman Conqueror Richard John
[*Edward Henry Elizabeth James Charles William George*]
And all the Kings & Nobles of the Earth & all their Glories.

(35–38)[44]

But in *Europe,* Blake's icon conflating Satan, the pope, and George III, as its shackling collar indicates, has usurped limited and unexpectedly limiting powers.[45] In Blake's counter-*Dunciad,* the conflict Pope decided in Dulness's favor is reengaged and the event left open at the close of *Europe.* Like Pope's Colley Cibber, "High on a gorgeous seat" (2:1), Blake's George wields power that may be more apparent than real. As he notes in the later verse, "To the Accuser who is the God of this World," "Truly My Satan thou art but a Dunce / And dost not know the Garment from the Man" (p. 269). *Europe*'s conclusion allows the hope that, in Paine's words, "this political popery, like the ecclesiastical popery of old, has had its day, and is hastening to its exit. The ragged relic and the antiquated precedent, the monk and the monarch, will moulder together" (*ROM,* p. 218).

Chapter 5

"The Perfect Englishman"

His life a lesson to the land he sways.
—William Cowper, *Table Talk*

The prospect of the apocalyptic counter-*Dunciad* that Blake anticipated terrified conservatives like Thomas James Mathias, who, in *The Imperial Epistle
from Kien Long, Emperor of China, to George the Third.* . . . (4th ed., London,
1798), predicts that the popularity of the British monarchy will overcome
the threat of French political theory and avert a Dunciadic conclusion:

> Close we that scene: for other scenes are near;
> Darkness, and discontent, distrust, and fear,
> And brooding policy in novel forms
> Call o'er the deep of empire clouds and storms.
>
> . . . .
>
> Though now awhile beneath the afflictive rod
> SUPERNAL POWER may bid THY Albion nod,
> Humbled in due prostration may she bend,
> And her far-fam'd beneficence extend:
> Then, all her ancient energies erect,
> Strength from herself and from her God expect
> And on her rocky ramparts bold, alone
> Maintain Her laws, and vindicate THY throne.   (325–28, 423–30)

In the event, of course, the throne of George III was vindicated, and
even before 1795 the conservative forces in Britain were rolling back the
radical threat. The returning light that reversed Pope's Dunciadic darkness was Mathias's, not Blake's. A forceful illustration of the conservative
reclamation of traditional iconography that was temporarily appropriated
or subverted by radicals like Blake may be found in James Gillray's *Light
Expelling Darkness.—Evaporation of Stygian Exhalations,—or—The Sun of the
Constitution, Rising Superior to the Clouds of Opposition* (fig. 102), published
30 April 1795. William Pitt, a rather hypertrophic Roman charioteer,
loosely holds the reins of the lion of Britain and the white horse of Han-

Figure 102. Gillray, *Light Expelling Darkness* (BMC 8644). Reproduced by permission of the Trustees of the British Museum.

over as they aggressively ascend a flower-strewn slope, driving before them members of the Opposition, including Fox and Sheridan. The Opposition is associated with the imagery of serpents, bats, and owls—icons of evil, ignorance, and stupidity. Here, Blake's political and religious enemies are clearly winning the battle of the books. Pitt's chariot scatters various writings whose titles imply that the Opposition comprises fanatical Francophiles seeking to overthrow Britain's monarchy. Beside the path of ascent are three papers: "Plan for inflaming the Dissenters in Scotland"; "A Scheme for raising the Catholicks in Ireland"; "Jacobin Prophecies for breeding Sedition in England." Ahead of the chariot fly a book, "*Irruption of the Goths and Vandals*. 2d Edition," and a tattered scroll, "Patriotick Propositions. Peace, Peace on any Terms. Fraternization Unconditional Submission No Law, No King, No God."

The conquering books include the "Magna Charta" on the chariot behind Pitt and two writings held by cherubs: the Bible and the family tree of the "Brunswick Succession," the base of whose trunk is "Ge III." "The Sun of the Constitution" is emphatically regal: the verbal "KING" at its top is reiterated iconographically by the crown of the royal arms at its bottom. The "mystery" of monarchy Blake and others denounced is here celebrated through the use of the arcane Hebrew word for wisdom at the sun's center.

At the time of its publication, Gillray's mock-epic print, like Mathias's poem, expressed the hope of conservatives rather than the certainty of victory. But even as early as 1794–95, when the outcome of revolutionary fervor in Britain seemed doubtful to contemporary conservatives and radicals alike, the struggle had turned in favor of the forces of stability. And George III was a principal cause and beneficiary.

George III's gradual "apotheosis," as one historian aptly labels it, bewilders those who rely excessively on the historiography of E. P. Thompson and his followers or who confine themselves to searching for intimations of romanticism in the last quarter of the eighteenth century. A Whig interpretation of literature operates just as strongly as a Whig interpretation of history to distort our view of the past.[1] In both interpretations the present exerts a teleological pressure on the past: the quest for anticipations of future outcomes privileges parts of the past and relegates countermovements to oblivion, and complex effects are traced to simple causes. Hence, George's "apotheosis" is the sudden result of Britain's war with France, Pitt's repressive legislation, or the rise of Napoleon. The truth is much more complicated.

Participants in a recent historiographic movement have demonstrated that the Whig interpreters greatly underestimated the influence of conservative reaction to the French Revolution and the consequent threat of revolution in Britain.[2] Some have persuasively argued that the monarchy and George III in particular enjoyed broad and growing support and certainly did not survive primarily by intermittently excessive oppression, which was often ineffective and probably unnecessary.[3]

Satirists of George III demonstrate the existence of a broadly accepted though often latent monarchical premise left relatively unexamined until the political crises beginning with the king's madness in 1788. Recognizing this premise goes a long way in explaining the apparent shifts in the political positions of such people as Burke, Coleridge, Gillray, Rowlandson, Southey, Wilkes, Wolcot, and Wordsworth. Blake's movement away from overt political themes in his Lambeth prophecies and toward psychological and spiritual epics may well have been a response to the increasingly undeniable popularity of the monarchy, which may also account for Shelley's desperate tone in his unpublished "England in 1819" and Byron's complex treatment of George III in *The Vision of Judgment*. The "apotheosis" of George III was far more than a simple public-relations success of Pitt and his successors. Rather, it was a natural development, albeit officially encouraged, of the reservoir of support for the king's two bodies that had existed since his accession. Ironically, the satirists' attacks in the early decades of his rule paved the way for George's transformation from satiric target to positive exemplar during the last half of his reign. The unanticipated consequences of earlier satirists' strategies and tactics were particularly important in aiding the growing identification of George III with John Bull.

The reservoir of support for monarchy is widely apparent even in Opposition satire issued during the civil war with America. A good example is the frontispiece to *Take Your Choice!* which John Almon published on 14 October 1776 (fig. 103). The author of the pamphlet was Major John Cartwright, defender of American independence, founder of the Society for Constitutional Information, and "one of the most radical reformers" of the time,[4] yet the frontispiece to his pamphlet is remarkably conservative in its assumptions. On the right, we find the present political situation: the pillar of despotism, crowned by monarchy, rests directly upon a military base surrounded by enchained emblems of Britannia, the Church, and the Law. Erstwhile supporting pillars either have almost disappeared ("Cinque Ports," "Boroughs," "Valour," "Services") or are in states of advanced decay ("Counties," "Opinion," "Wisdom," "Virtue"). As bad as the political situation is, however, public "Opinion" still lends it some aid. Hands that appear from behind the central pillar represent various secret influences: the papal tiara associated with the Quebec Act; the scroll reading "Boston Port Act Massachusetts Fishery Act" that refers to colonial oppression; and the bowing man in tartan dress signifying the "Scotch politics" that choreographs the dance of a king whose behavior has diminished his status

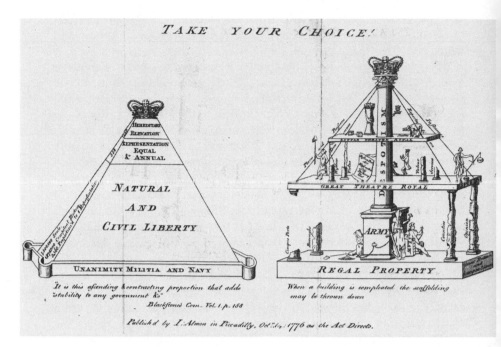

Figure 103. *Take Your Choice!* (Not in BMC). Courtesy of the John Carter Brown Library at Brown University.

to that of the commoners on the stage of the "Great Theatre Royal," that is, the House of Commons controlled by the Crown's use of "Places and Pensions," "Douceurs," "Expectations," and "Influence." The actions of the king's mortal body have alienated him from the regal body, which sits atop a Corinthian capital, an image that suggests oriental luxury far removed from the "Great Britain and 7,500,000 Slaves" that compose the foundation of "Regal Property" it oppresses.

However, the recommended choice on the left does not follow the recent American example of rejecting monarchy. Its authority is Blackstone, albeit Blackstone idealized: "It is this ascending & contracting proportion that adds stability to any government &," and the pyramid of power includes a House of Lords ("Hereditary Elevation") and is crowned with the monarchy, which is not separated by a capital from the rest of the political body and which is physically closer to the "7,500,000 Souls" that sustain it than the crown on the right is to its "Slaves." The present system needs only reform, not revolution. The message of the frontispiece may be a response to the probability remarked upon by Edmund Burke that, despite a vocal minority in opposition, most people outside Parliament supported Britain against America in the civil war. John Erskine, an opponent of the "calamitous civil war," admits in *Shall I Go to War with My American Brethren?* (London, 1769; Edinburgh, 1776) that "the greatest part of all characters and denominations, through Britain, approve the measures of administration, which I am not able to account for, without supposing the nation judicially infatuated" (p. iii). Many of those "judicially infatuated" apparently agreed with the anonymous author of *The Double Delusion; or, Faction the Cause of All the Confusion* (London, 1777): "That fatal Tree [the liberty tree], like the Tree of Knowledge in the Garden of Eden, bare [*sic*] [the Americans] bitter Fruits—the Knowledge of Good lost and Evil got" (p. 7).

Even when George III was held culpable, he usually did not bear primary responsibility for the American situation. In the 1777 print *The Royal George's Cruize in the Year 2777 with the Short Sighted Cockswain at the Helm, Sawney at the Cun, and the Devil at the Lead* (fig. 104), George says to Bute, "I trust all to you SAWNEY for I cannot see twice the Length of my NOSE." Bute, at the cun, or direction of steering, advises George III to follow him and his "trusty friend," the Devil. To another Scotsman the sturdy British tar in the foreground decries the imminent disaster: "D—— What are ye all about theare's [*sic*] the Breakers of America right a Head not a ships length from us, and we shall strike in a MINUTE." But no matter how blameworthy George might be personally, to most observers the monarchy was unquestioned. In the words of *Tyranny, the Worst Taxation: A Poetical Epistle to the Right Honourable Lord N{orth}* (London, 1778): "That K[in]gs

Figure 104. *The Royal George's Cruize in the Year 2777 with the Short Sighted Cockswain at the Helm, Sawney at the Cun, and the Devil at the Lead* (Not in BMC). Reproduced by permission of the Colonial Williamsburg Foundation.

are Men some Despots may forget. . . . 'Tis to the K[ing] you owe the
most Respect, / Not to the Man" (pp. 24, 26).

Military success in the war reinforced latent support for the monarchy
until defeats at Saratoga and Trenton in 1776–77. When the war turned
against Britain, the entry in 1778 of her traditional despotic enemies,
France and Spain, prompted a rallying around the throne. Many Britons,
like George Cockings in *The American War, a Poem: In Six Books* (London,
1782), saw the disasters of the civil war overshadowed by "the perfidious
Family Compact of the House of Bourbon," in the face of which Cockings
hoped "the powerful motives of religion, language, consanguinity, commerce, and mutual interest will once more unite us" (p. ii), a hope shared
by the anonymous poet of *The Triumph of Liberty and Peace with America*
(London, 1782). Compared to most countries, Britain was, in the words of
William Cowper's *Table Talk* (London, 1782), fortunate to have a monarch
who could rise above the temptations of despotism:

Oh! bright occasions of dispensing good,
How seldom us'd, how little understood!
To pour in virtue's lap her just reward;
Keep vice restrain'd behind a double guard;
To quell the faction that affronts the throne
By silent magnanimity alone;
To nurse with tender care the thriving arts,
Watch every beam philosophy imparts;
To give religion her unbridled scope,
Not judge by statute a believer's hope;
With close fidelity and love unfeign'd,
To keep the matrimonial bond unstain'd;
Covetous only of a virtuous praise,
His life a lesson to the land he sways;
To touch the sword with conscientious awe,
Nor draw it but when duty bids him draw;
To sheath it in the peace-restoring close
With joy beyond what victory bestows;
Blest country, where these kingly glories shine;
Blest England, if this happiness be thine!   (63–82)

To be sure, as the early Gillray(?) print *The State Tinkers* (1780) (fig.
105) shows, an audience certainly existed that was prepared to see George
III as bearing much of the responsibility for recent military and political
setbacks. Subscribed lines explain the image:

The National Kettle, which once was a good one,
For boiling of Mutton, of Beef, & of Pudding,

Figure 105. Gillray(?), *The State Tinkers* (BMC 5635). Courtesy of the Library of Congress.

By the fault of the Cook, was quite out of repair,
When the Tinkers were sent for,—Behold them & Stare.
The Master he thinks, they are wonderful Clever,
And cries out in raptures, 'tis done! now or never!
Yet sneering the Tinkers their old Trade pursue,
In stopping of one Hole—they're sure to make Two.

Verbal keys identify various tinkering ministers: North ("Ld North"), Sandwich ("Ld Sandwich"), and Lord George Germain ("Plan of Minden"). The tartan-clad Bute advises "the Master," George, who has undergone a symbolic recoronation much like the one seen in Blake's illustration of the papal George in *Europe*. In the Gillray print, George's crown sits on a feathered turban to suggest that he acts like an oriental despot, a charge symbolically made earlier in several prints of 1779 (BMC 5544–47). *The State Tinkers* is one of many recoronations or even decorations of George III that appeared in response to the unprecedented threats to the monarchy during the closing decades of the century. The choice by the conservative monarchist Gillray of "Tinkers" as his satiric vehicle is significant because since the Puritan revolution of the seventeenth century tinkers had been used to represent the danger that the political underclass posed to the stability of the state. Gillray implies that the ruling class creates a revolutionary threat to its own power by undercutting its own authority. The overclass is doing the underclass's work for it.

Tonally more typical than *The State Tinkers* of prints depicting recoronations in the 1780s is Gillray's 1782 *Guy Vaux* (fig. 106). The oddly French version of the name Guy Fawkes (or Faux) suggests that Gillray intended a homonymic pun on *valoir* to accuse the king of being equal in worth to a dummy, or guy (by extension from the effigies carried on Guy Fawkes Day). He may have further intended a homophonic pun on *veau,* or calf. George's political sins are implicitly those of omission. Wearing a fool's cap, the asinine king sleeps with bound wrists on a throne, beneath which is a barrel of "Gun Powder." His ass's ears not only indicate his political folly in tolerating the coalition but also, by recalling the punishment of Midas for his stupidly preferring Pan over Apollo, allude to his patronage of unworthy artists. Above the king, in an oval formed by the motto of the Order of the Garter, *"Honi soit qui mal y pense* [Shame to him who evil thinks]," appears an ass bearing a heavy crown. George's own crown and scepter stick out of a bag on the ground next to the throne.

The king is at the mercy of radical aristocratic conspirators who foolishly betray their own class (so identified by Cataline's ominously beheaded portrait), who seek to enact a modern version of the notorious but abortive Gunpowder Plot of 1605. The leader, Guy Vaux, is Fox, who lights the

Figure 106. Gillray, *Guy Vaux* (BMC 6007). Reproduced by permission of the Trustees of the British Museum.

way for his coconspirators the earl of Shelburne, carrying another barrel of gunpowder, Burke, wearing glasses, and Wilkes, second from the left and recognizable by his squinting resemblance to Hogarth's famous caricature. The print's general charge is that the aristocratic ministry threatens the monarchy and consequently the people. The representation of George (and Fox) marks an important step in the transition from rare animal images of the king, like that in *The Times* (see fig. 49), to the virtually subhuman caricatures of the monarch in some of Gillray's later works.

Gillray's message is similar to that of the 1778 poem *The Conquerors* (London), which laments a familiar threat to the throne, the "Butean hand" (p. 6):

An empire's gone—O dreadful, shameful sight!
A virtuous prince depriv'd—nay robb'd of right;
Drawn into woe by treach'rous bosom friends,
On shallow schemes and falsest hopes depends;
Sinking from high to low degen'rate state,
Long will this country mourn its wretched fate.   (p. 72)

The robberies of Gillray's print and the anonymous poem result in the decoronation of the February 1783 engraving *Blessed Are the Peacemakers* (fig. 107). Spain leads a procession to the house of "Inquisition." Behind him comes France, leading George III with a rope under a gateway, from whose top fall the British lion, crown, and unicorn. Next is the smiling Shelburne, holding the "Preliminaries" of the peace negotiations to end the war. America, the irreverent boy of *Poor Old England* (see fig. 72), now the master, prepares to scourge the king and Shelburne. America leads a stolid Dutchman, whose pose suggests his reluctance to join the procession.

What was most frequently desired was a stronger, not a weaker, king because threats of despotism came not from the throne but from aspiring politicians. Signs of increased regal strength and activity quickly obscured the defeat in America as the 1780s, after the overthrow of the Fox-North coalition, became a decade of repeated demonstrations of the regal body's resurrection.[5] The nadir of the royal body's fortunes, marked by the formation of the coalition in April 1783, inspired Gillray's *A Sun Setting in a Fog; with the Old Hanover Hack Descending* (fig. 108) and the anonymous *S{ta}te Miners* (BMC 6280). Gillray's title alludes to Shelburne's comment that "the sun of Great-Britain will set whenever she acknowledges the independence of America."[6] In *A Sun Setting,* published 3 June 1783, Fox rides the old Hanover hack (the king) into the darkening valley, where the setting sun, Britannia, represents the decline of the British monarchy. A signpost indicates that the king is moving "from the Pinacle of Glory" to "the Valley of Anihilation" as Fox says, "Aut Cromwell aut Nihil [Either

Blessed are the PEACE MAKERS

Figure 107. *Blessed Are the Peacemakers* (BMC 6174). Courtesy of the John Carter Brown Library at Brown University.

Figure 108. Gillray, *A Sun Setting in a Fog; with the Old Hanover Hack Descending* (BMC 6239). Reproduced by permission of the Trustees of the British Museum.

Cromwell or Nothing]—so come up Old Turnips." The horse's smoky flatulence is marked "Heigh-ho." Fox is associated with verbal allegations of foreign influence and evil motivations: "Lewis [*sic*] d'or, French commiss[ion], Spanish Anuity, Settlement, Pr Annu[ity], Enjoyments, and Hopes & Expectations." He wears a fleur-de-lis and "Spanish Leather" boots. In the basket behind him is the laurel-wreathed head of the king on a pike. On the head, a French cock, wearing another fleur-de-lis, crows. A sword thrusts through a crown, and a "Magna C[harta]" is torn.

Gillray's indirect allusion to the constitutional threat supposedly posed by Fox's ascendance becomes overt in *S[ta]te Miners,* a satire against the coalition, published on 21 December 1783. Fox, with a pickax marked "Oratory," and North, with the spade "Craft," undermine the rock of the constitution, inscribed, from top to bottom, "Constitution, Trade, Justice, Laws, Charter." George III, angrily asleep, and Britannia, despondently so, sit atop the weakened pillar. The cap of liberty falls from Britannia's broken spear, and above the king a fox uses an inverted crown as a urinal. Sitting atop the muzzled British lion in the background are three men, including the scourge-wielding Burke, identified by his glasses and Jesuit's dress. The two words of the title are separated by a shield on which a fox hangs. A cross-legged devil holds a headsman's ax.

The more direct attack in the later print is easily explained. It appeared, among many others, within days of the fall of the vastly unpopular coalition, undermined in the end by George III himself, who used Fox's ill-conceived India Bill as his tool. In November, Fox had introduced into the House of Commons legislative bills that proposed to transfer control of Indian patronage from the Crown and the East India Company to Parliament. George III let it be known through Temple that he disapproved of the bill, and the House of Lords consequently defeated it on 17 December. Having used his influence to undercut a ministry forced upon him, George dismissed Fox and North on 18 December for not being able to conduct the king's business. In performing one of the most questionably legal acts of his reign, George was hailed as savior of the constitution.[7]

George's remarkable triumph is the subject of William Dent's *The East India Air Balloon,* published 30 December 1783 (fig. 109). At the center of the print, Fox hangs suspended from a balloon, on which appears the East India House in Leadenhall Street. A banner across his shoulders reads, "Harm Watch—Harm Catch," and in his hand is a "[Bill of] Pains and Penalties." His tail is inscribed "the Man of the People." George III, dressed as Justice with her balanced scales, blows Fox away. The left scale holds half a royal crown, the right, "America." The king removes his blindfold because he has opened his eyes and influenced the vote on the India Bill. Beneath his feet are papers marked "Coalition" and "East India Bill."

Figure 109. William Dent, *The East India Air Balloon* (BMC 6289). Reproduced by permission of the Trustees of the British Museum.

The king stands on a solid, obviously man-made constitutional base inscribed "Auspicium melioris aevi [Divination of a better age]." George ignores North, who grovels in the wilderness of opposition and begs, "Sire —let me be in the Closet, even the Water Closet, rather than out of office." Before him is his "Letter of Dismission," and beneath him are the words "Quid feci? [What did I do?]."

In Dent's print, George has shed his satiric persona. *Coalition Arms* (fig. 110), published 8 March 1784, depicts an earlier stage of the same process. North, holding flags that refer to the demonically inspired coalition and the loss of America, and Fox, holding a pole surmounted by a tattered cap of liberty, step on the prostrate king, "who is extricating Himself from their Oppression." Following the shield's images clockwise from the upper right quadrant, we see images of gambling that allude to one of Fox's vices; Britannia inverted; Fox and North hanging from the gallows; and Burke, beneath his "Reform Bill," extracting the British lion's teeth.

The transformation of the king's satiric persona we saw earlier in the coalition print *The Royal Hercules Destroying the Dragon Python* (see fig. 96), in which the dragon wears shackles inscribed "Dissolution," is paralleled in the 1789 engraving *George and the Dragon* (fig. 111), in which the king has become a reincarnation of his sainted namesake. The mounted George is about to quell a dragon with the heads of Fox, North, and Burke. George is translated from political saint to god in Samuel Collings's(?) *The British Titans* (fig. 112), published 23 February 1784. Jove-like, George wears a crown of "Prerogative" and aims thunderbolts at Fox, whom he has just cast down from the clouds. Jove's eagle reproaches the falling Fox, who has dropped his ax of "Faction." The king's ministers join him in the clouds, including Pitt wearing a laurel wreath. Between Pitt and the king is Lieutenant Colonel Isaac Barre. Judicial robe and wig identify Thurlow among the others. On 19 December 1783, George III had asked Pitt, at the age of twenty-four, to form a new administration. On 25 March 1784, George took the very unusual step of dissolving Parliament. The election caused by the dissolution led to the defeat of many of "Fox's martyrs," as Fox's erstwhile supporters were called. The electoral results consolidated Pitt's control and again demonstrated the king's political prowess. *The British Titans* shows Fox falling into the abyss of Opposition to join Burke the Jesuit, supported by a demon on the left and North on the right. In the center is Lord John Cavendish, his left hand on the papers "East India Bill" and "Receipt Tax." Cavendish had been chancellor of the Exchequer in the Fox-North administration and a prominent "Fox's martyr." Beneath the design are these lines:

> First Typhon strove more daring than the rest,
> With impious hands the imperial bolts to wrest:

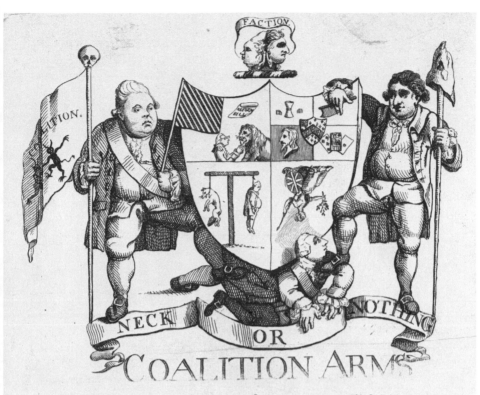

Lately granted by a new COLLEGE of ARMS to two *Illustrious Persons*
for their numerous and distinguished Virtues.

" Go and do thou likewise."

THEY ARE THUS EMBLAZONED:

FIRST QUARTER. A Standard with the Thirteen Stripes of the American States; Base, Edmund St. Omer's, like a skilful Dentist, drawing the Teeth of a Lion.

SECOND. Quarterly, First and Fourth, Implements of Gambling; Sinister Chief, a declining Axe; Dexter Base, the Head of Charles, Martyr; Fesse Point, Arms of *H—ll—d*.

THIRD. A Gallows, Two Halters charged Proper.

FOURTH. Britannia Renversed.

CREST. Janus, with the Motto Faction.

SUPPORTERS. Dexter, the Promoter of Independence with the Flag of Coalition. Sinister; the Man of the People, with a Liberty Cap worn Thread-bare; both Supporters trampling on an injured ——, who is extricating Himself from their Oppression.

Published by M. Smith, March 8, 1784; and sold at No. 46, in Fleet Street.   [Price One Shilling.]

Figure 110. *Coalition Arms* (BMC 6441). Courtesy of the John Carter Brown
Library at Brown University.

Figure 111. *George and the Dragon* (BMC 6405). Reproduced by permission of the Trustees of the British Museum.

First Typhon strove more daring than the rest, —
With impious hands the imperial Bolts to wrest:

THE BRITISH
TITANS.

Him and his Crew the red right arm of Jove,
Down to their native Hell indignant drove,

Figure 112. Samuel Collings(?), *The British Titans* (BMC 6419). Reproduced by permission of the Trustees of the British Museum.

Him and his Crew the red right arm of Jove,
Down to their native Hell indignant drove.

George III's victory through that of Pitt in the general election reflected the new prime minister's (and the king's, one should add) genuine
popularity, as even Paine begrudgingly admitted later in *Rights of Man:*
"Mr. Pitt was, at the time, what may be called a maiden character in politics. So far from being hackneyed, he appeared not to be initiated into the
first mysteries of court intrigue. Everything was in his favour. Resentment
against the coalition served as friendship to him, and his ignorance of vice
was credited for virtue. With the return of peace, commerce and prosperity would rise of itself; yet even this increase was thrown to his account"
(p. 283).

The popularity of the king and his new prime minister is the theme
of William Dent's *The Triumph of Virtue* (fig. 113), published on 14 June
1784. Dent's print alludes to John Dryden's *King Arthur or the British Worthy*
(1691), where "Grimbald, a fierce earthy goblin," opposes Philadel, "a
gentle aerial spirit, friendly to the Christians." In Dent's adaptation, the
crowned George III as King Arthur welcomes the laureled Pitt as Philadel. The promised return of the legendary Arthur to rule Britain is an apt
vehicle to celebrate the resurrection of the regal body. George III ignores
the despondent, demonic Fox as Grimbald, enchained and sans his "Asia"
crown. The withering plant behind him symbolizes his prospects.

Dent's image of the enchained Fox becomes the metaphor controlling
the anonymous 19 May 1784 satire on the king's renewed powers, *The Fetter
Manufactory by George King & Co.* (fig. 114), an acknowledgment of the regal
body's resurrection. On the left, the devil works the forge, saying, "Nothing but a Dissolution will do," while the king and probably Pitt hammer
out the fetters. George says, "This is my Prerogative," but the placement
of the fetters on the wall behind him and the position of the Devil suggest
that the king is not a truly independent agent. Pitt promises, "And I will
Support you Right or Wrong." On the right side of the print, a crowd of
fetters-bearing men promote the court candidates.

A more sophisticated recognition of the regal resurrection is Thomas
Rowlandson's *A Peep into Friar Bacon's Study* (fig. 115), published 3 March
1784, three weeks before the dissolution. George is the fabulous magician,
Friar Bacon, his necromantic cloak almost hiding his star and ribbon. With
each hand he points a wand at the visions he has called forth from the "bra-
zen head" at the center of the print. Verbally alluding to Robert Greene's
Friar Bacon and Friar Bungay (1594), the visions consist of three circles,
"Time Is Past," "Time Is," and "Time Was," each labeled "Constitution."
The first represents the distant past when England was ruled by unlimited

Figure 113. Dent, *The Triumph of Virtue* (BMC 6620). Reproduced by permission of the Trustees of the British Museum.

Figure 114. *The Fetter Manufactory by George King & Co.* (Not in BMC).
Reproduced courtesy of the Print Collection, Lewis Walpole Library, Yale
University.

Figure 115. Thomas Rowlandson, *A Peep into Friar Bacon's Study* (BMC 6436).
Reproduced by permission of the Trustees of the British Museum.

monarchy, with the House of Lords and the House of Commons as mere appendages. The second circle represents the disproportion of the present day, when the king is greater than the House of Lords, itself greater than the House of Commons. The third circle shows the idealized recent past with a balanced constitution, before George III reasserted the power of the throne. George demonstrates that he seeks to return to the relationship of the distant past when he asks, pointing with one wand to the king in the first circle and with the other to the House of Commons in the second, "To this[?] What is this[?]" Familiar metaphoric weapons from the anti-George arsenal appear in the necromantic accoutrements surrounding the king, such as the allusions to his vision found in the telescope, to his imperialism in the globe, and to his rigidity and dependence on mystery found in the large open book. The new ministry, demon directed, sneak down the "Back Stairs" while, from a doorway on the far left, Fox warns, "Beware." With him are North and Burke.

Ally and opponent alike agreed that by overthrowing the Fox-North coalition and appointing Pitt, George III had consolidated the throne's power. The king's position seemed secure. Even his earlier archenemy, Wilkes, whom George had once said he disliked more than any living man, had become the king's supporter and dependent during the electoral contest between Fox and Pitt. George's victories ushered in a period of relative political quiet beginning in the spring of 1784 and lasting until the onset of the Regency Crisis in the fall of 1788. The major development of this period, the growing significance of the Prince of Wales and his friends, also served to deflect satirists' attention away from the king. The diminished level of rancor aimed at the king appears in the ironic "preliminary discourse by Sir John Hawkins" introducing *Probationary Odes by the Various Candidates for the Office of Poet Laureat to His Majesty, in the Room of William Whitehead, Deceased* (London, 1785), written

> in an age of Reform; beneath the mild sway of a British Augustus; under the Ministry of a pure immaculate Youth; the Temple of Janus shut; the Trade of Otaheite open; not an American to be heard of, except the Lottery Loyalists; the fine Arts in full Glory; Sir William Chambers the Royal Architect; Lord Sydney a Cabinet Minister!— What a golden era! From this auspicious moment, Peers, Bishops, Baronets, Methodists, Members of Parliament, Chaplains, all genuine Beaux Esprits, all legitimate heirs of Parnassus, rush forward, with unfeigned ardour, to delight the world by the united efforts of liberal genius and constitutional loyalty. (pp. xii–xiii)

The "probationary odes" themselves generally demonstrate that the growing numbers of attacks, frequently more comic than satiric, on the king's mortal body indicate the royal body's enhanced security. The shift in emphasis is introduced in the "preliminary discourse" by ironically comparing the political faults of Charles I with the personal ones of George III:

> And finally, in the example of a Whitehead's Muse, expatiating on the virtues of our gracious Sovereign, have we not beheld the best of Poets, in the best of Verses, doing ample justice to the best of Kings?—The fire of Lyric Poesy, the rapid lightning of modern Pindarics, were equally required to record the Virtues of the Stuarts, or to immortalize the Talents of a Brunswick.—On either theme there was ample subject for the boldest flights of inventive genius, the full scope for the most daring powers of poetical creation; from the free unfettered strain of liberty in honour of Charles the First, to the kindred Genius and congenial Talents that immortalize the Wisdom and the Worth of George the Third. (pp. ix–x)

Previously, George's foibles and domestic interests had been satirized as distracting him from his regal responsibilities, as in William Mason's *A Congratulatory Poem on the Late Successes of the British Arms, Particularly the Triumphant Evacuation of Boston. To Which Is Added, an Ode to Mr. Pinchbeck, upon His Newly-Invented Patent Candle-Snuffers* (Dublin, 1776): "Enough if ONE a moment's audience spare / From buttons, snuffers, nut-crackers, and prayer" (p. 7). The list of misguided distractions and confused values lengthens in William Combe's(?) *An Heroic Epistle to an Unfortunate Monarch, by Peregrine the Elder* (London, 1778) to include George's fascination with scientific curiosities and his patronage of inferior, and often Scottish, artists and authors.

The lexicon of satirists of the 1780s may conveniently be sampled in three collaborative works produced by the circle of young Opposition members loyal to the monarchic premise but outside Pitt's administration: *The Probationary Odes* (9th ed., 1791), *Political Miscellanies* (1790), and *Political Eclogues* (1787). The principal collaborators, George Ellis, French Laurence, Joseph Richardson, and Richard Tickell, were members of the Foxite Opposition that organized around the reversionary interest of the Prince of Wales, the future George IV, once the prince was granted his own establishment in 1781 and attained his majority in 1783. The prince's first vote in the House of Lords had been for Fox's India Bill, and the prince shared Fox's unpopularity after the 1784 elections, in which the prince had supported Fox. One of the collaborators' primary purposes was to contrast the dashing, glamorous young heir with his stodgy, mundane father, who frittered away his time while the prince concerned himself with politics and more regal affairs.

Earlier satirists had not overlooked George III's character flaws mocked

in the 1780s—given the range of earlier attacks, any flaw's being overlooked is difficult to imagine—but the tone and emphasis differed. To be
sure, serious charges can still be found in the 1780s. For example, in the
"Irregular Ode" attributed to Edward, Lord Thurlow, can be found Blake's
and Paine's accusations that the king was a false father to America, but
here they are softened by a comic context:

> 'Tis mine to keep the conscience of the King;
> To me, each secret of his heart is shown:
> Who then, like me, shall hope to sing
> Virtues, to all but me, unknown?
> Say who, like me, shall win belief
> To tales of his paternal grief,
> When civil rage with slaughter dy'd
> The plains beyond th'Atlantic tide?   (p. 68)

In the overwhelming number of cases, however, the authors' eyes are
on more mortal weaknesses, such as the king's physical appearance, remarked in the ode facetiously attributed to Major John Scott:

> Grand is thy form,—'bout five feet ten,
> Thou well-built, worthiest, best of men!
> Thy chest is stout, thy back is broad,—
> Thy Pages view thee, and are aw'd!
> Lo! how thy white eyes roll!
> Thy whiter eye-brows stare!
>   Honest soul!
> Thou'rt witty, as thou'rt fair!

"Scott" goes on to mock George III's characteristically stammering speech,
which quickly became one of the satirists' most economical ways to tag
royal allusions:

> Oh! happy few! whom brighter stars befriend,
> Who catch the chat—the witty whisper share!
>   Methinks I hear
>   In accents clear,
> Great Brunswick's voice still vibrate on my ear—
>   "What?—what?—what?
>   "Scott!—Scott!—Scott!
>   "Hot!—hot!—hot!
>   "What?—what?—what?"
> Oh! fancy quick! oh! judgment true!
> Oh! sacred oracle of regal taste!   (p. 49)

But in the satirists' vision of reality expressed by the marquis of Graham in "his" ode, the king has debased his regal taste to the level of a farmer's interests, and he reaps the acclamation appropriate to the ironic golden age he has restored:

Ye feather'd choristers your voices tune,
'Tis now, or near the fourth of June;
All nature smiles—the day of Brunswick's birth
Destroy'd the iron-age, and made an heav'n on earth.
Men and beasts his name repeating,
Courtiers talking, calves a bleating;
   horses neighing,
   asses braying,
Sheep, hogs, and geese, with tuneful voices sing,
All praise their king,
George the Third, the Great, the Good.
France and Spain his anger rue;
Americans, he conquer'd you,
Or would have done it if he cou'd.
Shall not his gosling tune his throat;
Then let me join the jocund band,
Crown'd with laurel let me stand;
My grateful voice shall their's as far exceed,
As the two leg'd excels the base four-footed breed.   (p. 89)

The normal tone of the poetic collaborators is the bemused indulgence of a song found in *Political Miscellanies. By the Authors of the Rolliad and Probationary Odes* (1790):

Let great GEORGE his porkers bilk,
And give his maids the sour skim-milk;
With her stores let CERES crown him,
'Till the gracious sweat run down him,
Making butter night and day:
Well! Well!
Every king must have his way;
But to my poor way of thinking,
True joy is drinking.   (p. 127)

The laughing treatment of the king found its most popular advocate in John Wolcot, writing under the pseudonym Peter Pindar. Wolcot's strategy and tactics may be surveyed in a triad of poems published in 1787: *Ode upon Ode; or, A Peep at St. James* (March); *Apologetic Postscript to Ode upon Ode* (June); and *Instructions to a Celebrated Laureat, Alias The Progress of Curiosity,*

Alias A Birth-Day Ode, Alias Mr. Whitbread's Brewhouse (August). All three poems should be read as sequels to the *Probationary Odes* because they are addressed to Thomas Warton, who had been awarded the laureateship in 1785. The controlling premise of Wolcot's strategy is this assertion:

> Far from despising Kings, I like the breed,
> Provided *king-like* they behave:
> Kings are an instrument we need;
> Just as we razors want, to shave.   (*Apologetic*, p. 460)

Wolcot's objection to George III is not that the man is too much the monarch, the radicals' objection, but rather is that the monarch is too much the man:

> Hear what I have to say of Kings.——
> If, *unsublime,* they deal in childish things
> And yield not, of reform, a ray of hope;
> Each mighty Monarch straight appears to me.
> A *roaster* of *himself, Felo de se:*
> I only act as Cook, and *dish him up.*   (*Apologetic*, p. 456)[8]

For Blake, George III is sublime by virtue of his position; as a king he has become like unto a sky-god, a starry king. Wolcot professes to wish that George were what Blake attacks him for being:

> But perhaps, aloft on his imperial Throne,
> So distant, O ye Gods! from every one,
> The Royal Virtues are like many a Star,
> From this our pigmy System rather far;
> Whose Light, though flying ever since Creation,
> Has not yet pitch'd upon our Nation.   (*Instructions*, p. 477)

Wolcot's George is not dangerous; he is instead embarrassing because he is not large enough to fill the role that fate has given him:

> Whenever I have heard of Kings
> Who place in gossiping and news their pride;
> And knowing family-concerns, mean things;
> Very judiciously indeed I've cried:
>   "I wonder
> How their blind Stars could make so gross a blunder.
>
> "Instead of sitting on a Throne,
> In purple rich, of state so full;
> They should have had an Apron on,
> And, seated on a three-legged stool,

Commanded of dead Hair the sprigs
To do their duty upon Wigs.

"By such mistakes is Nature often foiled;
Such improprieties should never spring:
Thus a fine chattering Barber may be spoiled,
To make a most indifferent King."   (*Apologetic,* pp. 456–57)

Blake's satires generally rely on the tactic of enhancement to attack
George III; for Wolcot, diminution is the principal weapon. Even the usual
regal vices of extravagance and greed dwindle to trivial pursuits:

And why in God's name, should not Queens and Kings
Purchase a comb or corkscrew, lace for cloaks,
Edging for caps, or tape for apron-strings,
Or pins, or bobbin, *cheap* as other folks?   (*Ode,* p. 435)

Contemporary visual satirists reflected the verbal satirists' strategy and
tactics. As early as 1780, *Read, Mark, Learn & Inwardly Digest* (BMC 5687)
ridiculed George's manner of speech when the king says to Lord Amherst,
"I hear You made a fine Disposition You You You soon tame'd the Bull
[i.e., John Bull]." And the growing emphasis on a comic "Farmer George"
can be found in a number of prints of the mid-1780s, including the representative *Going to Market* (fig. 116), published 24 April 1786. In the
foreground we see George III, pitchfork in hand, directing two guardsmen
to take his turnips and carrots to market. The king, identifiable by the
ribbon of the Order of the Garter slipping down his leg, has exchanged his
regal dress for a simple frock. Behind him, Queen Charlotte stands in a
doorway, feeding chickens. On a hill in the background is Windsor Castle,
implicitly where George should be. The castle also serves as a reminder of
the site of George's farming activities on land reclaimed from marsh in the
Great Park at Windsor.

To satirists like Wolcot, "the Palace," rather than being the castle of a
king, "seemed the lodging of a Baker" (*Apologetic,* p. 460), where George
worried himself about how to make apple dumplings, to brew beer, or to
trace the provenance of a louse. The now conventional image of a weak-
eyed monarch looking through a glass is recalled:

Now Majesty into a Pump so deep
Did with an opera-glass of Dolland peep,
Examining with care each wondrous matter
That brought up water.

. . . .

Thus, to the world of *great* while others crawl,
Our Sovereign peeps into the world of *small:*

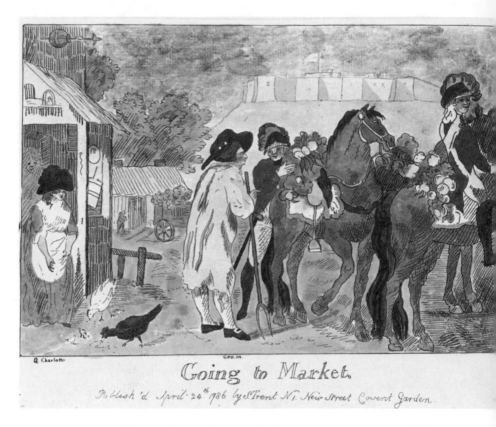

Going to Market.

Publish'd April 24th 1786 by S. Trent N.1. New Street Covent Garden.

Figure 116. *Going to Market* (BMC 6946). Reproduced by permission of the Trustees of the British Museum.

> Thus microscopic Geniuses explore
> Things that too oft provoke the public scorn;
> Yet swell of useful knowledges the store,
> By finding Systems in a Pepper-corn. (*Instructions*, pp. 484–85)

In mocking the king's alleged undermining of the dignity of the throne, Wolcot sought to enhance the attractiveness of the prince, whose extravagant way of life could perhaps be justified in no other way. Wolcot's design is clear in *Apologetic Postscript,* which, with its opening that allusively acknowledges debts to Pope and Horace, is the poet's apologia for his art. "Yes," he says, "I like Kings: and oft look back with pride / Upon the Edwards, Harries, of our isle" (p. 461), but the present monarch is not even worth mentioning, as the poet leaps to the future, when Prince George will sit on the throne:

> Muse, let us also *forward* look,
> And take a peep into Fate's book.
> Behold, the sceptre Young Augustus sways!
> I hear the mingled praise of millions rise:
> I see upraised to Heaven their ardent eyes,
> That for their Monarch ask a length of days.
> Bright in the brightest annals of renown,
> Behold fair Fame his youthful temples crown
> With Laurels of unfading bloom;
> Behold Dominion swell beneath his care,
> And Genius, rising from a dark despair,
> His long-extinguish'd fires relume!
> *Such* are the Kings that suit *my* taste, I own:
> Not those where all the *littlenesses* join;
> Whose souls should start to find their lot a throne,
> And blush to show their noses on a Coin. (pp. 461–62)

The prince quickly proved himself deserving more of mock-heroic treatment than of Wolcot's misdirected hopes. The prince's prodigality and licentiousness soon became too excessive to be celebrated by ridiculing his father's contrasting frugality and domesticity. The Regency Crisis forced their characters into sharply delineated focus. But even before the fall of 1788, events undercut attempts by the Opposition and its supporters in satire to diminish George III's popularity. The Opposition could do nothing to conceal the endomorphic reality of the disappointing heir, whose character and person are mocked in Robert Dighton's 1797 print *A Great Personage* (fig. 117), which juxtaposes the prince's swollen image with the words advertising a visiting pachyderm:

Figure 117. Robert Dighton, *A Great Personage* (Not in BMC). Reproduced by permission of the Henry E. Huntington Library and Art Gallery, San Marino, California.

To be SEEN:
the
ROYAL ELEPHANT
the largest Animal of the
kind ever seen in this
Country was brought
over by his
MAJESTY'S Ship
the
PRINCESS ROYAL.
N.B. Any lady may
STROKE him without
the least Danger.
has been exhibited
before the ROYAL FAMILY.

Contributing to George III's rising popularity were his reactions to two mad subjects he encountered before and after his own experience of 1788–89. On 2 August 1786, Margaret Nicholson, pretending to submit a petition outside St. James's Palace, tried to assassinate the king but managed only to bend the blade of her knife against his body. When asked if he was hurt, the king quickly replied that he was unwounded and expressed concern for his obviously deranged assailant. The king's courageous behavior, as well as the royal mercy he displayed in not having the madwoman arraigned for high treason, received almost universal praise in the verbal and visual reactions. When on 21 January 1790 another lunatic, John Frith, threw a rock at the royal coach as George III rode to open Parliament, the king again demonstrated understanding and mercy. Framing as they did the king's own bout with madness, the incidents enabled the king to set the standard for humane treatment of mentally deranged opponents, a standard, coupled with the popularity of the monarch, that greatly reduced the availability of the royal madness as a weapon for would-be satirists of the king.

That the Nicholson incident enhanced the king's political position was undeniable. One satirist tried to forestall any attempt to link the attack with the Opposition in the 1786 print *A Ministerial Fact; or, A Squib of the First Day* (fig. 118). Fox, dressed as a woman, is kept by a "beef-fed guard" from stabbing "god-like GEORGE" (in the words of "Margaret Nicholson," an ironic dialogue between Wilkes, "the regenerate man," and Lord Hawkesbury in *Political Eclogues,* 1790 ed., p. 108). The composed king holds off the raving Fox. Beneath the title we read: "Four presumptive Reasons—Because no two faces in the world are so much alike!—Because

Figure 118. *A Ministerial Fact; or, A Squib of the First Day* (BMC 6972).
Reproduced by permission of the Trustees of the British Museum.

the Political Proteus [Fox] was seen in a Miliners shop (where no doubt he bought the Cloak and bonnet) about a month ago!—Because he was seen by a Grenadier of the Guards coming out of a Cutler's shop (where no doubt he bought the knife) yesterday morning!—But the strongest reason to suppose him the Assassin is because he was an hundred miles from London at the time!!!"

As indirect admissions that the Nicholson attack helped the king and hurt the Opposition, satirists tried to lessen its effects by denying its seriousness. Hence, a footnote to *Political Eclogue*'s "Margaret Nicholson" wishfully observes:

> The public alarm expressed upon the event which is the subject of this Pastoral, was certainly a very proper token of affection to a Monarch, every action of whose reign denotes him to be the father of his people. Whether it has sufficiently subsided to admit of a calm enquiry into facts, is a matter of some doubt, as the addresses [of thanksgiving and congratulation] were not finished in some late Gazettes. If ever that time should arrive, the world will be very well pleased to hear that the miserable woman whom the Privy Council have judiciously confined in Bedlam for her life, never even aimed a blow at his August Person. (p. 113)

Wolcot is more overtly contemptuous. Writing exactly a year after what he calls, in *Instructions to a Celebrated Laureat*, "the tale of Margret's Knife, and Royal Fright," Wolcot reduces the incident to a display of cutlery: "The miraculous escape from a poor innocent insane woman, who only held out a small knife in a piece of white paper, for her Sovereign to view" (p. 495). The anonymous author of a poem in which the king is both recipient and annotator, *Ode Presented to the King at Blenheim . . . Notes by Farmer George* (London, 1786), tries to turn the incident into an occasion for mocking George's taste. In a footnote on "MARGARET's knife," Farmer George says that this event "is to be recorded, at my desire, by the pencil of Mr. West, who has promised, however, to give his Sovereign a better face than he has bestowed on his Apostles" (p. 2). And later we learn that "Tommy Warton" told him that the Greek root of his name "signified a Husband man" (p. 9).

The nature of anti-George III satires on the eve of the Regency Crisis is summarized by two works: David Williams's prose *Royal Recollections on a Tour to Cheltenham. . . .* (London, 1788) and an anonymous engraving of the same year, *Regum et Reginarum Hi Sunt Gloriosissimi Gestus* (Here are the most glorious deeds of kings and queens) (fig. 119). George, fictional author of Williams's piece, acknowledges Prince George's merits and

WHAT! WHAT! WHAT!

NIMROD

OTIUM CUM DIGNITATE

MIDAS

Underneath
are entombed the Remains
of the
Wonder Hunting Monarch
———
* * *
In Wisdom a second Solomon!
a Daniel!
One of the four Wise Kings of Europe!
Oh! ye Descendants of Midas
revere his memory,
for unto you it belongeth to save it from
annihilation.
Great was his knowledge! his lacteal knowledge!
his farming knowledge! & his saving knowledge!
but alas!
these Œconomical Virtues are no more
for the Grave levels all distinction
between the extravagance of a Cleopatra,
and
the parsimoniousness of a G_____.
milking his Cows one morning
before the Dairy Maids had risen
he received an unlucky kick on his Noddle
which
deprived him of Life
and
_____ the Nation
of an
_____ .

Whose farming knowledge, wonderful to say,
Hops from 'Grains could tell, and Straw from Hay:
Who milk'd and churn'd and skimm'd with noble skill,
Who knew a Sheep's Dung, from a Doctor's Pill.
This is the Wisdom makes e'n Monarchs great,
And saves the ruin of a falling State.

REGVM ET REGINARV

For a Description see the next leaf to the Title

Published as the Act directs, for C

Figure 119. *Regum et Reginarum Hi Sunt Gloriosissimi Gestus* (BMC 7322).
Reproduced by permission of the Trustees of the British Museum.

admits to unfairly slighting his heir. The king recapitulates past charges against himself and now recognizes that he has done much evil, including "the oppression of America," when "the Scots, like hungry locusts, surrounded me" (p. 6). But George has learned very little from his mistakes. He still opposes reforms of any sort, including John Howard's suggested prison reforms and especially ecclesiastical reforms, because they would lead to political change. He prophetically warns of the consequences of the rising natural-rights movement in France. Williams's George is a cynical fool who recognizes hypocrisy in others, especially Pitt, and admits it in himself, particularly in his religiosity. He cannot, however, understand why the common people avoid him during his many trips to the countryside, where he pays too much for a horse and investigates a mousetrap with his finger. The standard points are made about his taste, curiosity, greed, and folly. George III is a wise fool, not a Blakean despot.

Very similar in approach is *Regum et Reginarum,* an imaginary assassination of the royal rulers with a basically comic tone. We see two tombstones, the king's on the left surmounted by his profile. Beneath his profile, a scene depicts his occupation, and an oval contains an inscription. His head is labeled "Nimrod What! What! What!" in an allusion to George's actual pastime as a huntsman as well as to the "mighty hunter before the Lord," archetype of the tyrant, and key to understanding the significance of the stag hunt seen below.[9] Beneath a scepter and birch rod we read: "Underneath are entombed the remains of the Wonder Hunting Monarch— * * * In Wisdom a second Solomon! a Daniel! One of the four Wise Kings of Europe! Oh! ye Descendants of Midas revere his memory, for unto you it belongeth to save it from annihilation. Great was his knowledge! his lacteal Knowledge! his farming knowledge! & his saving knowledge! but alas! these Oeconomical Virtues are no more." Eight circles containing emblems ring the tombstone: a cup and ball, and a rattle marked "Otium cum Dignitate [Leisure with Dignity]"; a plow; a boy's head with crown and bells; "Midas," an ass; a man kicking a crown; a hunting cap, laurel, and whip; a cradle; a sun labeled "I am set."

The allusion to Nimrod notwithstanding, *Regum et Reginarum,* like *Royal Recollections,* reveals no serious discontent with the rule of George III. Both are essentially Peter Pindarian in tone. In their own lefthanded ways, they attest to the king's popularity because they find so little of real substance with which to find fault. What Robert Burd Gabriel says of Wolcot in "A Loyal Ode, Address'd to P. Pindyr, Esq.," the last poem in *The Blunders of Loyalty, and Other Miscellaneous Poems . . . The Poems Modernized by Ferdinando Fungus. . . .* (London, 1790), applies equally to Williams and the designer of *Regum et Reginarum:*

Ungentle bard!
Is it not hard,
That without thee
Men cannot see
The generous virtues of His Majesty!
But for the foible of a K[in]g
Thou canst not with thy wanted humour sing.
So, then, thy verse convinceth us he's wise,
Not impudence to punish, but despise.
Notice wou'd foster it to greater size.
'Tis thus chaste Virgil's charming epic line
In more majestic dignity doth shine,
Travestied humorously; so R[o]y[a]lty,
O Peter! owes some little thanks unthankfully to thee.   (pp. 37–38)

The reasons for the relative impotence of Opposition satirists were readily apparent to at least one contemporary, Sir Nathaniel William Wraxall. In the pro-Pitt *A Short Review of the Political State of Great Britain at the Commencement of the Year* (London, 1787), Wraxall considers George III to be a most fortunate monarch: "It has fallen to the lot of few Princes, of whom history has preserv'd any authentic record, to enjoy so considerable a portion of the personal attachment, respect, and adherence of their subjects, after the unprecedented disgraces and calamities of his reign, as George the Third appears to possess at the present moment" (p. 3). He attributes his luck to a variety of causes: the unpopularity of the alternative, the Prince of Wales; the unpopularity of the Fox-North coalition; the assassination attempt; the length of his reign, which makes him familiar to his subjects; and the fact that "his private virtues, and domestic character, drew a veil, even in the opinion of his enemies, across the errors of his Government and Administration. The father, and the husband, protected and sheltered the Prince" (pp. 6–7). During the course of his reign, George III had increasingly come to embody "the concept variously expressed as manners, politeness, or taste" with which Hogarth had identified him in *The Analysis of Beauty, Plate 2* (see fig. 19).[10]

With the onset of George's illness in the fall of 1788 and the crisis it precipitated, "the Prince" (George's regal body) came to the aid of "the husband and father" (George's mortal body). The Regency Crisis began a series of events that compelled Englishmen to articulate and confront their attitudes toward the monarchy. Followed closely by the French Revolution, the wars with France, and the rise of Napoleon, the Regency Crisis began the process in which George's subjects evaluated the heretofore largely unexamined premise of monarchy that governed their lives. The king's illness occurred during the centenary of Britain's Glorious Revolution. Just as George's subjects were congratulating themselves on the political stability seemingly established a hundred years before, the whole problem of legitimate succession was forced upon them again. During the Regency Crisis, the premise of the regal body was not seriously challenged; the question was which mortal body should rightly lay claim to that regal body.

The king's illness raised the hopes of the Prince of Wales's Foxite supporters that a regency would enable them to reach the promised land of power. The king's illness, however, put the Opposition in the awkward position of upholding hereditary right as the basis for the prince's claim to rule. Pitt, on the other hand, long attacked by the Opposition as the defender of excessive regal power, found himself in the enviable position of justifying George III's maintenance of power on the principle of parliamentary authority to determine the nature of a regency, should Parliament find one necessary.

Understandably, satirists shifted their attention from the king's foibles to his claim to rule as well as reign. His personal failings seemed largely irrelevant when measured against the larger issue. Much of the satire was directed at the politicians on either side rather than at the royal principals. In the 6 January 1789 print *House-Breaking, before Sun-Set* (fig. 120), we find Burke using "Tropes" to pick the lock, inscribed "GR" (George Rex), of the "Treasury" buildings. Aiding Burke are Fox, wielding the broken pickax of "Presumptive Right," and Sheridan, wearing an actor's mask, using a crowbar of "Begum Sophistry."[11] From a window above, Pitt fires balls of "Resolved 1, Resolved 2, and Resolved 3" from the blunderbuss "Constitution." In the background, the allegorical figure of "Truth," dressed as a sturdy citizen, holds his lantern to expose the burglars. In his right hand, he holds a noisemaker inscribed "Vox Populi [Voice of the People]," in his left, a crown-topped staff of "Loyalty." Beneath the crown in the sun overhead are the words "Obscured, but not lost."

Another 1789 print, *Frogs Chusing a King,* also mocks the king's aspiring opponents. The frogs, led by the bespectacled Burke and the bushy-tailed Fox, try to escape the impending punishment suggested by the noose, book, and ax above them. In the clouds overhead, Justice, referring to the Prince of Wales, who reclines irradiated on the mount at the left, assures Britannia, "The Son shall rise in due time." Beneath the prince lies the British lion guarding the regal crown and scepter. A more serious charge against the Opposition is the theme of *Revolutionists,* dated 30 October 1788 (fig. 121), in which the Jesuit Burke and others, under the flag of "Glorious Revolution" and the Prince of Wales's motto "Ich Dien" (I

Figure 120. *House-Breaking, before Sun-Set* (Not in BMC). Courtesy of the Library of Congress.

Figure 121. *Revolutionists* (Not in BMC). Courtesy of the Library of Congress.

serve) and ostrich feathers, attempt to scale the mount of "Constitution," on which sits George III, crowned, enthroned, and holding a book entitled *"Public Good."* The final ascent is protected by the "Pit of Circu[m]vention."

In the event, of course, Opposition expectations of a royal sunset were premature, and the prince and his followers soon found themselves re-illuminated by the return from eclipse of the Georgian sun depicted in Thomas Rowlandson's *The Eclipse at an End—and Political Tilting Discovered* (1789) (fig. 122). The artist visually puns on the etymology of lunacy by showing the traditionally regal solar icon emerging from an eclipse to re-veal the political contest below. On our left, Lord Chancellor Thurlow and Queen Charlotte are mounted on a jackass, ill disguised with the pelt of the British lion. The ass is branded "WP" (William Pitt). The disguise implies that Pitt and his riders have used assertions of loyalty to the throne as a "stalking-lion" for staying in power. Thurlow's irreverent grip on the queen and his reverent attitude toward the Prince of Wales reflect contemporary accusations that the minister had tried to protect his flank during the crisis by negotiating with the prince while retaining office. On our right, we see the prince and an unidentified supporter mounted on a horse wearing his master's ostrich feathers. The horse is hobbled to reflect the weakness of the Opposition's attack.

All the evidence proves that George's recovery pleased the vast ma-jority of his subjects, who celebrated his return to health with illumi-nations, rallies, addresses, commemorative art, and poetry, like William Cowper's "Annus Memorabilis, 1789: Written in Commemoration of His Majesty's Happy Recovery." William Knox's Loyalist analysis in *Consider-ations on the Present State of the Nation* (1789) was accurate:

> The truth of that aphorism of the moralists which represent mankind as unconscious of a value of a good they possess until they actually lose it, or find themselves in danger of being deprived of it, was never more fully proved than by the general affliction which the King's late illness occasioned; and the universal joy and exultation which broke forth upon his happy recovery. The dejection and despair which were visible in every face of the multitude, when the dark cloud of calamity hung over the nation; and the heartfelt expressions of joy which broke forth when the sky brightened, and their beloved luminary again cheered them with his benevolent rays, leave no room to suppose that political interests, or party artifice, had any share in their feelings. (pp. 1–2)

A Diary of the Royal Tour, in June, July, August, and September, 1789 (London, 1789) recounts a kind of public-relations campaign designed to reassure countrymen that the king had indeed returned to them.

Hostile witnesses also attest to George III's reinforced popularity. In *A*

THE ECLIPSE AT AN END — AND POLITICAL TILTING DISCOVERED.

Figure 122. Rowlandson, *The Eclipse at an End—and Political Tilting Discovered* (Not in BMC). Reproduced by permission of the Trustees of the Pierpont Morgan Library.

Discourse on the Love of Our Country, Delivered on November 4, 1789 (London, 1789; rpt., Boston, 1790), Richard Price complains, "In our late addresses to the King, on his recovery from the severe illness with which God has been pleased to afflict him, we have appeared more like a herd crawling at the feet of a master, than like enlightened and manly citizens rejoicing with a beloved sovereign, but at the same time conscious that he derives all his consequence from themselves" (p. 22). John Butler goes further in *The Political Fugitive* (New York, 1794), subscribing to the rumor that the amazing recovery of the king shows that *"he only affected a lunacy to prove the affections of his people"* (p. 101).

The brief respite from criticism that satirists were forced to grant George III was reflected in both the temporary silence of Wolcot and the 31 January 1790 publication of Isaac Cruikshank's *Frith the Madman Hurling Treason at the King* (fig. 123). Cruikshank uses Frith's attempt on the king's life as a vehicle for attacking the Opposition. Here, Frith is a bald and aged Burke about to stone the royal coach, in which sits George. Fox and Sheridan appear, respectively, as a woman and as a sailor who regret that Burke has been restrained by a constable and another man, perhaps intended to be the Prince of Wales. Above the head of Fox, who has a "Dying Speech," we read, "Creul [*sic*] Fortune thus our hopes Destroy." Sheridan looks away, saying, "Damn'd unlucky." Appearing in the interval between the storming of the Bastille on 14 July 1789 and the printing in November 1790 of Burke's *Reflections on the Revolution in France, Frith the Madman* suggests that the still unified Opposition seeks to imitate the violent methods of the French and overthrow a monarchy, thus outdoing their French model.

Before the appearance of Burke's *Reflections*, British sentiment toward the French Revolution had been generally favorable. Most Britons hoped that, coming as it did during the centenary of their own Glorious Revolution, the French Revolution would also accomplish a peaceful restructuring of government, thus enabling their age-old enemies to become more like enlightened Britons. In expressing his rather unpopular point of view in the *Reflections*, Burke was unfortunately all too prophetic in seeing not the English Glorious Revolution of 1688–89 but the English civil war of the 1640s as the proper analogue to current and future events in France.[12]

For Burke, the success of the French Revolution required creating "a degraded king" whose two bodies are severed in a brave new world where all the levels of natural and political hierarchy have collapsed:

On this scheme of things, a king is but a man; a queen is but a woman; a woman is but an animal; and an animal not of the highest order. All homage paid to the sex in general as such, and without distinct

Figure 123. I. Cruikshank, *Frith the Madman Hurling Treason at the King* (BMC 7624). Reproduced by permission of the Trustees of the British Museum.

views, is to be regarded as romance and folly. Regicide, and parricide, and sacrilege, are but fictions of superstition, corrupting jurisprudence by destroying its simplicity. The murder of a king, or a queen, or a bishop, or a father, are only common homicide; and if the people are by any chance, or in any way gainers by it, a sort of homicide much the most pardonable, and into which we ought not to make too severe a scrutiny. (p. 171)

Burke clearly states his own position earlier in the *Reflections:* "Though a king may abdicate for his own person, he cannot abdicate for the monarchy" (p. 105), because *qua* king he consists of two bodies, only one of which is under his control. With the coming of the French Revolution, earlier assertions that the king's two bodies are mismatched in the allegedly undignified George III take on far greater significance when repeated in the 1790s. Hence, the suggestion that disaster will ensue if George does not conduct himself in a more regal fashion is literally the central message of the 1792 etching *The Balance of Merit* (fig. 124), in which the angelic head advises, "George stand on thine own Feet and thou wilt weigh much Heavier." The hand of God, warning, "MENE, MENE, TEKEL, UPHARSIN," holds the balance, which now tilts in favor of the alleged Jacobins Fox and Sheridan. Fox holds a sword of "Revolution" and the "Bill on Libells." Ruddy-complexioned Sheridan holds a theatrical advertisement: "By Particular Desire of the National Assembly on Thursday 14th of July will be performed a Favourite Tragedy call'd the REVOLUTION Mirabeau. Mr. Renard [Fox] La Fayette, Mr. Sherry [Sheridan] and Principal Fish Woman by Mr. Horne T[ooke]. to which will be added Liberty a Farce with new Scenes & Decorations God save the King." Between the two men is the "National Cockade From Paris 1791." Behind Sheridan, the scrolls read, "Rights of Men," "Leveling of the Clergy," and "Reform of Parliament." In the opposing scale, the king, saying, "What What What," kneels beside Burke, who holds up a copy of *Reflections*. About to leave the scale is Thurlow ("by God I shall be off"), dismissed from office in June 1792. A box marked "10 Million" hangs over the other side. Pitt reaches toward the beam, saying, "A little higher and then ———."

Burke's analysis of the degradation of monarchy during the French Revolution is more pervasively apparent in another print that shows George failing to stand on his own two feet. Published on 19 July 1791, almost two years before the execution of Louis XVI, Gillray's *The Hopes of the Party, prior to July 14th—"From Such Wicked Crown & Anchor Dreams, Good Lord, Deliver Us"* (fig. 125) visualizes the English Jacobins as imitating seventeenth-century English regicides. The scene is a scaffold in the Strand before the "Crown & Anchor" tavern, meeting place of the Jacobins, on the

Figure 124. *The Balance of Merit* (Not in BMC). Reproduced courtesy of the Print Collection, Lewis Walpole Library, Yale University.

Figure 125. Gillray, *The Hopes of the Party, prior to July 14th* (BMC 7892).
Courtesy of the Library of Congress.

right. In this supposed fantasy of the Opposition, the king's two bodies have been severed—George has been divested of his crown and robes—and now he will lose his mortal crown as well. Reduced to a level below even that of mere man, he is a beast for slaughter—in this context specifically, a calf, alluding to the Calves' Head Club, which annually ridiculed the execution of Charles I in 1649 by eating calves' heads on its anniversary.

Sheridan holds the king's ear and nose, as one immobilizes a farm animal. The way Horne Tooke holds the king's legs suggests a more obscene indignity. In Tooke's pocket is his "Petition of Horne Tooke." He exults,

O, such a day as this, so renown'd so victorious,
Such a day as this was never seen
Revolutionists so gay;—while Aristocrats notorious,
Tremble at the universal glee.

Sheridan says to Fox, the executioner, "Hell & Damnation, dont be afraid give a home stroke, & then throw off the Mask—Zounds, I wish I had hold of the Hatchet." The bloated Fox, whose mask has fox's ears, responds, "Zounds! what the devil is it that puts me into such a hell of a Funk?—damn it, it is but giving one good blow, & all is settled!—but what if I should miss my aim?—ah! it's the fear of that which makes me stink so!—& yet, damnation! what should I be afraid of? if I should not succeed, why nobody can find me out in this Mask anymore than the Man who chop'd the Calf's-head off, a Hundred & Forty Years ago—and so here goes!"

Fox's hypocrisy is mirrored in the figure of the dissenting minister Joseph Priestley, holding "Priestly on a Future State." Priestley's presence recalls the role of religion in the Puritan regicide of the last century as well as Burke's emphasis throughout the *Reflections* on the identification of political radicalism and religious dissent. Priestley offers the king frosty consolation: "Don't be alarmed at your situation, my dear Brother; we must all dye once; and, therefore what does it signify whether we dye today or tomorrow—in fact, a Man ought to be glad of the opportunity of dying, if by that means he can serve his Country, in bringing about a glorious Revolution:—& as to your Soul, or any thing after death don't trouble yourself about that; depend on it, the Idea of a future state, is all an imposition: & as everything here is vanity & vexation of spirit, you should therefore rejoice at the moment which will render you easy & quiet." Sir Cecil Wray, holding a little cask marked "For Small Beer" and from whose pocket protrudes "Plan of Chelsea Hospital by Sir Ceci[l] Wray," says to Sheridan, "Here do give me a little room Joseph [thereby conflating the hypocritical character Surface in Sheridan's *School for Scandal* with his creator] that I may be in readiness to catch the droppings of the Small Beer when it is tapp'd; I never can bear to see the Small Beer wasted Joseph!"

Thus, the king is reduced even further, to the level of an inanimate object, and the motif of cannibalism, metaphorically present in the Calves' Head Club allusion, is directly introduced.

From a lamp's bracket over the "Crown & Anchor" tavern dangle the caricatured corpses of Queen Charlotte and Pitt, accused, as in Rowlandson's *The Eclipse at an End,* of trying to consolidate power during the king's recent illness. A wildly cheering mob surrounds the scaffold, unaware of the sinister side of Fox, the modern-day Cromwell, and his regicide gang. Behind them all, houses are already burning, and over the whole scene presides a figure of French Liberty, seated on the clouds of smoke above Temple Bar, the Christopher Wren gateway that terminated Fleet Street from 1670 until 1878. The deadly nature of this Liberty is indicated by having her cap on a pole, the visual analogue of the two skulls on poles that flank it. The statues below her are of Charles I and Charles II.

If George III is about to join the other images of death in this Jacobin fantasy, he will not do so as a complete innocent. His very passivity implies a certain amount of culpability. His utterance shows that he is shamefully unaware of what is happening around him: "What! What! What!—what's the matter now." Gillray's allusion to the dramatic character Joseph Surface and the mask on Fox alert us to the controlling metaphors of his print: the theater and the masquerade. The scaffold forms a stage on which the captive king plays the central role, his mortal crown at the midpoint of the engraving. As in other prints we have looked at that employ an explicitly theatrical or masquerade vehicle, the king is part of the show, in Gillray's treatment here sharply separated from the audiences within and without the confines of the design. He is the only one unaware of what's happening and why. He is far removed from the analogue he parodies, "the royal actor" who "adorns" the "tragic scaffold" in Marvell's "An Horatian Ode" (1650), who "nothing common did or mean / Upon that memorable scene" (53–58). George III, Gillray suggests, does not know how to play his assigned role. And in an age when the relationship between the king's two bodies had been demystified, when the monarch was increasingly seen as an agent of politics rather than as a surrogate for divinity, his mortal body's actions, as Dryden had observed in *Absalom and Achitophel,* could jeopardize the existence of his regal body. Certainly the actions of his monarch offended Gillray, a conservative monarchist who expected regal authority to supplement his own authority as satirist in controlling the *demos* he so often tried to contain by mockery.

It is unlikely that Gillray is simply expressing the radicals' delusion that the king would not resist their regicide conspiracy, but even if that were true, he has made a major rhetorical error in recalling the tradition of seeing the king as contributing to the decline of respect for his office. But perhaps such an error was inevitable. Two hundred years earlier, the satirist Joseph Hall, in *Virgidemiarum Sex Libri* (1597–98), had warned that any dramatic representation of the monarchy would lead to diminution of its dignity by suggesting that performance determined legitimacy rather than the reverse. If kingship were just a role, more than one actor could audition for the part. Hall certainly would have objected to the development of post-Restoration satiric prints as inherently subversive: even when their object is to praise the monarch at the expense of his opponents, their form is inevitably that of a tableau or mise-en-scène, in which the hero can be said to merely play a part.

In light of recent events in France, even seemingly comic depictions of the king's mortal foibles could carry a monitory message about his regal conduct. In the 1792 print *The Royal Dairy or George Split Farthing Selling His Skim Milk* (fig. 126), the primary subject is the familiar allegation of the royal couple's greed, here manifested in the profitable sale of milk. On the left, the caricatured queen says, "Come Come give me the money my Bags are not full yet & I am afraid they never will you give those Lubbers too much Measure." The king, also caricatured, encourages the buyers: "What What What Come my Lads hold up your Pitchers it have [*sic*] only been skimd once I have made a good Breakfast of it myself Sugar is so Dear." Before the king lies a yoke for carrying milk pails, suggesting that even that labor is not too common for George. The significance of the monarch's activities is revealed by the telling comment of one of the crowd: "Oh Lud Oh Lud he is nothing but a Man."

The growing emphasis on the king's being "nothing but a Man," reflected in Blake's stripping him in *Europe,* may account for the increasingly scatological nature of satires during 1792. In *Louis Dethron'd; or Hell Broke Loose in Paris!* (fig. 127), published in August, we are reminded that even kings need a privy, the scene of Pitt's announcement: "Dreadful Express! dreadful Express! Bury your Money and Jewels! The French Hell Hounds have broke loose again and have run down the poor King! Fifty Noble Heads dancing upon Poles every day in Paris!" Pitt's state of undress suggests either that he has been caught with his pants down or that he is prepared for a sansculottic revolution in Britain. The terrified king responds, "Stark mad! stark mad! Didn't kill the King I hope, Billy? Lord have mercy upon me, the infernal yell sounds in my ears this moment!" In a graphic representation of anal retentiveness, the queen, whose breasts and belly appear to be composed of money bags, puts her sacks of wealth into the toilet, saying, "Make haste with the other bags—Swelly [Juliana Elizabeth Schwellenberg, keeper of the robes to the queen] and I read this upon the Cards a week ago."

The creator of *Louis Dethron'd* was probably influenced by Gillray's

Figure 126. *The Royal Dairy or George Split Farthing Selling His Skim Milk* (Not in BMC). Reproduced by permission of the Henry E. Huntington Library and Art Gallery, San Marino, California.

Figure 127. *Louis Dethron'd; or Hell Broke Loose in Paris!* (Not in BMC).
Reproduced by permission of the Henry E. Huntington Library and Art Gallery,
San Marino, California.

more overtly scatological *Taking Physick:—or—The News of Shooting the King of Sweden!* (fig. 128), which had appeared in April. Here the very caricatured royal couple are using the toilet, as a terrified Pitt, showing them the "News from Sweden," remarks, "Another Monarch done over!" The shocked king can utter only "What? Shot? What? what? what?—Shot! shot! shot!" The physical effect the news has on the king is suggested by the defecating lion of the royal arms on the wall over the latrine. Once again the physicality of the king is emphasized. In other prints of the 1790s, including Blake's, we have seen George III symbolically decrowned and dethroned, often to be satirically recoronated. In Gillray's *Taking Physick,* the king's new crown suggests a fool's cap and his new throne a toilet. The king's one body apparently dominates the other. *Throne* was a slang term for a toilet, as for example, in Smollett's *Humphry Clinker* (1771), where we find "Frogmore enthroned on an easing-chair, under the pressure of a double evacuation" (Melford letter of 3 October). In British graphic satire, the idea of identifying a throne with a toilet to undercut authority goes at least as far back as Hogarth's 1751 print *Paul before Felix* BURLESQUED (BMC 3173), in which courtiers hold their noses in response to the way Felix has defiled the seat of power. Hogarth and Gillray's images remind us of the observation Montaigne makes in *Essays,* book 3, chapter 13 ("Of Experience"): "When seated upon the most elevated throne in the world, we are but seated upon our breech" (Charles Cotton translation, 1685–86, 6th ed. 1743). Even more to Gillray's point is a couplet from Swift's "The Problem" (1746)—"We read of kings, who in a fright, / Though on a throne, would fall to shite" (19–20)—or Benjamin Franklin's aphorism in *Poor Richard's Almanack* (1737)—"The greatest monarch on the proudest throne, is oblig'd to sit upon his own arse."

Long before the execution of Louis XVI on 21 January and the French declaration of war against Britain on 1 February 1793, the satirists seemed to have diminished George III's status to a point beyond the possibility of salvation. But the very means the satirists had employed to denigrate George soon bore unanticipated consequences: the recurrent masking motif implied the possibility that the king could play a different role by changing masks or perhaps even reveal his true self by discarding the various masks given him over the years by the satirists who visually made and unmade the king. Scatology served as a means to separate the man from the masks of position and authority, but such familiarity with the king's person could breed identification as well as contempt. Domestication of the regal image brought the viewer up to the king's level as much as it brought the king down to his subject's.

George's status had been rising since at least 1784, when his regal body's popularity was widely acknowledged. Subsequent emphases on his

Figure 128. Gillray, *Taking Physick:—or—The News of Shooting the King of Sweden!* (BMC 8080). Courtesy of the Library of Congress.

mortal body prepared the way for a remarkable satiric development in the following decades, as the British reacted to a French revolution that increasingly vindicated Burke's prophecy. The king's two bodies were regenerated and remerged. Gillray, for example, whose oeuvre betrays a virtual obsession with toilet and fecal imagery in his political and more strictly social satires, such as *National Conveniences* (1796, BMC 8906), transformed the scatological vehicle that was introduced by Hogarth in *The Punishment Inflicted on Lemuel Gulliver* (1726, BMC 1797) as a means of punishment and that was later developed by others, such as the anonymous designer of *Bro{the}r Robert under His Last Purgation* (1742, BMC 2533), during the 1740s as a figure for purification. Scatology becomes a symbol of desirable potency in Gillray's characteristically "carnival-grotesque form," *The French Invasion;—or—John Bull, Bombarding the Bum-Boats* (fig. 129), published 5 November 1793 under the pseudonym "John Schoebert." The ambiguous title allows Gillray to use a celebration of the recent British participation in the coalition against France as his overt subject and as the satiric vehicle for a preemptive response to a feared invasion by France, a national concern he had treated directly on 30 March in *Dumourier Dining in State at St. James's, on the 15th of May, 1793* (BMC 8318). In a remarkable transformation, George has shifted from target to tactic in this scatological flexing of the national sphincter, as Britain, represented by the vigorous body of George, excretes the "British Declaration" of boats into the mouth and face of France, depicted as an angry old man (whose nose is "Cherbourg," whose mouth is "St. Malo," and whose chin is "Bretagne"). Gillray ingeniously exaggerates what Mikhail Bakhtin calls "the material bodily element"[13] by recalling George's oft-noted girth to invoke the traditional British contrast between wellfed Englishmen and starving Frenchmen, depicted, for example, in Hogarth's *The Gate of Calais, or The Roast Beef of Old England* (1749, BMC 3050). Gillray ironically feeds France with British defecation. In choosing to portray France as a wizened old man, Gillray stresses the longevity of the Anglo-French antagonism and denies to the French revolutionists and their British sympathizers their claim to the iconography of rebirth and rejuvenation. Revolutionary France is an enemy easy to defeat. *The French Invasion* is a revision of an earlier depiction in *Britannia* (25 June 1791, BMC 8045), probably by Gillray, of Britain as a poor old woman with a dove of peace. In retrospect, the intervening *Taking Physick* (see fig. 128) seems to have purged Britain of her enervating inactivity in the face of the revolutionary threat. Like her leader, Britain has been paradoxically translated into a higher being by grossly physical activity.

Gillray's conception of France was probably inspired by a passage in Burke's *Reflections:* "Your new commonwealth is born, and bred, and fed, in

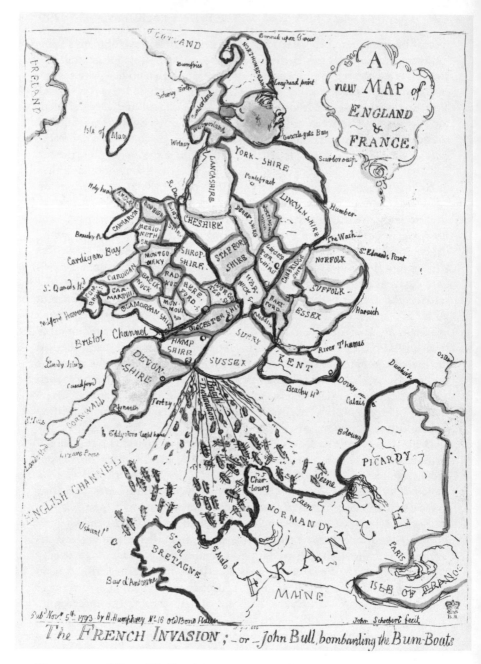

Figure 129. Gillray, *The French Invasion;—or—John Bull, Bombarding the Bum-Boats* (BMC 8346). Reproduced by permission of the Trustees of the British Museum.

those corruptions, which mark degenerated and worn out republics. Your child comes into the world with the symptoms of death; the *facies Hippocratica* [Hippocrates' description of the face of a dying man] forms the character of its physiognomy, and the prognostic of its fate" (p. 299). Gillray's France appears to be modeled closely on Hippocrates' description, found in *The Book of Prognostics:* "A sharp nose, hollow eyes, collapsed temples; the ears cold, contracted, and their lobes turned out: the skin about the forehead being rough, distended, and parched." Elsewhere, Burke refers to the "premature baldness of the national assembly" (p. 356). Hippocrates, in the fifth century B.C., invented the theory of characterology, the belief that one's personality was revealed by physical or psychological characteristics. In his figure of France, Gillray uses one of the oldest modes of visual representation, characterology, to create one of the most recent modes, caricature, but a caricature of a polity, not of a person—caricature on the grand scale.

Though he still wears a belled fool's cap, in an amusing anticipatory reversal of Byron's phrase, "of foolscap subjects to be king" (*Don Juan* 11:438), in Gillray's scatological attack, George is now the festive wielder as well as the victim of satire. The hat serves as a visual pun on clown as fool and clown as rustic to create a comic monarch who fertilizes an unfruitful land with manure. The "carnival-grotesque form" allows the artist to combine reassurance with threat: George is comical and therefore not intimidating on the domestic scene, yet he is still potent on the foreign stage. George's mortal body has remerged with his regal body to form the national figure of John Bull. Gillray, who, like Hogarth, habitually distrusts any authority, regal or demotic, except his own as satirist, typecasts a foolish king as the perfect emblem of an equally foolish, though powerful, people. This is indeed "a New Map of England & France" because it reflects the changed conception of statehood that had developed between the close of the sixteenth and the end of the eighteenth centuries, the transition from kingdom to nation. In the famous Ditchley portrait of Elizabeth I (1592?), attributed to Marcus Gheeraerts the Younger, the monarch bestrides the map of England; similarly, on Abraham Bosse's 1651 title page for Thomas Hobbes's *Leviathan,* the figure of the sovereign still looms over the landscape, but now his subjects give him form. In Gillray's print, the land incorporates its king and vice versa.[14] Gillray visually disputes Paine's assertion that "a nation is not a body, the figure of which is to be represented by the human body" (*ROM,* p. 203), and even more pointedly Paine's attack on cults of "personality . . . [because] the putting any individual as a figure for a nation is improper" (*ROM,* p. 228).

With scatology as a vehicle, Gillray's icon marks the confluence of two satiric traditions that had been developing during the last thirty years, for the most part independently of each other but with occasional overlaps: John Bull and Farmer George. This development could not have reached its successful conclusion without the king, who, in his first speech to Parliament after his accession, had uttered the widely reported words, "Born and educated in this country, I glory in the name of Briton." (The reports differed from the draft of the speech, which shows that he said "Britain" rather than "Briton.") Like Farmer George, John Bull was born in satire, created by Dr. John Arbuthnot in a series of pamphlets first published from March through July of 1712 and later published together in 1727 as *The History of John Bull*.[15] In Arbuthnot's allegory, John Bull is the personification of Britain: good-hearted, hardworking, stolid, often victimized but never vicious, honest though quarrelsome—not unlike Farmer George, a later country squire. During 1762, when Bute was the primary target and satirists often sought to underscore the king's role as victim, several prints, at times very casually, linked George and John Bull. George acts as an analogue of John Bull when Bute victimizes both in prints that include *John Bull's House Sett in Flames* (see fig. 24), Paul Sandby's untitled "Satire on Lord Bute, the Duke of Bedford, Earl Talbot, Lord Mansfield, Hogarth, Smollett, and Others" (see fig. 25), and *A Catalogue of the Kitchen Furniture of John Bull Esq. Leaving Off House-Keeping Now Selling by Auction* (BMC 3990). The only example that anticipates the John Bull–Farmer George confluence is *The Three Roads to John Bull's Farm* (BMC 3926), but so early (1762) an association of the king and agriculture is merely an arbitrary metaphor, and it makes nothing of George's domestic virtues or his interest in the common people. George's identification with his subjects occurs in the 1784 print *John Bull Enraged!* (BMC 6581), in which a bull, one of whose horns is marked "Prerogative," tramples the Foxites. Two years later, George appears as a man *of* as well as *for* the people in *The Commercial Treaty; or, John Bull Changing Beef and Pudding for Frogs and Soup Maigre!* (BMC 6995), where he is a cook trading British beef for the French frogs offered by the foppish Louis XVI. Here, through the semiotics of dress and occupation, the king of Britain is associated with the majority of his subjects, while the ruler of France represents the ruling aristocracy of his land.

A less positive association of king and countrymen appears in Gillray's *Anti-Saccharrites,—or—John Bull and His Family Leaving Off the Use of Sugar* (fig. 130), published 27 March 1792. Beneath the title Gillray writes, "To the Masters & Mistresses of Families in Great Britain, this Noble Example of Oeconomy, Is respectfully submitted." The subject of the print is the boycott of sugar as a protest against the slave trade, but Gillray questions the motivation behind a seemingly noble act. Gillray's conservative objection to the king's personal frugality reflects Adam Smith's observation in

Figure 130. Gillray, *Anti-Saccharrites,—or—John Bull and His Family Leaving Off the Use of Sugar* (BMC 8074). Reproduced by permission of the Trustees of the British Museum.

An Inquiry into the Nature and Causes of the Wealth of Nations that the expenditure on a monarch's dignity should be in proportion to the riches of the land he rules.

> In an opulent and improved society, where all the different orders of people are growing everyday more expensive in their houses, in their furniture, in their tables, in their dress, and in their equipage; it cannot well be expected that the sovereign alone should hold out against the fashion. He naturally, therefore, or rather necessarily becomes more expensive in all those articles too. His dignity even seems to require that he should become so. . . . We naturally expect more splendor in the court of a king, than in the mansion-house of a doge or burgo-master. (1:814)

By calling the royal family the John Bulls, Gillray extends the accusation of miserliness from the king and queen to the nation at large. The caricatured king pronounces his unsweetened tea "O delicious! delicious!" while the even more caricatured queen encourages the royal daughters, "O my dear Creatures, do but Taste it! You can't think how nice it is without Sugar:— and then think how much Work you'll save the poor Blackeemoors by leaving off the use of it!—and above all, remember how much expence it will save your poor Papa!—O its charming cooling Drink!"

In *Anti-Saccharrites* we can see the unanticipated consequences of decades of previous satiric attacks. Wraxall complains in *A Short Review* (1787) that the satirists have degraded the king to the level of a commoner:

> I must with equal impartiality, censure and condemn that daring and licentious spirit, which pervades them thro' every page; and which, after having demolish'd all the intermediate barriers, has laid it's [*sic*] sacrilegious hand upon the throne itself. . . . But, because the *Monarch,* in his public and regal capacity, is accountable to his subjects, and an object of their fair disquisition—was it generous or magnanimous, to pursue the *man* thro' every walk of private retirement? Is it becoming the honest rage, and inherent dignity of satire, to hold up a Sovereign —I will not say to the ridicule, but to the contumely and derision of his people? To pervade, and drag into open day, all the little personalities and weaknesses, inseparable from mortality, however elevated it's [*sic*] station? To follow him, with unremitted persecution, from St. James's to Windsor, and from Windsor to Kew? With indefatigable and subtle industry, to depicture him in every disgraceful attitude or position, from the crowded levee, to the kitchen-garden, or the grocer's shop?—It was not thus that Junius, with the arm of genius laid his strong hand upon the Monarch, in an earlier period of his reign. He disdain'd to persecute the *man,* tho' he attack'd the *King.* (pp. 33–36)

However, neither Wraxall nor the satirists could have known that the royal vices of the 1780s were to become the national virtues of the 1790s. By degrading the king, the satirists were unintentionally and ironically "generous or magnanimous" because they made possible the later identification of Farmer George with John Bull that rhetorically became so desirable and effective a few years later. When Burke, in *Reflections,* acknowledges the generally accepted view of the British character, he might as well be describing either satiric icon: "I know that we are supposed a dull sluggish race, rendered passive by finding our situation tolerable; and prevented by a mediocrity of freedom from ever attaining to its full perfection" (p. 145). The satirists discovered that their fictional creation had to respond to their audience's needs and wishes. They were reminded that successful rhetoricians can lead an audience only where it is willing to go. Demand compelled supply.

The war with revolutionary and Napoleonic France from 1793 to 1815, with brief intermissions, was a modern war between completely mobilized nations, not a war like those earlier sports of kings fought by professional and even mercenary soldiers alone. What was needed to help rally the British in 1793 was not simply a call to defend the throne but a call to defend themselves exemplified by the unifying image of the throne. The people could be brought so easily to the throne in part because the satirists had already brought the throne to the people. In showing the king to be "nothing but a Man," the satirists had in effect democratized the monarchy by demystifying the monarch, though Loyalists had to be careful lest rhetorical democratization undermine the hierarchical premise supporting hereditary monarchy. An instance of democratization controlled by comic distancing appears in Gillray's 1803 engraving *John Bull and the Alarmist* (fig. 131), where George III is a Hogarthian John Bull holding a bulldog-headed "Crab-stick" in one hand and a full beer mug in the other. On the wall at the upper left is a broadside, "The Roast Beef of Old England." The subscribed verses refer to the coronation chair bearing the royal arms as John Bull's "old Easy Chair." To John Bull–George III comes Richard Sheridan, "the Alarmist." Although ministerial papers like *The Sun* and *The True Briton* certainly sought to promote a cult of George III, they were accepting rather than creating a figure; they were more opportunistic than calculating, taking advantage of the accident of George's human character, which satirists had developed into the fictional character of Farmer George. The character (in both senses) of the Prince of Wales would have given neither the satirists nor the ministerial apologists the same opportunity.

By implication, to turn against the king was to turn against oneself (in a communal sense), to commit suicide.[16] The faults and problems of the king were shared by his people, were not the cause of their faults and problems. Such identification is the underlying theme of Hewitt's 1794 engrav-

Figure 131. Gillray, *John Bull and the Alarmist* (BMC 10088). Reproduced by permission of the Trustees of the British Museum.

ing *Favorite Chickens, or The State of Johnny's Farm-Yard in 1794* (fig. 132), where we see a conflation of John Bull and Farmer George foolishly subsidizing his Continental allies against France while he ignores his own house burning behind him. The Russian bear looks on as Johnny feeds coins to a flock of Prussian eagles. The white horse of Hanover devours coins from a basket. In the foreground, the British lion is an impotent watchdog, immobilized by chains. The Gallic cock pecks at his closed eyes.

The conflation of king and subject enabled conservative satirists, like the creator of the 1795 print *Billys Hobby Horse or John Bull Loaded with Mischief* (fig. 133), to divert blame for military failures abroad and agricultural dearth at home from monarch to minister. Though John Bull does not look like George III here, the identification is clear from the milestone "To St James's" and Bull's words: "What, What, What Maister Billy is it come to this you load me with Taxes I must rise for want of Bread." To reflect Britain's growing commercialization since his birth in satire, John Bull has moved from the farm to the city. "Gee up Johnny I'll stick Close [*sic*] to you my Boy," says his rider, Pitt, who flogs him with a scourge of four lashes ("War War War"; "Tax Tax Tax"; "Opression Opression"; "Monopoly"). In Pitt's pocket is a paper, "The Art and Mistery of Managing Neddys." Markings on Pitt's saddle and saddlecloth allude to the cost of his administration. In the background, before a signpost to "St. Georges Fields," where the London Corresponding Society had held a large protest meeting on 29 June, a group of respectable citizens hear a speaker. Members of the group hold aloft sticks or swords. Above them are their demands: "Petition to the Ki[n]g Petition to the People Reform in Parliament—out with a Vile Minister—Annual Parliaments & a Speedy Peace —no Monopoly."

E. P. Thompson and his followers have made radical and reformist groups like the London Corresponding Society familiar to us. Less familiar until very recently have been the various Loyalist organizations celebrated in the 1794 engraving *A Picture of Great Britain in the Year 1793* (fig. 134), attributed to Isaac Cruikshank. *A Picture* is "dedicated to the Associations for Preserving Liberty and Property against Republicans and Levellers," some of whom are identified by banners behind the wall of order. From left to right, they read: "Edinburgh Association, Lloyds Coffee House Association, Country House Ass.———n Exeter, Parish of St. Martins Assn, Parish of St James's Assn, Merchant Taylo[rs] Hall Association, St. Albans Tavern Association, and Association for Preserving Liberty & Property." The wall bears three plaques: "Honi Soit qui mal y pense; Britannia and the Constitution. The Law and Security. Liberty and Property. Religion and Concord; Amor Patriae [Love of Country]." Paralleling the emphasis on the king's mortal body in the John Bull–George III prints, *A Picture* exempli-

FAVORITE CHICKENS,
or the
State of Johnny's Farm-Yard in 1794

Figure 132. Hewitt, *Favorite Chickens, or The State of Johnny's Farm-Yard in* 1794 (BMC 8488). Reproduced by permission of the Trustees of the British Museum.

Figure 133. *Billys Hobby Horse or John Bull Loaded with Mischief* (BMC 8664).
Reproduced by permission of the Trustees of the British Museum.

Figure 134. I. Cruikshank, *A Picture of Great Britain in the Year 1793* (BMC 8424). Reproduced by permission of the Trustees of the British Museum.

fies how the king's regal body could serve as a positive norm by which to castigate his opponents, both practical and theoretical.

The design's focal point is the temple of "the British Constitution." Fronting its dome is a profile of George III wearing a laurel, framed with the words "By the Grace of God." George III is the mediating image between "Deus," the eye of God in the upper left corner, who pronounces, "The wicked shall Perish I will cut them off," and Chaos in the upper right, which is anticipated by a demoness, who encourages the forces of evil with the words, "My dear Children persevere thus till Chaos comes again." Pillars labeled "King," "Lords," and "Commons," support the temple's dome, and under the dome sits Britannia, the British lion reclining beside her. The rock sustaining the temple has been so undermined that barrels of gunpowder can be placed beneath the constitution. A gunpowder trail points to Fox and Sheridan, Jacobin leaders of the evil forces who have already overthrown one barrier. Before the fallen barrier lie a skull, bones, and books of "Law" and "God."

Associated with the forces of order, the rock (or stone) temple, books, and God remind us that A Picture was part of the argument of images with Blake in his contemporary satires. Blake would have joined Fox and Sheridan here as a member of the Devil's party, propelled by the infernal smoke machine of a hellgate in the lower right corner. Above Fox and Sheridan, two more demons undermine the temple's foundation. The one using the pitchfork of "Reform" says, "Better to reign in hell than serve in Heaven." Fox holds in his left hand a paper, "The Hazard of the Die!" and with his right extends a torch inscribed "Speech at the Whig Club." Beneath his foot, a paper reads, "No King. No Religion No Laws." He says to the red-faced Sheridan, "Thy visage & Design are refulgent! delectable!" and Sheridan responds, "The light of my Countenance directs thee." Behind them march their supporters, the forces of Evil, carrying banners: "British Convention Scotland," "London Corresponding Society," "Equal Representation," "Derby Meeting," "Sedition," "Murder Treason," "Anarchy Rapine." Fox's torch is about to be snuffed with "truth" by Pitt, who says, "I will Extinguish the Torch of Sedition & frustrate the plots of Incendiaries." His gesture parallels that of a hovering angel, who holds a palm leaf and assures the forces of Good, "I will guard those from harm who serve God & keep the Law." Beneath the design, quotations from John Milton's *Paradise Lost* associate Fox, Sheridan, and their supporters with Satan's legions. As Samuel Johnson in his political pamphlets had done before him, Cruikshank here appropriates the words of the great political radical and literary authority for a conservative message.[17]

A Picture is a representative example of how a conservative satirist could combine caricature, available to him since the 1740s, with the older emblematic tradition Blake seeks to subvert or appropriate in the war of icons that was waged in the 1790s. The conservative satirist still has at his command the old images that religion, politics, and (increasingly) British literature offered him as tactics to suggest that his side defended long-recognized general truths against the onslaught of upstart Jacobins, whose very particularity implied the ephemeral quality of their cause. True, their Loyalist opponents are individuals as well (though not so particularized as to be caricatured), but above them all loom the larger issues and implications whose representation only timeless emblems befit. The contemporary struggle, seemingly time- and space-bound, is, from the images that frame the furiously engaged men, set in perspective. Though the outcome of the present crisis is still in doubt in *A Picture,* the emblematic icons reassure the viewer by reminding him of visual verities, including the king's royal body, which is by position ontologically equivalent to the other figures placed in its half of the design. George III is not particularized; he is rendered emblematic. The face of kingship, poised on the spear of Britannia, who points to it with her right hand, is the vanishing point of the lines of battle formed by the two walls below—the vanishing point both of the design and of the satire's message, because, from the eternal perspective of the emblematic royal body, the significance of the present political actors disappears.

Invocation of the king's regal body and the constitution to appeal to British patriotism was, as Charles Pigott concedes, powerful rhetoric. "No nation," he complains, "ever seemed more stupidly rooted in admiration of the glare and parade of royalty than the English" (*The Jockey Club,* p. 11). As a result, just a bit of rhetorical legerdemain can shake John Bull out of his usual lethargy: "Only tell him that the constitution is in danger, he doesn't pause to enquire into its principles, which might perhaps discover to the astonishment of his weak mind, that the idol of his adoration was the cause of his misfortunes—the word is enough for him;—his honor as an Englishman is at stake;—the memory of all personal grievances vanishes like a charm, and if you add the necromantic sounds, CHURCH AND KING, the bull is at once metamorphosed into a lion, and his spirit becomes savage and irresistible" (p. 141). John Butler laments that the emblematic status George achieves in representations like *A Picture* is deserved, in part because the king's subjects stupidly support the monarchy: "The present monarchy of England is an over-grown monster, supported like a Colossus, in his emblematic attributes, with one foot upon the throne, and the other upon the people . . . whose duplicity is awarded with the oppressive tyranny of political profligacy" (*The Political Fugitive,* p. 23).

The king's popularity helps to explain how easily satirists transformed particular events into more general attacks on the monarchy's real or alleged opponents. Within days of a mob attack on George's coach as he rode to open Parliament on 29 October 1795, Gillray produced *The Republican-Attack* (fig. 135), in which the mob has been revised to include Fox, Sheridan, and their followers. Although Gillray also satirizes Pitt, who drives the coach over Britannia, support for the throne was so strongly rallied by the attack that the Opposition accused the ministry of intentionally provoking the incident. By 1800, members of the Opposition had to acknowledge the king's popularity, as Sheridan did when the demented James Hadfield tried to shoot the king at Drury Lane Theatre on 15 May 1800. The king acquitted himself superbly, displaying obviously sincere concern for the queen's feelings. The royal family saw the comedy through, after which they were treated to three choruses of "God Save the King" and one of "Rule Britannia." Following the farcical afterpiece, another chorus of "God Save the King" preceded verses that Sheridan composed for the occasion:

From every latent foe
From the Assassins blow
God Save the King
Ov'r him thine Arms extend
For Britains sake defend,
Our Father Prince & Friend.

Rowlandson celebrated the event with *Britannias Protection or Loyalty Triumphant* (fig. 136), published on 4 June, the king's birthday. A majestic George III, his eminence signified by his dress, stands beside a column marked "Fortitude" and before a curtain which reads, "God Save the King." Hadfield drops his pistol before Britannia's threatening spear. A demon drags him off in a halter, taunting him, "Hadfield for thy diabolical attempt, thou shall meet with thy reward."

Napoleon's acquisition of complete power in 1799 made him another agent of George's elevation. Napoleon's rise forced into unavoidably sharp contrast the difference between a revolutionary "man of the people" and a hereditary monarch. The conservative warnings were vindicated—a new Cromwell had arisen, more despotic than any true monarch. Moreover, Napoleon was a satirist's dream because he made possible praise of the king without taking George III out of the satiric character developed during his reign. Thus, in Charles Williams's 1803 engraving *The Rival Gardeners* (fig. 137), George III is still recognizably Farmer George with a comical speech habit. The satiric tradition of attacks on George was strong enough to absorb Napoleon, who becomes an alternative farmer in the prophetic anticipation of Napoleon's crowning himself in 1804. "The Channel" separates the real from the would-be monarch, who is kept from crossing by the

Figure 135. Gillray, *The Republican-Attack* (BMC 8681). Reproduced by permission of the Trustees of the British Museum.

TACK.

On the 29.th of October 1795, the King in his way to the House of Lords to open Parliament was violently attacked by the populace, stones thrown at the carriage, and in passing through Palace Yard, one of the windows was broken; it was said by a bullet discharged from an air gun.

Earl of Westmoreland

Duke of Norfolk

Pitt

Page 68 No 132.

Figure 136. Rowlandson, *Britannias Protection or Loyalty Triumphant* (BMC 9542). Reproduced by permission of the Trustees of the British Museum.

"British Oak" of the English navy. Each gardener has a planted tub, but the crown of Napoleon's weed wilts, while George's oak flourishes. Not even plunder, "Manure from Italy & Switzerland," can revive the plant, whose crown Napoleon holds. Napoleon observes, "Why I dont know what is the reason—my Poppies [the rows of "Military Poppies" next to him] flourish charmingly—but this Corona Imperialis [Imperial Crown] is rather a delicate kind of plant, and requires great judgement in rearing." George advises him, "No-No-Brother [the conventional way one monarch addresses another] Gardener—though only a ditch parts our grounds—yet this is the spot for true Gardening,—here the Corona Britanica [British Crown], and Heart of Oak, will flourish to the end of the World." The semiotics of dress suggests that Napoleon's claim to power is based on military force, while George's rests on a more demotic foundation. The plainly dressed British king, the true man of and for the people as well as the true monarch, needs no crown because his authority derives from his identification with his subjects.

As George III's satiric character became a tactic rather than a target, it consequently turned into a comically positive figure. Magnifying glasses or telescopes previously used to attack George's alleged political shortsightedness increasingly serve as devices to diminish another while enhancing George. George no longer needs visual aids because of his own weakness; the insignificance of his opponents demands them. This distancing technique is seen in Gillray's famous 1803 print *The King of Brobdingnag, and Gulliver* (fig. 138), where George, as Swift's ideal monarch, peers through a spyglass at the tiny Napoleon he holds in the palm of his hand. George admonishes his ridiculous adversary, "My little friend Grildrig, you have made a most admirable panegyric upon Yourself and Country, but from what I can gather from your own relation & the answers I have with much pains wringed & extorted from you, I cannot but conclude you to be, one of the most pernicious, little odious reptiles, that nature ever suffer'd to crawl upon the surface of the Earth."

Gillray's print inspired a number of adaptations, including the 1803 engraving *The Brodignag* [sic] *Watchman Preventing Gullivers Landing* (fig. 139), perhaps by Temple West, in which the king remains a symbol of state authority but now in the figure most familiar both on the level of personal experience and as a comic stereotype on the stage and therefore presumably the figure least threatening to his subjects. The dehumanizing metaphor aimed at Napoleon in Gillray's original and in the later adaptation is reified in two other 1803 prints that exploit the tradition of mocking George's scientific interests as well as his weak vision. In *A British Chymist Analizing a Corsican Earth Worm!!* (fig. 140), George studies the distillation of a retort that contains a glaring Napoleon.[18] The retort sits atop a furnace whose tap

Figure 137. Charles Williams, *The Rival Gardeners* (BMC 9968). Reproduced by permission of the Trustees of the British Museum.

Why I dont know what is the reason_ my Poppies
flourish charmingly_ but this *Corona Imperialis*
is rather a delicate kind of a plant, and requires
great judgement in rearing.

Figure 138. Gillray, *The King of Brobdingnag, and Gulliver* (BMC 10019).
Reproduced by permission of the Trustees of the British Museum.

Figure 139. Temple West(?), *The Brodignag* [sic] *Watchman Preventing Gullivers Landing* (BMC 10130). Reproduced by permission of the Trustees of the British Museum.

I think I can now pretty well ascertain the ingredients of which this insect
is composed — viz — Ambition, and self sufficiency, two parts — Forgetfulness
one part, — some light Invasion Froth, on the surface and a prodigious quantity
of fretful passion, and conceited Arrogance in the residue !!

London Pub: July 1803 by W. Holland, Cockspur Street Poll Mall.

July. 1803.
West.

A British Chymist Analizing a Corsican Earth Worm!!

Figure 140. Temple West(?), *A British Chymist Analizing a Corsican Earth Worm!!*
(BMC 10031). Reproduced by permission of the Trustees of the British Museum.

faces the king. George concludes from his investigation, "I think I can now pretty well ascertain the ingredients of which this insect is composed— viz,—Ambition, and self sufficiency, two parts—Forgetfulness one part, —some light Invasion Froth on the surfase [sic] and a prodigious quantity of fretful passion, and conceited Arrogance in the residue!!" The emphasis on Napoleon's impotence increases in *Amusement after Dinner, or The Corsican Fairy Displaying His Prowess!* (fig. 141), where the bemused king and queen observe the antics of a fairy who boasts, "If I could but get over this dish of Blanche Mange [a flavored and sweetened milk pudding, here topped with British ships]—I would soon Invade the Pine Apple," topped by a British royal crown.

Gillray develops the idea of Napoleon as a player or pretender who aspires to an illusory crown in *Pacific-Overtures,—or—A Flight from St. Cloud's—"Over the Water to Charley."—A New Dramatic Peace Now Rehearsing* (fig. 142), published in 1806. On stage, in a position that visually alludes to Rowlandson's *Britannias Protection* (see fig. 136), George III stands before the royal box to better observe, or perhaps direct, Napoleon's performance, "Now Rehearsing." George is no longer, as he is in *The Hopes of the Party* (see fig. 125), simply part of the show. He now also shares the perspective of audiences both inside and outside the print's design. Indeed, he and the statue of Pitt are the only figures within the design that share the intended judgment of the external audience. The British politicians in the pit ignore the performance above them.

Napoleon, standing on a cloud, tries to dictate the "Terms of Peace" that Talleyrand holds. George responds, "Very amusing Terms indeed!— and might do vastly well with some of the new-made little Gingerbread kings—but WE are not in the habit of giving up either 'Ships, or Commerce, or Colonies,' merely because little Boney is in a pet to have them!!!" Napoleon's apostate supporter Talleyrand parallels the statue behind George commemorating the late Pitt, whose hand rests on the pillar "Integrity." The pedestal supporting the statue reads, "Non sibi sed Patriae vixit [He lived not for himself but for his country]." Talleyrand's supporting base is as fluid as Pitt's is solid.

Opposed emblems of security and insubstantiality continue the iconic argument: George, his feet on the solid stage, stands before an anchor, emblem of hope as well as synecdoche of naval strength reflected in "the Royal Sovereign," itself symbolizing the ship of state identified with the monarchy; Napoleon floats on the appearance of substance, and the crowns on the caps of the skeletal soldiers behind Talleyrand reflect his illusory monarchic claim. The king's empty box, labeled "G. IIId. whom God long preserve" and surmounted by a crown, outweighs the boxes filled with Napoleon's self-interested followers. George's absence from the box

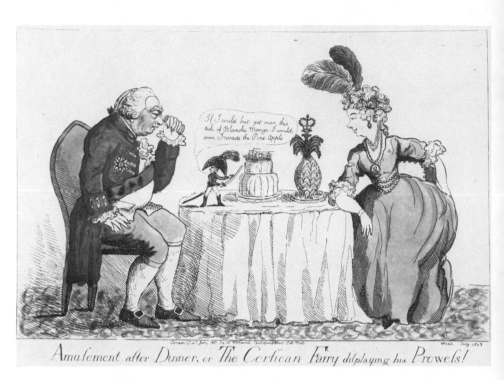

Figure 141. Temple West(?), *Amusement after Dinner, or The Corsican Fairy Displaying His Prowess!* (BMC 10034). Reproduced by permission of the Trustees of the British Museum.

Figure 142. Gillray, *Pacific-Overtures,—or—A Flight from St. Cloud's—"Over the Water to Charley."—A New Dramatic Peace Now Rehearsing* (BMC 10549).
Reproduced by permission of the Trustees of the British Museum.

suggests that his strength resides not in his mortal body but in his regal body, which remains ever constant and available. The open book on the front of the royal box indicates that George and Napoleon are but temporary players on a stage of life that will survive the mortal bodies of both. It reads, "Shakespeare—I know You all." As he and others had done earlier with Milton and Swift, Gillray here adds literary authority and emblematic tradition to universalize his message.

Gillray's choice of a theatrical metaphor as his satiric vehicle reflects larger issues of British and French artistic contention. Less well known than Napoleon's promotion of a neoclassical revival to legitimate his rule is George's counterpatronage of a British revival. For example, he spent £500,000 to build a new Gothic castle at Kew.[19] Gillray's allusion to Shakespeare underscores the rising interest in native British literature that accelerated during George's reign. The increasing value that the verbal and visual arts placed on nativism seemed appropriate support for Britain's unique political system, exemplified in George III's two bodies.[20] As the neoclassical statue of Pitt indicates, modern Britain represented the ideal fusion of classicism and nativism opposed to Napoleon's supposititious claim to power. Loyalists' emphasis on British constitutional precedent and tradition abetted recovery of the earlier mode of allegorical visual satire that, combined with the more recent caricatural mode, made possible at the end of the eighteenth and beginning of the nineteenth centuries the golden age of British engraved satire.

Traditional emblems praising the king dominate George Cruikshank's *God Save the King* (fig. 143), an allegorical illustration of the national anthem and published in 1807 in part to celebrate abolition of the slave trade. In the headpiece, George III, on the throne, is flanked by Liberty on his left and by Africa, America, Asia, and Europe bearing him gifts on his right. One of two African children waves a flag, which reads, "Slave Trade Abolished." On the right, a castle and church overlook the pastoral prosperity that results from Britain's hierarchy of church and state. The tailpiece below shows the regal sun rising over a naval scene observed by the British lion and unicorn. Traditional iconography receives more innovative treatment in Gillray's 1805 print *St. George and the Dragon. A Design for an Equestrian Statue, from the Original in Windsor-Castle* (fig. 144). George is about to deliver the finishing blow to a winged, fire-breathing, saurian Napoleon, who has attempted to ravish the maiden Britannia. Napoleon's regal crown has already been cracked by an earlier strike; his mortal crown is now about to be broken as well.

Gillray's coronal pun calls attention to the concept of the king's two bodies, exemplified in the image of George translated into that of St. George, the mortal rendered immortal, and perverted in the image of

Figure 143. George Cruikshank, *God Save the King* (BMC 10778). Reproduced by permission of the Trustees of the British Museum.

Figure 144. Gillray, *St. George and the Dragon. A Design for an Equestrian Statue, from the Original in Windsor-Castle* (BMC 10424). Reproduced by permission of the Trustees of the British Museum.

Napoleon transmogrified into a monster by his presumptuous claim to two bodies. Like an inhabitant of Dante's *Inferno,* Napoleon is damned by achieving his aspiration. He has two bodies, here monstrously merged. The mortal George's claim to a second body, since it is a valid claim, elevates the man; Napoleon's false claim leads to his degeneration, reminiscent of Satan's in *Paradise Lost.* George III's translation anticipates his fully realized apotheosis in Southey's *A Vision of Judgment* (1821) and was at least in part a response to Napoleon's alleged attempt to assert his own apotheosis, the subject of Gillray's *Apotheosis of the Corsican-Phoenix* (fig. 145), published in 1808. Napoleon's unnatural aspirations have once again perverted him into a monstrosity. He sits amidst the flames of a burning world atop the "Pyrenean Mountains." The conflagration he has started in his vain wish for an apotheosis loses him his scepter, crown, and orb. Above the man-bird Napoleon ascends the true bird of Peace, the positive norm of Gillray's satire. The fiery globe and the irenic bird recall the imagery of Hogarth's much earlier celebration of George III in *The Times* (see fig. 23) to once again merge the traditions of nativist art and politics in the patriotic cause. As Blake remarks to William Hayley in a letter of 28 May 1804, they were living in a time of competing national apotheoses: "I suppose an American would tell me that Washington did all that was done before he was born, as the French now adore Buonaparte and the English our poor George; so the Americans will consider Washington as their god."

Nationalism could turn into jingoism. To commemorate George's very popular and successful opposition to Catholic Emancipation, Gillray combines comedy and sublimity in *A Kick at the Broad-Bottoms!—i.e.—Emancipation of "All the Talents. &c." Vide, the Fate of ye Catholic Bill* (fig. 146), published in 1807. Partly because of its political-religious subject, *A Kick* grants the king the respect usually reserved for the deity. His face concealed, he demonstrates his power by ejecting the Grenville ministry. As in so many of the prints we have looked at, power resides in the Crown, here placed atop a Bible at the left side of the print. It does not need to be worn by a man for it to exert its influence; the particular king is merely the agent of kingship. Moreover, the power's sublimity is not undercut even if wielded by a comic character whose speech instantly identifies him: "What!—what!—bring in the Papists!—O you cunning Jesuits, you!—what you thought I was like little-Boney & would turn Turk, or anything?—but if you have no Faith or Conscience—I have!!—ay, & a little Old Protestant Spunk too!—So Out with you all!!—out!—with all your Broad-bottom'd-Popish Plots!!!—Out with you!—out!—out!—out!" Gillray developed his metaphors of the popish plot and a deified George III in *The Pillar of the Constitution* (fig. 147) to observe the king's birthday in 1807. Light emanating from George III's eye, barely visible in

Figure 145. Gillray, *Apotheosis of the Corsican-Phoenix* (BMC 11007). Reproduced by permission of the Trustees of the British Museum.

Figure 146. Gillray, *A Kick at the Broad-Bottoms!—i.e.—Emancipation of "All the Talents"* (BMC 10709). Reproduced by permission of the Trustees of the British Museum.

Figure 147. Gillray, *The Pillar of the Constitution* (BMC 10738). Reproduced by permission of the Trustees of the British Museum.

the upper right corner, reveals the plot to blow up the temple of the constitution with gunpowder. The beam of light crosses the central pillar of the
constitution, whose iconography of a Bible, a blank scroll (probably the
Magna Charta), and a crown shows that monarchy is threatened by the attempt to achieve Catholic Emancipation. A rose and a thistle flank the
crown. Above it are oak leaves. Again, the king is virtually concealed,
while his numerous though impotent opponents are revealed in all their
particularities.

By the time the nation celebrated the jubilee commemorating the beginning of the fiftieth year of George's reign on 25 October 1809, the king
had completed his transformation from target to tactic. That the jubilee
was initiated by suggestions from outside the government is noteworthy.
The length of his reign as well as the repeated depictions of him had made
the king more familiar to his subjects than any monarch before him. By
1809, very few Britons had lived under any other reign; the identification
of king and country seemed an increasingly natural one to make. And as the
outcome of the movement for Catholic Emancipation had shown, the king
had not yet become a mere figurehead, reigning without ruling. The king
could still be counted on to defend his subjects' prejudices in the face of
upstart politicians, as he does in Gillray's *An Old English-Gentleman Pester'd
by Servants Wanting Places* (fig. 148), published 16 May 1809. George is
still at the center of the political action, saying, "Well Gentlemen, I have
taken a peep at you all: but I am afraid that you won't do—for some of
you are too Heavy & Broad-bottom'd for Service; & the rest seem to have
no Bottom at all.—so Gentlemen, I think I shall be content with my Old
Servants."

The recuperation of the king's satiric fortunes led to a reclamation of
royal imagery. The king's interest in hunting that had prompted earlier
satirists to liken him to Nimrod, the mythical founder of political tyranny,
now turned in the monarch's favor. He is the successful huntsman of domestic and foreign political foes. In Gillray's 1803 *Death of the Corsican-Fox,
—Scene the Last, of the Royal-Hunt* (fig. 149), George stands beside the Hanoverian horse beneath the royal oak. He holds up a Napoleon-headed fox
to Pitt, mounted and shouting "Tally ho" in the background. The hounds
who have earthed, or run down, the fox bear collars with the names of
British naval heroes. In *Royal Fox Hunt* of 12 July 1806 (fig. 150), Rowlandson, probably influenced by Gillray's print, comments on Fox's entry into
office as foreign secretary in William Wyndham Grenville's "ministry of all
Talents" following the death of Pitt in January. On the left, rival politicians
lament, "Oh its impossible to Earth or Kill him many, many Years have we
tried but in Vain, he is too Cunning for us we are worn to Skeletons Alas.
Alas wt shall we do." Safe in the royal arms, Fox responds, "Here I am

Figure 148. Gillray, *An Old English-Gentleman Pester'd by Servants Wanting Places* (BMC 11330). Reproduced by permission of the Trustees of the British Museum.

Figure 149. Gillray, *Death of the Corsican-Fox,—Scene the Last, of the Royal-Hunt* (BMC 10039). Reproduced by permission of the Trustees of the British Museum.

Figure 150. Rowlandson, *Royal Fox Hunt* (Not in BMC). Reproduced by permission of the Beinecke Library, Yale University.

snugg little I value you Touch me who dare." His savior observes, "Oh how he Stinks," as Sheridan, now treasurer of the navy, advises, "My Darling Reynard keep a fast hold." George III is a comic every-Englishman figure, victimized by politicians who pick his pocket or are ready to perform an obscene act to gain office. However, he does retain the power to control the hunt.

Satirists also recovered the traditional royalist emblem of the sanctified monarch-farmer that Dryden had used to eulogize Charles II in *Threnodia Augustalis:*

> The Royal Husbandman appear'd,
>   And Plough'd, and Sow'd, and Till'd,
> The Thorns he rooted out, the Rubbish clear'd,
>   And Blest th'obedient Field.
> When, straight, a double Harvest rose;
> Such as the swarthy Indian mowes;
> Or happier Climates near the Line,
> Or Paradise manur'd, and drest by hands Divine.   (356–63)

We can trace the recovery of the emblem in three Gillray prints. *Ecclesiastical, and, Political, State of the Nation* (fig. 151), published 2 June 1780, a few days before the anti-Catholic Gordon Riots, faults the king for not being a proper monarch-farmer. The occasion of the engraving was the government's attempt to extend the Catholic Relief Act of 1778 to Scotland. The print's design shows a blindfolded George under the direction of the pope seated on clouds. Lord North, astride a bull, guides the king's plow toward Scotland, across the "River Tweed." The print is dedicated "to the Respectable Association of Protestants & to every Worthy Supporter of both Church & State . . . by their Humble Servt the Publisher," and beneath the design we have an "Explanation."

> The State Husbandman Plowing up the glebe of the Constitution, whilst the Popish Emissaries take the Advantage of the supineness of the Established Church who is fast asleep in the Vineyard where its grand Adversary the Pope, and all his host of Devils, are permitted to Sow the Seeds of their Pernicious Doctrine: Opposition attempts to stop their Progress, but the band of Unanimity is broke, & they have fallen off. Truth descends, showing a Scroll of Melancholy proofs of popish cruelty, Soliciting the Aid of her Friends, to vanquish the Inveterate Enemy, who threatens the Ruin of thair [*sic*] Religion, thair Posterity & thair much injured Country.

A quarter-century later, Gillray again turned to the monarch-farmer emblem in a pair of engravings, the 1806 *"More Pigs than Teats,"—or—The*

Figure 151. Gillray, *Ecclesiastical, and, Political, State of the Nation* (BMC 5678). Reproduced by permission of the Trustees of the British Museum.

New Litter of Hungry Grunters, Sucking John-Bulls-Old-Sow to Death (fig. 152) and the 1807 *The Pigs Possessed:—or—The Broad Bottom'd Litter Running Headlong into ye Sea of Perdition.—a Supplement to More Pigs than Teats 1806* (fig. 153). In the first, the greedy office seekers dismay the onlooking John Bull: "O Lord—O Lord!—well!—I never had such a dam'd Litter of hungry Pigs in all my life before!—why, they's beyond all count!—where the devil do they think I shall find Wash & Grains for all their Guts?—zookers, why they'll drain the poor old Sow to an Otomy [a cadaver for an anatomy, hence *otomy,* class]!—'e'cod She'll make but bad Bacon for Boney, when they's all done sucking o' her—!!!" In *The Pigs Possessed,* John Bull transforms into a comically Christ-like Farmer George, who saves his land by driving out the fattened Gadarene supporters of Catholic Emancipation: "O you cursed ungrateful Grunters!—what, after devouring more in a twelve-month, than the good old Litter did in twelve years, you turn round to kick and bite your old Master!—but if the Devil or the Pope has got possession of you all—pray get out of my Farm yard!—out with you all—no hangers behind!—you're all of a cursed bad-breed; so out with you alltogether!!!"

The orgy of national self-congratulation that was the jubilee included, of course, fulsome praise of the monarch who made the celebration possible: "That the inhabitants of this country have duly appreciated the merits of their Sovereign, and paid a just tribute to his manifold virtues, these pages will amply testify. The general sentiment so unequivocally exhibited in the Jubilee Year of his Reign, more eloquently declares the affection of the people at large, than volumes of studied panegyric" (*An Account of the Celebration of the Jubilee. . . . ,* London, p. xi). At the height of his personal and institutional popularity, George in 1810 lapsed into his final state of blind madness, a condition that lasted until his death on 29 January 1820 and that marks the point at which the British monarchy moved from an effective to a dignified status.

But through the power of satire, George III remained on the political scene after he had become mad and even after his death. Earlier in his satiric career, he had been mocked as an irresponsible would-be Cincinnatus figure in "Sir George Howard's" *Probationary Ode:*

> Oh! Europe's pride! Britannia's hope!
>   To view his turnips and potatoes,
> Down his fair Kitchen-garden's slope
>   The victor monarch walks like Cincinnatus.   (p. 98)

But now, like George Washington, he had left power for the plow.[21] Once his son became regent on 6 February 1811, George III became available to satirists as a politically disinterested tutelary spirit overlooking his be-

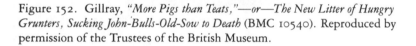

Figure 152. Gillray, *"More Pigs than Teats,"*—or—*The New Litter of Hungry Grunters, Sucking John-Bulls-Old-Sow to Death* (BMC 10540). Reproduced by permission of the Trustees of the British Museum.

Figure 153. Gillray, *The Pigs Possessed:—or—The Broad Bottom'd Litter Running Headlong into ye Sea of Perdition.—a Supplement to More Pigs than Teats* 1806 (BMC 10719). Reproduced by permission of the Trustees of the British Museum.

loved country, a role he plays in Charles Williams's 1816 engraving *Political Balance—Unexpected Inspection—or A Good Old Master Takeing a Peep into the State of Things Himself* (fig. 154). Although physically marginalized on the extreme right of the print, in a tower marked "Windsor," George III uses his glass to serve as the moral and political center of this attack on the exploitation of the poor during the economic distress following the end of the Napoleonic Wars. In effect, George is awarded the satirist's perspective of the outsider commenting on the actions of others. The mad king, whose crown tops a round hat, is the sole opponent of the recently passed laws intended to artificially raise the prices of basic commodities: "Heigh! Heigh! Fellow! pull away those d——d heavy Corn Laws and Butter and Cheese Laws; let the prices find the *level* & come *within the reach* of my distress'd people; I say pull them of [*sic*] *directly* Fellow, d'ont you see Old England is *sunk* almost out of sight, you thought I could not see did you Fellow Heigh! Heigh!" George's principal opponent is the wealthy man who gloats, "How rich I shall get by plundering the Poor, now my old Master is *blind* and there is no one to watch me." The tearful face within a descending sun expresses the isolated king's inability to arrest the slide of "Old England" into the "Abyss of Corruption."

As the copperplate illustration of George III on the apex of *"England's Firm Pyramid"* (fig. 155), in the anonymous *The Palace of John Bull, Contrasted with the Poor "House That Jack Built,"* shows, perhaps only by exchanging effectiveness for dignity could George ever have become "the PATRIOT KING." Accompanying verses make the message clear:

Behold ENGLAND'S PYRAMID gracefully peering
O'er a beautiful Champaign—Fields reaping—Sheep shearing;
  The PEOPLE all joyous,
  Peaceful and prosperous,
The PYRAMID circle, their GLORY and PRIDE;
The COMMONS and NOBLES supporting each side;
  Their venerable SOVEREIGN
  ON the PYRAMID'S TOP,
  Lost EUROPE recovering
  And raising her up,
  HALF A CENTURY swaying
  A SCEPTRE of LOVE,
  O'er a PEOPLE obeying
  A KING they approve.
Lo! to Britain's great FATHER—the PATRIOT KING,
All orders their tribute bring.
Tho' now in his Palace, retir'd from their gaze,

Figure 154. Charles Williams, *Political Balance—Unexpected Inspection—or A Good Old Master Takeing a Peep into the State of Things Himself* (BMC 13497). Reproduced by permission of the Trustees of the British Museum.

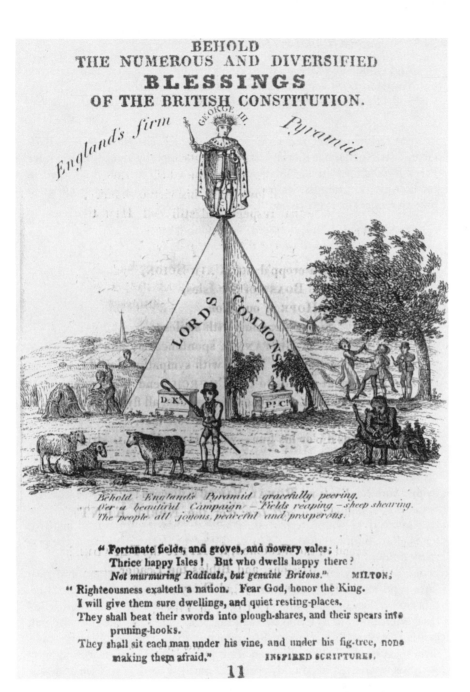

Figure 155. *England's Firm Pyramid* (BMC 13558). Courtesy of the Special Collections, University of Maryland-College Park Libraries.

And clouded by Heaven his reason's bright rays,
Yet HIS PEOPLE still love HIM, his virtues admire,
Still His SCEPTRE respect and still call HIM their SIRE.

(pp. 10–11)[22]

For Williams and the anonymous author of *The Palace of John Bull*, George III's ineffective mortal body prompts sympathy and admiration; for Percy Bysshe Shelley, in "England in 1819," which was not published in his lifetime, it prompts derision and hatred. Shelley's sonnet is closer in tone to straightforward vituperation than to satire:

An old, mad, blind, despised, and dying King;
Princes, the dregs of their dull race, who flow
Through public scorn,—mud from a muddy spring;
Rulers who neither see nor feel nor know,
But leechlike to their fainting country cling
Till they drop, blind in blood, without a blow.
A people starved and stabbed in th'untilled field;
An army, whom liberticide and prey
Makes as a two-edged sword to all who wield;
Golden and sanguine laws which tempt and slay;
Religion Christless, Godless—a book sealed;
A senate, Time's worst statute, unrepealed—
Are graves from which a glorious Phantom may
Burst, to illumine our tempestuous day.[23]

Shelley's desperate tone results from his implicit acknowledgment that the identification between king and country, which previous satirists had helped to create, has become an accepted fact. Since about 1793, the undeniable popularity of George III forced radicals to accommodate their rhetoric to the Loyalist defense of monarchy. The king *is* England in 1819; for Shelley, both are mad and obtuse. Grammatically, the king is the primary noun of the compound subject—"King . . . Princes . . . Rulers . . . people . . . army . . . laws . . . Religion . . . senate"—of the plural verb "Are" and its predicate nominative "graves" in the penultimate line. Significantly, the "people," albeit "starved and stabbed in th'untilled field" (i.e., victimized at Peterloo by the king who should be the husbandman of his subjects, the farmer of his country), share responsibility for their own oppression. Shelley's Blakean attempt to subvert royalist iconography with his references to "muddy spring," "untilled field," "Golden and sanguine laws," "a book sealed," and a rival sun is itself undercut by the doubtful implications of "may," crucially placed in the concluding couplet. That one word acknowledges, perhaps unintentionally, the residual power of the monarchy and the king who still reigns even if he can no longer rule. Byron more directly acknowledges the *potential* power of the throne in an epigram that he sent to Lady Melbourne in a letter of 21 September 1813:

> 'Tis said *Indifference* marks the present time,
> Then hear the reason—though 'tis told in rhyme—
> A King who *can't*—a Prince of Wales who *don't*—
> Patriots who *shan't,* and Ministers who *won't*—
> What matters who are *in* or *out* of place
> The *Mad*—the *Bad*—the *Useless*—or the *Base*?[24]

Prospects for George III's would-be satirists only worsened with the king's death because he immediately became a candidate for beatification. Sorrow at his death was widespread and sincere: more than thirty thousand of his subjects attended what was to have been the private funeral at Windsor for the "sainted remains of our dear king."[25] His nation grieved for the ruler whose *"character was minutely and essentially British.* He comprehended in himself, to an almost unexampled extent, those high, holy, and valuable qualities, which, by the general consent of the wise and good among us, are considered as constituting *the perfect Englishman."*[26] George's transformation to "a bright example of what a King, a Christian, and a man should be" was now complete.[27] Moreover, as such an exemplary figure, George III could be used to measure George IV's shortcomings. George IV faced the problem that Johnson outlines at the opening of *Rambler* 86 (1751): "One of the ancients [perhaps Pliny] has observed, that the burthen of government is encreased upon princes by the virtues of their immediate predecessors. It is, indeed, always dangerous to be placed in a state of unavoidable comparison with excellence, and the danger is still greater when that excellence is consecrated by death, when envy and interest cease to act against it, and those passions by which it was first vilified and opposed, now stand in its defence, and turn their vehemence against honest emulation" (4:87). Would-be satirists of the late king faced the same problem.

In the anonymous *Advice from the Other World—or A Peep in the Magic-Lanthorn* (fig. 156), published in August 1820, the dead king has sent the late Pitt as his minister to the errant George IV to warn him of the revolutionary effects his misrule will have. Pitt points to the warning "Thou Art Weigh[ed] in the ballance and [found] wanting" and says, "I am come from your father, to warn you of the consequence of your evil life—take warning and repent look through this lanthorn." George IV begs, "O Lord O Lord!! *take away the lanthorn* Billy, and I'll never act wrong while I live. O Lord O Lord!!" He responds to the vision projected by the lanthorn, "Che Sara Sara [what will be, will be]," that Pitt holds before him. George IV's moral and political failings are indicated by the bottle of "Noyau" beside his chair and the "Addresses" ignored beneath his "Gout"-stool.

Figure 156. *Advice from the Other World—or A Peep in the Magic-Lanthorn* (Not in BMC). Reproduced by permission of the Henry E. Huntington Library and Art Gallery, San Marino, California.

George III's ghost itself appears in two more 1820 prints, *Richard Coeur de Diable!!* (October) and *His Most Gracious Majesty Hum IVth & His Ministers Going to Play the Devil with the Satirists.* In *Richard* (fig. 157), a parody of Hogarth's famous *Garrick in the Character of Richard III* (1745, 1746), the ghost of his late father joins those of his late daughter, Princess Charlotte, and her stillborn son to haunt the unrepentant, "devil-hearted" George IV, on the right. Until her death in childbirth on 6 November 1817, Charlotte, "the Daughter, whom the Isles loved well" (Byron, *Don Juan* 11:614), had been heir presumptive to the throne.[28] On the left, ministers plunder the treasury. The head of the blind George III, like those of the other spirits, is irradiated. Charlotte warns her father, "Will not the Spirit of thy *Relatives* once loved though coming from the grave induce the K[in]g to *banish* from his counsels *treacherous foes*? 'Awake! Arise! or be for ever fallen!!!' " The frightened George IV cries out, "By holy Paul—*Shadows* to night have struck more terror to the Soul of Richard, than can the substance of ten thousand foes, arm'd all in proof, and led by *Caroline*!!!"

In *His Most Gracious Majesty* (fig. 158), the dead king's shade, now the satirists' ally, at the lower left, tries unsuccessfully to warn George IV to learn from the experiences of his father: "O my Son! my dear Son! if you prosecute them you will make their fortunes—but if you will conduct yourself like a man and a gentleman, you will destroy thir profession. farewell!" The foolish Hum IV ignores the advice: "Zounds & fury down with them! Here! Sid! you old tottering h[u]mb[u]g, desire the Bishops to come along with the tinder-box and matches! whip behind G[i]ff[or]d! don't you see! they are rediculing my very Bomb! I tell you again, I am K[in]g and be d[amne]d to you all, and will do just as I please!!!"[29]

In Byron's essentially carnivalesque treatment of George III in *The Vision of Judgment* (1822), the grotesquely realistic depiction of the late king satirizes George IV, the tacit target of the subtext, as well as Robert Southey and George III, the overt targets. Byron's immediate reaction to the king's death had been at least partially sympathetic: "I see the good old King is gone to his place—one can't help being sorry—though blindness —and age and insanity are supposed to be drawbacks—on human felicity —but I am not at all sure that the latter at least—might not render him happier than any of his subjects." In his satire, however, Byron puts "the said George's Apotheosis in a Whig point of view, not forgetting the Poet Laureate for his preface and his other demerits."[30] The immediate occasion, however, of Southey's *Vision of Judgment* (1821) gave Byron the opportunity to mock more than one particular poem. His portrayal in his "finest ferocious Caravaggio style" of a caricatured George III serves as a vehicle for undermining the ruling hierarchy's political and religious practices, if not premises.[31] Southey himself does not appear until stanza 85 of the 106

Figure 157. *Richard Coeur de Diable!!* (Not in BMC). Courtesy of the Library of Congress.

Figure 158. *His Most Gracious Majesty Hum IVth & His Ministers Going to Play the Devil with the Satirists* (Not in BMC). Reproduced by permission of the Henry E. Huntington Library and Art Gallery, San Marino, California.

stanzas in the poem because he is the creation rather than the creator of the political culture that produced his abominable verse. Byron's true object in *The Vision* is not to parody the superstructure of Southey's *Vision* but rather to expose the ideology underlying the earlier poem.[32]

Southey's *Vision,* as its dedication to George IV and its twelve-part organization suggest, serves to legitimize and sanctify the ruling system and its cultural products. Beatification of the late king in this epyllion, or little epic, is an excuse for glorifying his successor, as Southey does at the opening of his dedication: "Only to Your Majesty can the present publication with propriety be addressed. As a tribute to the sacred memory of our late revered Sovereign, it is my duty to present it to Your Majesty's notice; and to whom could an experiment, which, perhaps, may be considered hereafter as of some importance in English Poetry, be so fitly inscribed, as to the Royal and munificent Patron of science, art, and literature?"

Byron's assault on the authority of Southey and his royal patron begins with his revision of the laureate's title. The satirist's substitution of the definite for the indefinite article implies that *his* is the final vision. The attribution of the poem to "Quevedo Redivivus" challenges Southey's self-congratulatory claims for nativist tradition, and "Suggested by the Composition so Entitled by the Author of Wat Tyler" embarrassingly subverts the laureate's legitimacy as court spokesman.

Two anti-Southey prints had anticipated many of Byron's satiric tactics. The controlling metaphor of Charles Williams's *A Poet Mounted on His Court-Pegasus* (1817) (fig. 159) applies to the new poet laureate Mathias's witty accusation in *The Pursuits of Literature* (1794–97) that Priestley made words as easily as he made water. Saying, "God Save the KING!!" Southey straddles the source of his inspiration, the annual cask of sack that came with his office. From it flows "Adulation," "Apostacy," "Flattery," "Meaness [*sic*]," "Servility," and "Sycophancy," which swamp his earlier works. The money bag of his pension replaces his manhood because he has accepted the wreath of nettles (tied with a ribbon marked "Net/tle") from the Devil behind him, who points to "Wat Tyler A Dramatic Poem." Beneath the design we read,

> Aye, aye, hear him—
> He is no mealy mouthed court Orator
> To flatter vice, and pamper lordly pride!!
> vide Wat Tyler.

Williams's depiction of Southey parodies the "floating Bacchus" illustration in Dryden's translation of Virgil's *Georgics,* book 2, thereby underscoring the putative source of Southey's genius and emphasizing the discrepancy between Southey and his honorable predecessor as poet laureate.

Figure 159. C. Williams, *A Poet Mounted on His Court-Pegasus* (BMC 12877).
Reproduced by permission of the Trustees of the British Museum.

George Cruikshank's *A New Vision, by Robert Southey, Esq.! LL.D.!! Poet Laureate!!! &.!!!! &.!!!!! &.!!!!!!* (fig. 160), a frontispiece to an 1821 parody of Southey's poem, is more graphic in its excremental vision. Southey's cask spews his "Vision of Judgement" into a chamber pot shaped like a crown, while the object of Southey's worship, an irradiated George IV, dances on a figure, historically identifiable as John Sewell, president of the Constitutional Society, and perhaps intended to symbolically represent Southey's earlier, radical self, stuffed into another chamber pot. The laureate, visibly burdened by his office, addresses the king: "Sing we Now Apollo's praise." Like Byron, the artist and the author of the parody recognize that George IV is the true subject of Southey's *Vision.*

To Southey's celebration of the king's two bodies Byron responds with a recapitulation of the late king's career in satire. In his preface, Byron faults George III for not having been that old-fashioned ideal of eighteenth-century political discourse, a "patriot king" who protects his political off-spring, "inasmuch as several years of his reign passed in war with America and Ireland." Contextual and textual evidence indicates that Byron believed in the ideal and that he measured George III and his son against the standard of a "patriot" prince. In his "Sonnet to George the Fourth" (1819), Byron observes:

> To be the father of the fatherless,
> To stretch the hand from the throne's height, and raise
> *His* offspring, who expired in other days
> To make thy sire's sway by a kingdom less,—
> *This* is to be a monarch, and repress
> Envy into unutterable praise.
> Dismiss thy guard, and trust thee to such traits,
> For who would lift a hand, except to bless?   (1–8)

Byron expresses similar political feelings in *Don Juan* (1823):

> He saw however at the closing session [of Parliament]
> That noble sight, when *really* free the nation,
> A king in constitutional possession
> Of such a throne as is the proudest station,
> Though despots know it not—till the progression
> Of freedom shall complete their education.
> 'Tis not mere splendour makes the show august
> To eye or heart—it is the people's trust.   (canto 12, st. 83)

And in *The Vision,* Byron's objection to George III is not that he was a king but that he was an ineffective king, a tool of others, as his revision of "worse" to "weaker" in the following couplet suggests: "A better

Sing we Now Apollo's praise

A *NEW* VISION, By ROBERT SOUTHEY, Esq.! LL.D.!! Poet Laureate!!! &c.!!!! &c.!!!!! &c.!!!!!!

Figure 160. G. Cruikshank, *A New Vision, by Robert Southey, Esq.! LL.D.!! Poet Laureate!!! &.!!!! &.!!!!! &.!!!!!!* (BMC 14226). Reproduced by permission of the Trustees of the British Museum.

farmer ne'er brush'd dew from lawn, / A weaker king never left a realm undone!" (61–62).

Despite his apparent belief in the "patriot" ideal, Byron mocks the premises of power that support the throne. Byron's ideological attack is reflected in his subversions of form. Hence, the Christian machinery of Southey's royalist epyllion is immediately exploded: St. Peter's "keys were rusty, and the lock was dull" (2); "The angels all were singing out of tune" (9). From St. Peter's glancing reference to *Georgium sidus*—" 'There's another star gone out, I think!' " (128)—Byron proceeds to divorce church and state by pointing out the contradiction between royalist claims for political hierarchy and Christian faith in spiritual equality: " 'And who *is* George the Third?' replied the apostle: / *'What George? what Third?'* " (138–39). Southey's George III is beatified, Byron implies, not for his personal virtues but because he was a monarch; Byron's George III faces damnation for his position but is redeemed by his person. Satan points out that the king's two bodies must be separated if he is to be saved:

> He merely bent his diabolic brow
>   An instant; and then raising it, he stood
> In act to assert his right or wrong, and show
>   Cause why King George by no means could or should
> Make out a case to be exempt from woe
>   Eternal, more than other kings, endued
> With better sense and hearts, whom history mentions,
> Who long have "paved hell with their good intentions."   (289–96)

Such separation takes place in the course of Byron's *Vision*. In the middle of Southey's poem, section 7, "The Beatification," George III escapes his mortal body with its blinding limitations:

> Thither the King drew nigh, and kneeling he drank the water.
> Oh what a change was wrought! In the semblance of age he had
>   risen,
> Such as at last he appear'd, with the traces of time and affliction
> Deep on his faded form, when the burthen of years was upon him.
> Oh what a change was wrought! For now the corruptible put on
> Incorruption; the mortal put off mortality. Rising
> Rejuvenescent he stood in a glorified body, obnoxious
> Never again to change, nor to evil and trouble and sorrow,
> But for eternity form'd, and to bliss everlasting appointed.

In Byron's revision, George III was merely a man among men, his eternal salvation threatened by his former status and the ludicrous attempts to obscure his corruptibility. He remains blind because he was physically so but also because his metaphoric blindness—"an old man / With an old soul, and both extremely blind" (181–82)—continues the long-standing satiric depiction. Like Shelley, Byron recognizes that many of the king's subjects share responsibility for the nation's political madness and blindness. Byron's disjunction of the two bodies opens with a revision of historical chronology, which appropriates the sun image, so that freedom, not George IV, is George III's rightful political successor:

In the first year of freedom's second dawn
    Died George the Third; although no tyrant, one
Who shielded tyrants, till each sense withdrawn
    Left him nor mental nor external sun;
A better farmer ne'er brush'd dew from lawn,
    A weaker king never left a realm undone!
He died!—but left his subjects still behind,
One half as mad—and t'other no less blind.

. . . .
                                Of all
The fools who flocked to swell or see the show,
Who cared about the corpse? The funeral
    Made the attraction, and the black the woe.
There throbbed not there a thought which pierced the pall;
    And when the gorgeous coffin was laid low,
It seemed the mockery of hell to fold
The rottenness of eighty years in gold.

. . . .
But the unnatural balsams merely blight
    What nature made him at his birth, as bare
As the mere million's base unmummied clay—
Yet all his spices but prolong decay.   (57–64, 73–80, 85–88)

Through the tradition of "The king is dead—long live the king," George III achieves political immortality in Southey's *Vision* because his son continues his policies:

Then as his waken'd mind to the weal of his country reverted,
What of his son he ask'd, what course by the Prince had been
    follow'd.
Right in his Father's steps hath the Regent trod, was the answer:
Firm hath he proved and wise, at a time when weakness or error
Would have sunk us in shame, and to ruin have hurried us headlong.
True to himself hath he been, and Heaven has rewarded his counsels.
                                    (sec. 3, "The Awakening")

Byron is far more concerned with the personal virtues of George III, which pointedly do not survive him in his son:

> But where's the proctor who will ask his son?
> In whom his qualities are reigning still,
> Except that household virtue, most uncommon,
> Of constancy to a bad, ugly woman.   (93–96)

The triple hit strikes the dead king, his late queen, and their heir. Even Satan, admitting historical reality, must say of George III, "I grant his household abstinence; I grant / His neutral virtues, which most monarchs want" (359–60). George's eulogists made much of his self-denial for the sake of country in his dynastic marriage to the unseen Charlotte at his reign's beginning and of his subsequently observing the sanctity of marriage.

In tacit but sharp contrast stood his son's own treatment of *his* wife, Caroline Amelia Elizabeth of Brunswick-Wolfenbuttel. To get his father to pay for his debts, the future George IV agreed to marry his cousin, whom he began to mistreat even before their wedding on 8 April 1795, which he attended drunk. He deserted her three months after the birth of their daughter, Charlotte, on 7 January 1796, and only by appealing to George III was Caroline able to regain access to her daughter. When he became regent in 1811, the prince, accusing her of immorality, forbade Caroline any access to or influence over their daughter. In 1814 he granted Caroline permission to go abroad, where she soon established a scandalous liaison with an Italian, Bartolomeo Bergami (who preferred his name to be spelled Pergami). At the prince's accession in 1820, her name was left out of the state prayers, and a bill for divorce was brought against her upon her return to London. She immediately became the darling of the political opposition, including Byron, and popular support for her cause led to the dropping of the bill. She died on 7 August 1821, several days after being forcibly and publicly excluded from the coronation on 29 July. George IV's objection to having her body pass through London led to a bloody confrontation between the Life Guards and a crowd at Hyde Park Corner.[33]

By 1822 Byron's use of George III to judge the actions of his son was, of course, a familiar satiric tactic. Byron, however, is more subtle in *The Vision* than was the anonymous author of *A Groan from the Throne* (London, 1820), yet another case in which the afterlife is no barrier to the continuation of George III's satiric career. George Cruikshank's cover illustration shows a cloud inscribed "Desist" over George III's ghostly head (fig. 161). Set "in the ancient Isle of Blefescu, so celebrated in Gulliver's Travels . . . , the characters are ideal, of course, though the events are *true*" (p. 3). The late king's *deus ex machina* voice ends Queen Caroline's persecution:

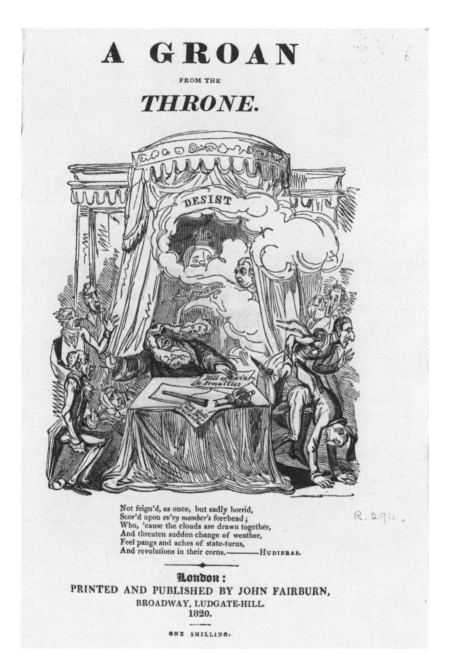

Figure 161. G. Cruikshank, *A Groan from the Throne* (BMC 13894). Reproduced by permission of the Trustees of the British Museum.

"Mark me and tremble! while I now declare,
"Unnumber'd evils *you* have cause to fear;
"Call back the K——g, let *him* his crimes repent,
"Or sad misfortunes *he* may yet lament."   (p. 28)

In Byron's poem, the implicit judge is himself the object of explicit judgment.

Byron constantly revises George III so that the satiric tradition linked to his mortal body subverts the royalist apologetics associated with his regal body. In Byron's *The Vision,* Junius and Wilkes are named, thus given equal political and spiritual status with George, whereas in Southey's *A Vision* they remain anonymous accusers, not worthy of true identities. Byron recounts many of the old traits of George's satiric persona, such as his being Bute's puppet (564), but paradoxically this persona saves his soul. Speaking for his fellow satirists before him, Byron acknowledges George III's transition from target to tactic by appropriating his telescope (842) to transform it into a satirist's "telescope of truth" and by granting him the insight denied Southey and George IV.[34] George's one judgment rendered in this vision of judgment comically countermands George IV's creation of Southey as poet laureate in 1813, undermines the legitimacy of the court poet, his culture, and his patron, and serves as an act of literary repentance that earns the now comically heroic George III the right to slip forever from the satirists' grasp:

The monarch, mute till then, exclaimed, "What! what!
Pye come again? No more—no more of that!"   (735–36)

Notes

CHAPTER I. The Tradition of Regal Satire

1. James I, *Political Works*, ed. C. H. McIlwain (London, 1918), quoted in *POAS* 1:xxxix.

2. King George to Lord North, 11 April 1780, in *Correspondence of King George the Third*, ed. Sir John Fortescue (London, 1928), 5:41–42.

3. For the assumption that Blackstone was a Whig and not a Tory, as Daniel J. Boorstin, for example, calls him in *The Mysterious Science of Law (An Essay on Blackstone's "Commentaries")* (Cambridge, Mass.: Harvard Univ. Press, 1941), see J. G. A. Pocock, *Virtue, Commerce, and History: Essays on Political Thought and History, Chiefly in the Eighteenth Century* (Cambridge: Cambridge Univ. Press, 1985), p. 276. Even Blackstone's opponents, like Jeremy Bentham, in *A Fragment on Government* (London, 1776), acknowledged him as "an Author whose works have had beyond comparison a more extensive circulation, have obtained a greater share of esteem, of applause, and consequently of influence (and that by a title on many grounds so indisputable) than any other writer who on that subject has ever yet appeared" (p. iii).

4. See J. G. A. Pocock, *The Machiavellian Moment: Florentine Political Thought and the Atlantic Republican Tradition* (Princeton, N.J.: Princeton Univ. Press, 1975), for an extended treatment of the reception of Machiavelli in the eighteenth century.

5. The major change in constitutional theory from James I's view that sovereignty resides solely in the king to the post-Restoration premise that it resides in the king, lords, and commons has been dated back to Charles I's *Answer to the Nineteen Propositions of Parliament* (June 1642). On the development of the theory of coordination of sovereignty, see Corinne C. Weston and Janelle R. Greenberg, *Subjects and Sovereigns: The Grand Controversy over Legal Sovereignty in Stuart England* (Cambridge: Cambridge Univ. Press, 1981), and Weston, "Co-ordination: A Radicalising Principle in Stuart Politics," in James Jacob and Margaret Jacob, eds., *The Origins of Anglo-American Radicalism* (London: Allen and Unwin, 1983), pp. 85–104. For a reminder that the theory of coordination was not universally accepted, see J. A. W. Gunn, *Beyond Liberty and Property: The Process of Self-Recognition in Eighteenth-Century Political Thought* (Kingston and Montreal: McGill-Queen's Univ. Press, 1983), chap. 4.

6. On the king's two bodies, see Ernst Hartwig Kantorowicz, *The King's Two Bodies: A Study in Mediaeval Political Theology* (Princeton, N.J.: Princeton Univ. Press, 1957).

7. See Gunn, *Beyond Liberty*, chap. 2.

8. The role of censorship, which encouraged indirect political discourse, must not be ignored: J. G. A. Pocock, *The Ancient Constitution and the Feudal Law: A Study of English Historical Thought in the Seventeenth Century* (Cambridge: Cambridge Univ. Press, 1957); Annabel Patterson, *Censorship and Interpretation: The Conditions of Writing and Reading in Early Modern England* (Madison: Univ. of Wisconsin Press, 1984); and Steven Zwicker, *Politics and Language in Dryden's Poetry: The Arts of Disguise* (Princeton, N.J.: Princeton Univ. Press, 1984).

9. For commentaries on Marvell's poetry, see John M. Wallace, *Destiny His Choice: The Loyalism of Andrew Marvell* (Cambridge: Cambridge Univ. Press, 1968); Annabel Patterson, *Marvell and the Civic Crown* (Princeton, N.J.: Princeton Univ. Press, 1978); and Warren L. Cherniak, *The Poet's Time: Politics and Religion in the Work of Andrew Marvell* (Cambridge: Cambridge Univ. Press, 1983).

10. Zwicker, *Politics and Language*, notes a "repeated and almost Jacobean stress on the divinity of kings" in *Absalom* (p. 101). Zwicker's observation is qualified by Michael McKeon, "Historicizing *Absalom and Achitophel*," in Felicity Nussbaum and Laura Brown, eds., *The New Eighteenth Century: Theory, Politics, English Literature* (New York: Methuen, 1987), pp. 23–40. McKeon reminds us that in the poem Dryden implicitly accepts a contractual theory of monarchy and does not explicitly embrace a patriarchalist position. Perhaps, as Howard D. Weinbrot suggests in " 'Nature's Holy Bands' in *Absalom and Achitophel:* Fathers and Sons, Satire and Change," *Modern Philology* 85 (1988): 373–92, Dryden avoided such an explicit statement to maintain his pose of moderation. Weinbrot's essay is the fullest treatment of the familial theme in the poem. The poem's generic status as a satire aimed in part at the king reflects the demystification of the monarchy effected in 1649 and underscored in 1660. The king's mortal body could now pose a threat to his regal body. The subversion of the authority of the monarchy through verbal and visual representations during the Renaissance, which is discussed in Stephen Orgel, *The Illusion of Power* (Berkeley and Los Angeles: Univ. of California Press, 1975), becomes much more evident after the Restoration.

11. On Dryden's poetry, consult Earl Miner, *Dryden's Poetry* (Indianapolis: Univ. of Indiana Press, 1967); Steven Zwicker, *Dryden's Political Poetry* (Providence, R.I.: Brown Univ. Press, 1972); and George McFadden, *Dryden the Public Writer, 1660–1685* (Princeton, N.J.: Princeton Univ. Press, 1978).

12. On the Glorious Revolution as a radical turning point in constitutional theory, see Lois G. Schwoerer, *The Declaration of Rights, 1689* (Baltimore: Johns Hopkins Univ. Press, 1981), and Schwoerer, "The Contributions of the Declaration of Rights to Anglo-American Radicalism," in Jacob and Jacob, *Origins of Anglo-American Radicalism*, pp. 105–24.

13. The subscribed key identifies many of the print's elements: "A. The church of England almost over throwne by the infernal councel of the most Christian Turk [Louis XIV]"; "B. The royal Orange Tree, representing the Prince of Orange"; "C. Gods Providence Influencing both from Heaven"; "D. A Bishop representing the Lords Spiritual"; "E. A Knight of the Garter representing the Lords Temporal"; "F. Three or 4. representing the Commons of England"; "G. The

French king murthering his owne subjects"; "H. His most Christian Scourge of Europe his councel"; "I. The K. and Q. with the Child"; "K. The Late Cha: Jec. [Jeffries]"; "L. Lassciveous Peters the Jesuit"; "M. The Popes Nuncio"; "N. The whole Head of Papists and Jesuits running from the hand of Justice"; "O. The Armes of Danmark, Sweadland, and of ye Palatinate Princes, in League with the Empire against the French perfidious usurpation, who have declared the Prince of Orange Generalissimo of all the Protestant forces, and Protector of the Protestant Religion." For fuller descriptions of BMC prints, check the BMC listings. For general studies of prints relevant to satires about the Georges, consult Thomas Wright, *Caricature History of the Georges* (1868; reprint, New York: Benjamin Blom, 1968); Mary Dorothy George, *English Political Caricature: A Study of Opinion and Propaganda* (Oxford: Oxford Univ. Press, 1959), vol. 1 (to 1792) and vol. 2 (to 1832).

14. Gordon J. Schochet, *Patriarchalism in Political Thought: The Authoritarian Family and Political Speculation and Attitudes, Especially in Seventeenth-Century England* (Oxford: Oxford Univ. Press, 1975).

15. F. P. Lock, *Swift's Tory Politics* (London: Duckworth, 1983), p. 108.

16. See Gunn, *Beyond Liberty,* chap. 1. For a study of political satire during 1713–64, see Vincent Carretta, *"The Snarling Muse": Verbal and Visual Political Satire from Pope to Churchill* (Philadelphia: Univ. of Pennsylvania Press, 1983).

17. Two essays in, respectively, vols. 2 (1983) and 3 (1984) of *Parliamentary History: A Yearbook* (New York: St. Martin's Press) discuss the vexed questions of Jacobitism and party distinctions: J. C. D. Clark, "The Politics of the Excluded: Tories, Jacobites, and Whig Patriots, 1715–1760," pp. 209–22, and Marie Peters, " 'Names and Cant': Party Labels in English Political Propaganda c. 1755–1765," pp. 103–27.

18. See J. A. W. Gunn, *Factions No More: Attitudes to Party in Government and Opposition in Eighteenth-Century England* (London: Frank Cass, 1972), and Frank O'Gorman, *The Rise of Party in England, 1760–1782* (London: Allen and Unwin, 1975).

19. Lock, *Swift's Tory Politics,* pp. 167, 170.

20. Tobias Smollett, *The Adventures of an Atom* (Athens: University of Georgia Press, 1989), p. 11.

21. Horace Walpole, *Memoirs of the Last Ten Years of the Reign of George the Second,* ed. John Brooke (New Haven, Conn.: Yale Univ. Press, 1985), 3:118.

22. BMC 2447, reproduced in Carretta, *"The Snarling Muse,"* p. 47. All references to *The Craftsman* are to the fourteen-volume collected edition (London, 1737).

23. BMC 2551, reproduced in Carretta, *"The Snarling Muse,"* p. 194.

24. For a convenient, recent review that includes coverage of the Hanoverian connection (pp. 41–44), see Jeremy Black, "British Foreign Policy in the Eighteenth Century: A Survey," *Journal of British Studies* 26 (1987): 26–53.

25. BMC 1937, reproduced in Herbert M. Atherton, *Political Prints in the Age of Hogarth: A Study of the Ideographic Representation of Politics* (Oxford: Oxford Univ. Press, 1974), pl. 16.

26. The accusation of "petticoat government" had also been used to undercut Charles II's patriarchal authority. The charge was particularly telling if someone other than a wife wore the petticoat.

27. BMC 2613, reproduced in Carretta, *"The Snarling Muse,"* p. 205.

28. Philip C. Yorke, *The Life and Correspondence of Philip Yorke, Earle of Hardwicke* (Cambridge: Cambridge Univ. Press, 1913), 1:382–83. Black, "British Foreign Policy," pp. 39–41, discusses recent challenges to the myth of royal political impotence in domestic and foreign affairs during the eighteenth century.

29. By midcentury, the term *Tory* had undergone some redefinition and confusion. Hanoverian Tories recognized George II as the *de jure* as well as *de facto* ruler of Great Britain and were eager to convince him that they could serve him as loyally as the Whigs. Jacobite Tories, caricatured by Fielding in Squire Western, endured their *de facto* ruler while longing for their *de jure* king across the water. A further distinction was made between City (or radical) Tories, whose support came from the middling sort dependent on trade and commerce, and Country Tories, celebrated in Smollett's *Humphry Clinker,* who continued to see political power as agriculturally based. What gave City and Country Tories their common label, besides a shared political rhetoric inherited from Bolingbroke through *The Craftsman,* was their joint belief in a strong monarch who would protect their interests from the depredations of their common enemy, the aristocracy. The social and economic interests of City and Country Tories were quite different. The clearest split between the two, exploited brilliantly by John Wilkes, occurred when the king seemed to betray City Tories' economic interests and to ally himself with aristocrats rather than the Great Commoner, William Pitt. See Marie Peters, "The Monitor on the Constitution, 1755–1765: New Light on the Ideological Origins of English Radicalism," *English Historical Review* 86 (1971): 706–25; Linda Colley, "Eighteenth-Century English Radicalism before Wilkes," *Transactions of the Royal Historical Society* 31 (1981): 1–19. On the natural political alliance of the king and the burghers against the nobles, see Adam Smith, *An Inquiry into the Nature and Causes of the Wealth of Nations* 3:3.

30. See Marie Peters, *Pitt and Popularity: The Patriot Minister and London Opinion during the Seven Years' War* (Oxford: Oxford Univ. Press, 1980).

CHAPTER 2.   "The Royal Dupe"

1. Horace Walpole, *Memoirs of the Reign of King George the Third* (1894; reprint, Freeport, N.Y.: Books for Libraries Press, 1970), 1:3–4.

2. John Brooke, *King George III: A Biography of America's Last Monarch* (New York: McGraw-Hill, 1972), p. 43. For a very helpful review of recent biographical work on George, see Ian Christie, "George III and the Historians: Thirty Years On," *History* 71 (1986): 205–21. Christie's *Wars and Revolutions: Britain, 1760–1815* (Cambridge, Mass.: Harvard Univ. Press, 1982), one of the most reliable of the many surveys covering the period, includes a bibliography of the best secondary works, arranged by topic, on George's reign. Christie should be supplemented by Frank O'Gorman, "Fifty Years after Namier: The Eighteenth Century in British

Historical Writing," *Eighteenth Century* 20 (1979): 99–120, and his "Recent Historiography of the Hanoverian Regime," *Historical Journal* 29 (1986): 1005–20.

3. On Hogarth's engravings, in addition to their BMC listings, see the appropriate catalog entries in Ronald Paulson, *Hogarth's Graphic Works*, rev. ed. (New Haven, Conn.: Yale Univ. Press, 1970).

4. Frank J. McLynn, "Jacobites and the Jacobite Risings," *History Today* 33 (1983): 45–47, briefly discusses the most important books and controversies about Jacobitism. McLynn, *The Jacobites* (London: Routledge and Kegan Paul, 1985), is disappointingly superficial. The best surveys are by Bruce Lenman: *The Jacobite Risings in Britain, 1689–1746* (London: Eyre Methuen, 1980) and *The Jacobite Cause* (Glasgow: Richard Drew, 1986). Satirists continued to treat the Jacobite threat as real long after it had ceased to be—see below.

5. *Horace Walpole's Correspondence*, ed. Wilmarth S. Lewis et al. (New Haven, Conn.: Yale Univ. Press, 1937–83), 21:472.

6. For a fuller discussion of Bolingbroke's influence on the development of Country ideology and satire, see Carretta, *"The Snarling Muse,"* pp. 20–61.

7. *Memoirs of Thomas Hollis* (London, 1780), 1:98–99.

8. *Letters of Samuel Johnson*, ed. R. W. Chapman (Oxford: Oxford Univ. Press, 1952), 1:137–38. Although its historiographical assumptions are challenged by more recent research, the standard study of Johnson's political beliefs remains Donald J. Greene, *The Politics of Samuel Johnson* (New Haven, Conn.: Yale Univ. Press, 1960).

9. On Churchill as a political poet, in addition to the works cited in Carretta, *"The Snarling Muse,"* pp. 274–75, n. 11, see Lance Bertelsen, *The Nonsense Club: Literature and Popular Culture, 1749–1764* (Oxford: Oxford Univ. Press, 1986), pp. 160–253.

10. *Horace Walpole's Correspondence* 22:97. On the justification for the fears of the aristocracy, see John Cannon, "The Isthmus Repaired: The Resurgence of the English Aristocracy, 1660–1760," *Proceedings of the British Academy* 68 (1982): 431–53.

11. *Letters of Samuel Johnson* 1:138.

12. The fullest account of George III's education and his earliest political beliefs is Brooke, *King George III*, pp. 55–58.

13. Christie, "George III and the Historians," p. 210.

14. *Horace Walpole's Correspondence* 22:42, 53. On the political turmoil at the beginning of George III's reign, see John Brewer, *Party Ideology and Popular Politics at the Accession of George III* (Cambridge: Cambridge Univ. Press, 1976). For thorough discussions of the attacks on Bute, see Brewer, "The Faces of Lord Bute: A Visual Contribution to Anglo-American Political Ideology," *Perspectives in American History* 6 (1972): 95–116, and his "Misfortunes of Lord Bute: A Case-Study in Eighteenth-Century Political Argument and Public Opinion," *Historical Journal* 16 (1973): 3–43. On the dominant tone of midcentury politics, see Gordon S. Wood, "Conspiracy and the Paranoid Style: Causality and Deceit in the Eighteenth Century," *William and Mary Quarterly* 39 (1982): 401–41. Wood overlooks the influence of "the king can do no wrong" doctrine on the search for causes of unpopular political decisions.

15. For the nature of the attacks on Walpole, see Carretta, *"The Snarling Muse,"* chaps. 2–6.

16. Brewer, *Party Ideology,* pp. 142, 147.

17. Newcastle, quoted in Brewer, *Party Ideology,* p. 227. For the developments in historiography, iconography, and satire referred to in this paragraph, see Carretta, *"The Snarling Muse,"* passim.

18. See John A. Phillips, *Electoral Behaviour in Unreformed England, 1761–1802: Plumpers, Splitters, and Straights* (Princeton, N.J.: Princeton Univ. Press, 1982), and Frank O'Gorman, "The Unreformed Electorate of Hanoverian England: The Mid-Eighteenth Century to the Reform Act of 1832," *Social History* 11 (1986): 33–52.

19. A good survey of the subject is Robert R. Rea, *The English Press in Politics, 1760–1774* (Lincoln: Univ. of Nebraska Press, 1963).

20. See George Nobbe, *The North Briton: A Study in Political Propaganda* (New York: Columbia Univ. Press, 1939).

21. See above, chap. 1, nn. 17, 18. George III was anti-anti-Tory in that he did not accept the argument of the Old Corps Whigs, successfully made to his Hanoverian predecessors, that Tories, former Tories, and others outside the Old Corps ranks could not be trusted to serve the king's interests.

22. See Ronald Paulson, *Hogarth: His Life, Art, and Times* (New Haven, Conn.: Yale Univ. Press, 1971), 2:354–99.

23. For Sandby's relationship to Hogarth and *The Times,* see Paulson, *Hogarth* 2:371–72, 373, 377.

24. Jefferson's draft is reproduced in Garry Wills, *Inventing America: Jefferson's Declaration of Independence* (New York: Random House, 1978), pp. 374–79; the quotation is from p. 378. Similar anti-Scot sentiments are found in John Adams's *Autobiography: The Adams Papers,* ed. L. H. Butterfield (Cambridge, Mass.: Harvard Univ. Press, 1961), 3:352.

25. John Wilkes, in Adrian Hamilton, ed., *The Infamous "Essay on Woman": or, John Wilkes Seated between Vice and Virtue* (London: Deutsch, 1972), pp. 17–18.

26. Robert Halsband pointed out to me the likely pronunciation.

27. Reproduced in Carretta, *"The Snarling Muse,"* p. 230.

28. P. D. G. Thomas, "George III and the American Revolution," *History* 70 (1985): 16. See, too, Christie, "George III and the Historians," passim.

29. BMC entries that depict George III as a fool during the first dozen years of his reign include 3846, 3880, 3881, 4298, 4324, and 4417.

30. BMC 2458 is reproduced in Carretta, *"The Snarling Muse,"* p. 45.

31. In my discussion of the Mortimer allusions in anti-Bute satires, I am indebted to Lance Bertelsen, who kindly shared with me his findings and thoughts on the Mortimer-Bute connection. Bertelsen has since published some of his research in "The Significance of the 1731 Revisions to *The Fall of Mortimer,*" *Restoration and Eighteenth-Century Theatre Research,* 2d ser., 2 (1987): 8–25.

32. BMC entries that depict George III as blind, blindfolded, or shortsighted during the first dozen years of his reign include 3843, 3849, 3885, 3886, 3926, 3927, 3928, 3961, 3965, 3968, 3979, 4153, 4164, 4239, 4245, and 4303. Those that depict him as childish include 3936, 3981, 4163, 4195, and 4376.

33. Carretta, *"The Snarling Muse,"* chap. 5, discusses the politics of miseducation in *Dunciad* 4.

34. Carretta, *"The Snarling Muse,"* p. 243.

35. Douglas Grant, in the edition of Churchill's work cited herein, suggests that "the hardy Poet" is Andrew Marvell (p. 526). Perhaps because he took so much from Pope the poet, Churchill disliked Pope the man and consequently might have denied that Pope is referred to here.

36. Mary Wollstonecraft, *A Vindication of the Rights of Woman* (London, 1792), ed. Miriam Kramnick (Harmondsworth: Penguin, 1975), p. 314.

37. Terry Castle, *Masquerade and Civilization: The Carnivalesque in Eighteenth-Century English Culture and Fiction* (Stanford, Calif.: Stanford Univ. Press, 1986), p. 5.

38. *Boswell's Life of Johnson,* ed. G. B. Hill, rev. L. F. Powell (Oxford: Oxford Univ. Press, 1934), 2:353.

39. For a discussion of Junius (also Burke and Johnson) as a writer, see James T. Boulton, *The Language of Politics in the Age of Wilkes* (London: Routledge and Kegan Paul, 1963). Much of Junian research is concerned with the authorship question: Francesco Cordasco and Gustave Simonson, *Junius and His Works: A History of the Letters of Junius and the Authorship Controversy* (Fairview, N.J.: Junius-Vaughn, 1986), and Cordasco, *Junius: A Bibliography of the Letters of Junius, with a Checklist of Junian Scholarship and Related Studies* (Fairview, N.J.: Junius-Vaughn, 1986).

40. Figure 40 is a fanciful late-eighteenth-century reconstruction of the event, whose significance is retained even though the king's horse has been lost and East Indians have been relocated to New York.

CHAPTER 3.   "The Royal Brute of Britain"

1. For a general bibliography, see Ronald M. Gephart, comp., *Revolutionary America, 1763–1789: A Bibliography,* 2 vols. (Washington, D.C.: Library of Congress, 1984). For the pamphlet literature, see Thomas R. Adams, *The American Controversy: A Bibliographical Study of the British Pamphlets about the American Disputes, 1764–1783,* 2 vols. (Providence, R.I.: Brown Univ. Press, 1980). And for the poetry, see Martin Kallich, *British Poetry and the American Revolution: A Bibliographical Survey of Books and Pamphlets, Journals and Magazines, Newspapers and Prints, 1755–1800,* 2 vols. (Troy, N.Y.: Whiston, forthcoming). For a more specialized study, see Bruce Granger, *Political Satire in the American Revolution, 1763–1783* (Ithaca, N.Y.: Cornell Univ. Press, 1960).

2. Montesquieu, *The Spirit of the Laws,* bk. 3, sec. 7.

3. See, for example, William D. Liddle, "A Patriot King, or None: American Public Attitudes towards George III and the British Monarchy, 1754–1776" (Ph.D. diss., Claremont Graduate School and University Center, 1970); James E. Bradley, *Popular Politics and the American Revolution in England: Petitions, the Crown, and Public Opinion* (Macon, Ga.: Mercer Univ. Press, 1986); and John Sainsbury, *The Disaffected Patriots: London Supporters of Revolutionary America, 1769–82* (Kingston and Montreal: McGill-Queen's Univ. Press, 1986).

4. See T. H. Breen, *The Character of the Good Ruler: A Study of Puritan Political Ideas in New England, 1630–1730* (New Haven, Conn.: Yale Univ. Press, 1970).

5. Evert Augustus Duyckinck, *Cyclopaedia of American Literature* (Philadelphia, 1875), p. 142.

6. Bernard Bailyn, *The Ideological Origins of the American Revolution* (Cambridge, Mass.: Harvard Univ. Press, 1967); Gordon Wood, *The Creation of the American Republic, 1776–1787* (Chapel Hill: Univ. of North Carolina Press, 1969).

7. John Brewer, "English Radicalism in the Age of George III," in J. G. A. Pocock, ed., *Three British Revolutions: 1641, 1688, 1776* (Princeton, N.J.: Princeton Univ. Press, 1980), pp. 361–62.

8. Alison Olson, "Parliament, Empire, and Parliamentary Law, 1776," in Pocock, *Three British Revolutions*, pp. 289–322.

9. See George Rude, *Wilkes and Liberty: A Social Study of 1763 to 1774* (Oxford: Oxford Univ. Press, 1962).

10. Pauline Maier, "John Wilkes and American Disillusionment with Britain," *William and Mary Quarterly*, 3d ser., 20 (1963): 373–95.

11. The classic study of the subject is Edmund S. Morgan and Helen M. Morgan, *The Stamp Act Crisis: Prologue to Revolution* (Chapel Hill: Univ. of North Carolina Press, 1953).

12. See Edgar P. Richardson, "Stamp Act Cartoons in the Colonies," *Pennsylvania Magazine of History and Biography* 96 (1972): 275–97.

13. Kenneth Silverman, *A Cultural History of the American Revolution* (New York: Thomas Y. Crowell, 1976).

14. Arthur M. Schlesinger, "Liberty Tree: A Genealogy," *New England Quarterly* 25 (1952): 435–52.

15. See Paul Korshin, "The Development of Abstracted Typology in England, 1650–1820," in Earl Miner, ed., *Literary Uses of Typology* (Princeton, N.J.: Princeton Univ. Press, 1977), pp. 147–203.

16. Clarence Brigham, *Paul Revere's Engravings* (New York: American Antiquarian Society Rpt., 1969), p. 22.

17. See Caroline Robbins, *The Eighteenth-Century Commonwealthman: Studies in the Transmission, Development, and Circumstance of English Liberal Thought from the Restoration of Charles II until the War with the Thirteen Colonies* (Cambridge, Mass.: Harvard Univ. Press, 1961).

18. Brewer, *Party Ideology*, p. 185.

19. The most convenient edition of Thomas Jefferson's *Summary View* is the Library of America volume *Jefferson Writings* (New York: Literary Classics of the United States, 1984).

20. Jefferson, *A Summary View*, p. 110.

21. On David Hume's *History of England*, see Carretta, *"The Snarling Muse,"* chap. 7.

22. John Cannon does not identify the king as *"that man"* in his edition of Junius's letters.

23. On John Almon, see Deborah Rogers, *Bookseller as Rogue: John Almon and the Politics of Eighteenth-Century Publishing* (New York: Peter Lang, 1986). Rogers does not deal with Almon's role in the history of engraved satires.

24. "The king had been caught up in the escalation of events as much as any British politician. His involvement in the making and implementation of policy had been at the behest or request of his ministers, not on his own initiative. Demands for the support of their sovereign by the Rockingham and Chatham administrations had been followed by the seeking of his advice during the ministries of Grafton and North. George III's personal inclination towards 'firmness' had often been tempered by the insistence of ministers for more moderate lines of policy. To portray the king as a hardliner is evidently misleading. At each moment of crisis, right up until the outbreak of war, his hopes were centred on a political solution, and he always bowed to his cabinet's opinions, even when skeptical of their success. The detailed evidence of the years from 1763 to 1775 tends to exonerate George III from all real personal responsibility for the American Revolution" (P. D. G. Thomas, "George III and the American Revolution," p. 31). The most recent study of Paine is Owen Aldridge, *Thomas Paine's American Ideology* (Newark: Univ. of Delaware Press, 1984).

25. See Alan Dugald McKillop, "Ethics and Political History in Thomson's *Liberty,*" in James L. Clifford and Louis Landa, eds., *Pope and His Contemporaries: Essays Presented to George Sherburn* (Oxford: Oxford Univ. Press, 1949), pp. 215–29.

26. See Christopher Hill, "The Norman Yoke," Christopher Hill, ed., in *Puritanism and Revolution: Studies in Interpretation of the English Revolution of the Seventeenth Century* (London: Secker and Warburg, 1958), pp. 50–122.

27. The most recent example was Louis XVI, born in 1754, who had come to the throne in 1774. Paine's attacks on George III tend to be more personal in *The Crisis,* where he mocks the king's interest in buttons and accuses him of having an affair with a young Quaker woman.

28. For a recent discussion of the king as a false father devouring his own children, see Ronald Paulson, *Representations of Revolution (1789–1820)* (New Haven, Conn.: Yale Univ. Press, 1983), pp. 76–79.

CHAPTER 4.   "Monarchy Is the Popery of Government"

1. William Godwin, *An Enquiry concerning Political Justice and Its Influence on Modern Morals and Happiness,* ed. Isaac Kramnick (Harmondsworth: Penguin, 1976), pp. 420–21.

2. Among the numerous productions by the industrious students of Blake, very few focus on him as an eighteenth-century political satirist. For a comprehensive bibliography on Blake studies, see Mary Lynn Johnson, "William Blake," in Frank Jordan, ed., *The English Romantic Poets: A Review of Research and Criticism* (New York: Modern Language Association of America, 1985), pp. 113–253. The general works most relevant to my concerns are David V. Erdman, *Blake: Prophet against Empire: A Poet's Interpretation of the History of His Own Times,* rev. ed. (Princeton, N.J.: Princeton Univ. Press, 1969); Erdman, ed., *The Illuminated Blake: The Complete Illuminated Works of William Blake, with an Introduction and Plate-by-Plate Commentary* (Garden City, N.Y.: Doubleday, 1974); Leslie Tannenbaum, *Biblical Tradition in Blake's Early Prophecies: The Great Code of Art* (Princeton, N.J.: Prince-

ton Univ. Press, 1982); and John Howard, *Infernal Poetics: Poetic Structures in Blake's Lambeth Prophecies* (Rutherford, N.J.: Fairleigh Dickinson Univ. Press, 1984).

3. The best introduction to the *Poetical Sketches* is Robert F. Gleckner, *Blake's Prelude: Poetical Sketches* (Baltimore: Johns Hopkins Univ. Press, 1982).

4. On the question of irony, see Gleckner, *Blake's Prelude,* pp. 96–112.

5. See Erdman, *Blake: Prophet,* p. 67.

6. See Robert Willman, "Blackstone and the 'Theoretical Perfection' of English Law in the Reign of Charles II," *Historical Journal* 26 (1983): 39–70.

7. The best reading of the politically inspired revisions of "London" is E. P. Thompson, "London," in Michael Phillips, ed., *Interpreting Blake: Essays* (Cambridge: Cambridge Univ. Press, 1978), pp. 5–31.

8. The plate that refers to George III and that Blake canceled from *America* is reproduced in Blake, p. 58.

9. On Nebuchadnezzar as a type of the proud king humbled, see Joseph Wittreich, *"Image of That Horror": History, Prophecy, and Apocalypse in King Lear* (San Marino, Calif.: Huntington Library, 1984), p. 102.

10. See Ida Macalpine and Richard Hunter, *George III and the Mad-Business* (New York: Random House, 1969).

11. On the Gordon Riots, see Christopher Hibbert, *King Mob: The Story of Lord George Gordon and the London Riots of 1780* (Cleveland: World Publishing, 1958).

12. A recent, provocative treatment of Gillray's work that takes into account previous scholarship is Paulson, *Representations,* chap. 6.

13. Wollstonecraft, *Vindication,* pp. 96, 99. The classic study of the Regency Crisis is John W. Derry, *The Regency Crisis and the Whigs, 1788–1789* (Cambridge: Cambridge Univ. Press, 1963).

14. Macalpine and Hunter, in *George III,* pp. 42, 48, 53–54, 64–68, 69, 76–79, 92, 133, 144, 146, 151, 159, 160, 281, discuss the widely reported use of the straitwaistcoat to restrain the king.

15. Erdman, *Blake: Prophet,* p. 36, notes Blake's friendship with Stothard.

16. Brooke, *King George III,* pp. 302, 303–4, describes the king's patronage of Sir William Herschel.

17. David Williams is the subject of Gunn, *Beyond Liberty,* chap. 5, and of Whitney R. D. Jones, *David Williams: The Anvil and the Hammer* (Cardiff: Univ. of Wales Press, 1986).

18. The shaved head is associated with madness, for example, in the last scene of Hogarth's *The Rake's Progress* and in the anonymous 1789 print *The Funeral Procession of Mrs. Regency. Vide the Pamphlet,* in which a bald Burke appears in a straitjacket.

19. David V. Erdman, *"America:* New Expanses," in Mary Lynn Johnson and John E. Grant, eds., *Blake's Poetry and Designs* (New York: Norton, 1979), p. 581.

20. Johnson and Grant, *Blake's Poetry,* p. 113.

21. Adams, *American Controversy,* pp. xii–xiii.

22. See Jay Fliegelman, *Prodigals and Pilgrims: The American Revolution against Patriarchal Authority, 1750–1800* (Cambridge: Cambridge Univ. Press, 1982), and

Stephen C. Behrendt, "Blake's *America* and the American Revolution," *Eighteenth Century: Theory and Interpretation* 27 (1986): 26–51.

23. Johnson and Grant, *Blake's Poetry*, p. 107. Stuart Curran, "The Political Prometheus," *Studies in Romanticism* 25 (1986): 429–55, refers to the "representation of a female Prometheus being tortured by the male American eagle in *Visions of the Daughters of Albion*" (p. 444). Presumably, he detects a similar allusion to Prometheus on plate 13 of *America*.

24. Paine's opponents frequently and intentionally misspelled his name to emphasize the effects of his writings and to exercise the satirist's right to control an enemy by appropriating his identity.

25. David Bindman, *William Blake: His Art and Times* (London: Thames and Hudson, 1982), p. 122.

26. Wollstonecraft, *Vindication*, p. 299.

27. Erdman, *Illuminated Blake*, pp. 31, 142–43, associates head clutching with despair and fear as well.

28. For more on the religious implications of Blake's book image, see Tannenbaum, *Biblical Tradition*, chap. 5.

29. The title alludes to John Shebbeare's royalist political allegory, *The History of the Excellence and Decline of the Constitution, Religion, Laws, Manners, and Genius of the Sumatrans* (London, 1763), as well as to the theme of his *Seventh Letter to the People of England. A Defence of the Prerogative Royal, as It Was Exerted in His Majesty's Proclamation for Prohibiting the Exportation of Corn* (London, 1767).

30. Israel Mauduit, another ministerial pamphleteer.

31. At this time, John Montagu, fourth earl of Sandwich, was first lord of the admiralty, and Lord George Germain, formerly Lord George Sackville, was president of the board of trade.

32. The Hanoverian monarchs discontinued the practice of trying to cure victims of scrofula by touching them (hence the name "the king's evil"). "The king's evil" quickly became a code phrase for belief in the magical and mystical powers of monarchy associated with the Stuarts, in part because the Pretenders claimed the power. Samuel Johnson had unsuccessfully been "touched" by Queen Anne in 1712.

33. Sandwich earned his sobriquet from John Gay's *Beggar's Opera* because he had hypocritically turned on his erstwhile companion Wilkes in the House of Lords over Wilkes's *Essay on Woman*.

34. Samuel Gillam's reading of the Riot Act to a Wilkesite mob precipitated the "Massacre" at St. George's Fields in May 1768.

35. On Blake and the Druids, see Peter F. Fisher, "Blake and the Druids," *Journal of English and Germanic Philology* 58 (1959): 589–612.

36. Richard Thomson, ed., *A Faithful Account of the Processions and Ceremonies Observed in the Coronation of the Kings and Queens of England: Exemplified in That of Their Late Most Sacred Majesties King George the Third, and Queen Charlotte: With All the Other Interesting Proceedings Connected with That Magnificent Festival* (London, 1820), pp. 91–92.

37. The first line of this quotation is the motto of the Scottish royal family.

38. On the appeal of female monsters, see Susan Gubar, "The Female Monster in Augustan Satire," *Signs: Journal of Women in Culture and Society* 3 (1977): 380–94, and the exchange between Gubar and Ellen Pollak in *Signs* 3 (1977): 728–32, 732–33.

39. Erdman, *Blake: Prophet,* pp. 210–25, rather arbitrarily labels Rintrah as Pitt and Palamabron as Parliament.

40. Wollstonecraft, *Vindication,* p. 264.

41. Paine may be responding, in an argument of images, to Burke's earlier description in *Reflections* of Richard Price as "this arch-pontiff of the *rights of men*" (p. 96).

42. David V. Erdman, "William Blake's Debt to James Gillray," *Art Quarterly* 12 (1949): 165–70, offers two other possible models: *The Impeachment; or, The Father of the Gang Turned King's Evidence* (1791, BMC 7861) and *The Infant Hercules* (1784, BMC 6402), both of which he attributes to Gillray. Thomas Rowlandson created *The Infant Hercules*.

43. Erdman, *Illuminated Blake,* p. 169.

44. The bracketed line was deleted in final copies: see Blake, p. 812.

45. The collar also recalls the restraints used on George during his madness.

CHAPTER 5.   "The Perfect Englishman"

1. E. P. Thompson's magnum opus is *The Making of the English Working Class* (Harmondsworth: Penguin, 1968). Thompson's assumptions are challenged by J. C. D. Clark, "Review Article: Eighteenth-Century Social History," *Historical Journal* 27 (1984): 773–88; Clark's own assumptions are questioned by Joanna Innes, "Review Article: Jonathan Clark, Social History, and England's 'Ancien Regime,' " *Past and Present* 115 (1987): 165–200.

George's elevation is the subject of Linda Colley, "The Apotheosis of George III: Loyalty, Royalty, and the British Nation, 1760–1820," *Past and Present* 102 (1984): 94–129; see also Herbert M. Atherton, "The British Defend Their Constitution in Political Cartoons and Literature," in Harry C. Payne, ed., *Studies in Eighteenth-Century Culture* 11 (1982): 3–31.

2. See F. K. Donnelly, "Ideology and Early English Working-Class History: Edward Thompson and His Critics," *Social History* 2 (1976): 219–38. As Clive Emsley rightly observes in "Repression, Terror, and the Rule of Law in England during the Decade of the French Revolution," *English Historical Review* 100 (1985): 301–25, "The body of literature on England during the 1790s is considerable, distinguished and ever expanding. Yet most of this work has been written from the point of view of the radicals and reformers" (p. 301). A brief, reliable overview of both conservative and radical positions, with a good bibliography, is H. T. Dickinson, *British Radicalism and the French Revolution, 1789–1815* (Oxford: Basil Blackwell, 1985), which should be supplemented by Ian R. Christie, *Stress and Stability in Late Eighteenth-Century Britain: Reflections on the British Avoidance of Revolution* (Oxford: Oxford Univ. Press, 1984); J. C. D. Clark, *English Society, 1688–1832: Ideology, Social Structure, and Political Practice during the Ancien Regime* (Cambridge:

Cambridge Univ. Press, 1985); and Thomas Philip Schofield, "Conservative Political Thought in Britain in Response to the French Revolution," *Historical Journal* 29 (1986): 601–22.

3. See Emsley, "Repression"; Jeremy Black, *The English Press in the Eighteenth Century* (Philadelphia: Univ. of Pennsylvania Press, 1987), chap. 6, especially pp. 184–88, 196.

4. Carl Cone, *The English Jacobins: Reformers in Late Eighteenth-Century England* (New York: Charles Scribner's Sons, 1968), p. 51.

5. John Cannon, *The Fox-North Coalition: Crisis of the Constitution, 1782–1784* (Cambridge: Cambridge Univ. Press, 1969).

6. Shelburne's comment is repeated, for example, in Paine's *Crisis* (29 October 1782).

7. Christie, "George III and the Historians," defends the constitutionality of the king's actions.

8. Wolcot plays on the derivation of *satire* from *satura*, a kind of olio, just as he uses his actual training as a physician to play on the tradition of the satirist as a curer of evils.

9. See Pope's use of Nimrod in Pope, 1:138, 139, 155, 155n, and 165n.

10. Pocock, *Virtue, Commerce, and History*, p. 196.

11. A reference to Sheridan's famous "Begums Speech" of 7 February 1787 on the Begams of Oudh, a subject to which he returned on 3 June 1788.

12. The best introduction to the *Reflections* is F. P. Lock, *Burke's "Reflections on the Revolution in France"* (London: Allen and Unwin, 1985).

13. Mikhail Bakhtin, *Rabelais and His World,* trans. Helene Iswolsky (Bloomington: Indiana Univ. Press, 1984), pp. 34, 36. Bakhtin's introduction (pp. 1–58) discusses at length the "concept of grotesque realism" (p. 18).

14. The Ditchley portrait is reproduced and discussed in Richard Helgerson, "The Land Speaks: Cartography, Chorography, and Subversion in Renaissance England," *Representations* 16 (1986): 51–85. Margery Corbett and R. W. Lightbown reproduce and analyze the title page of *Leviathan* in *The Comely Frontispiece: The Emblematic Title Page in England, 1550–1660* (London: Routledge and Kegan Paul, 1979), pp. 218–30.

15. See also A. M. Broadley, "The Evolution of John Bull," *Pearson's Magazine* (1909), pp. 543–51. Peter Mellini and Roy T. Matthews, in "John Bull's Family Arises," *History Today* 37 (1987): 17–23, completely ignore George's role in the development of John Bull.

16. In a comic context, Thomas Dibdin exploits the association of identification and suicide in his prologue to George Colman the Younger's play *John Bull; or, The Englishman's Fireside* (London, 1805):

> JOHN BULL is—*British Character* at large;
> 'Tis he, or he—where'er you mark a wight
> Revering law, yet resolute for right;
> Plain, blunt, his heart with feeling, justice, full,
> That is a Briton, that's (thank heaven!) JOHN BULL.

And John, till now, we set it down for certain,
Has always ta'en his seat *before* the curtain.

. . . .

Shou'd you condemn, sans mercy, the poor elf,
'Twere suicide for JOHN to kill *himself*.

17. On the great interest in Milton during the 1790s, see Stuart Curran, *Poetic Form and British Romanticism* (Oxford: Oxford Univ. Press, 1986), pp. 158–61.

18. The anonymous designer of *A British Chymist Analizing a Corsican Earth Worm!!* also shows the king to be a fortuitous beneficiary of the recently developed redefinition of a British eccentricity that has now become a virtue. See Margaret C. Jacob, "Scientific Culture in the Early English Enlightenment: Mechanisms, Industry, and Gentlemanly Facts," in Alan Charles Kors and Paul J. Korshin, eds., *Anticipations of the Enlightenment in England, France, and Germany* (Philadelphia: Univ. of Pennsylvania Press, 1987), pp. 134–64.

19. Colley, "Apotheosis of George III," p. 108.

20. For a general study, see Gerald Newman, *The Rise of English Nationalism: A Cultural History, 1740–1830* (New York: St. Martin's Press, 1987); see also Linda Colley, "Whose Nation?: Class and National Consciousness in Britain, 1750–1830," *Past and Present* 113 (1986): 97–117.

21. Garry Wills, *Cincinnatus: George Washington and the Enlightenment* (Garden City, N.Y.: Doubleday, 1984), p. 13, traces the revival of the legend to Washington's resigning his commission as commander in chief on 23 December 1783. Marcus Cunliffe, "The Two Georges: The President and the King," *American Studies International* 24 (1986): 53–73, does not discuss the Cincinnatus figure.

22. *The Palace of John Bull* was first published between 23 January (the death of Edward, duke of Kent) and 29 January 1820 (the death of George III).

23. *Shelley's Poetry and Prose,* ed. Donald H. Reiman and Sharon B. Powers (New York: Norton, 1977), p. 311. Mary Shelley supplied the title "England in 1819" for the posthumous 1839 edition.

24. *Byron's Letters and Journals,* ed. Leslie Marchand, 12 vols. (Cambridge, Mass.: Harvard Univ. Press, 1973–81), 3:117.

25. *The Castle and the Tomb or The Patriot Monarch: or, A Visit to Windsor on Occasion of the Funeral Procession of George III,* pp. 17–18, quoted in Colley, "Apotheosis of George III," p. 94.

26. J. W. Cunningham, *A Sermon Preached in the Parish Church of Harrow on the Hill, on Sunday the 6th of February, 1820, on the Death of His Most Gracious Majesty George the Third* (London, 1820), pp. 8–9. Emphases are Cunningham's.

27. William Hardwicke, *A Sermon Preached in the Parish Churches of Wisbech Saint Peter, in the Isle of Ely, and of Outwell in the County of Norfolk, on Wednesday, February 16th, 1820, on the Death of His Late Most Excellent Majesty, George the Third* (Wisbech, 1820), p. 12.

28. Byron's fullest account of the political and spiritual hopes invested in Princess Charlotte and her offspring appears in *Childe Harold's Pilgrimage,* canto 4, stanzas 167–72.

29. In addition to prosecution, George IV foolishly tried to buy up runs of

visual satires and to bribe artists into nonproduction, thereby encouraging others to try to deserve bribes. The "Bomb" (pronounced *bum*) to which George IV refers is the huge mortar given to him by the Spanish regency in 1816 to commemorate Wellington's victory. "Sid" is Sidmouth, Henry Addington, first viscount, the home secretary; "G——ff——d" is Robert Gifford, the attorney general.

30. *Byron's Letters and Journals* 7:41, 8:229.

31. *Byron's Letters and Journals* 8:240.

32. On the literary form of Byron's *Vision,* see Emrys Jones, "Byron's Visions of Judgment," *Modern Language Review* 76 (1981): 1–19, and Leon Guilhamet, *Satire and the Transformation of Genre* (Philadelphia: Univ. of Pennsylvania Press, 1987), pp. 55–67. On the poem's politics, see Carl Woodring, *Politics in English Romantic Poetry* (Cambridge, Mass.: Harvard Univ. Press, 1970), pp. 192–99; Stuart Peterfreund, "The Politics of 'Neutral Space' in Byron's *Vision of Judgment,*" *Modern Language Quarterly* 40 (1979): 275–91; and Malcolm Kelsall, *Byron's Politics* (Totowa, N.J.: Barnes and Noble, 1987), pp. 119–45.

33. See Thomas W. Laqueur, "The Queen Caroline Affair: Politics as Art in the Reign of George IV," *Journal of Modern History* 54 (1982): 417–66.

34. Byron uses the phrase "telescope of truth" in the nonsatiric vision "The Dream" (1816), line 180. The satiric career of George III, ultimately saved by his mortal body despite his regal body, would have been an apt emblem of the transition that Leo Braudy traces in "From Monarchs to Individualists," *The Frenzy of Renown: Fame and Its History* (Oxford: Oxford Univ. Press, 1986), pp. 315–89.

Index